HIT or Miss

Lessons Learned from Health Information Technology Projects

Third Edition

HIMSS Book Series

Participatory Healthcare: A Person-Centered Approach to Healthcare Transformation
Jan Oldenburg

The Journey Never Ends: Technology's Role in Helping Perfect Health Care Outcomes
David Garets and Claire McCarthy Garets

Glaser on Health Care IT: Perspectives from the Decade that Defined Health Care Information Technology
John P. Glaser

Leveraging Data in Healthcare: Best Practices for Controlling, Analyzing, and Using Data
Rebecca Mendoza Saltiel Busch

HIT or Miss

Lessons Learned from Health Information Technology Projects

Third Edition

Edited by Jonathan Leviss

CRC Press is an imprint of the
Taylor & Francis Group, an **informa** business
A PRODUCTIVITY PRESS BOOK

CRC Press
Taylor & Francis Group
6000 Broken Sound Parkway NW, Suite 300
Boca Raton, FL 33487-2742

Printed on acid-free paper

International Standard Book Number-13: 978-0-367-14346-6 (Hardback)

Library of Congress Cataloging-in-Publication Data

Names: Leviss, Jonathan, author.
Title: HIT or miss : lessons learned from health information technology projects / Jonathan Leviss.
Description: 3rd edition. | Boca Raton : Taylor & Francis, 2019. | "A CRC title, part of the Taylor & Francis imprint, a member of the Taylor & Francis Group, the academic division of T&F Informa plc." | Includes bibliographical references and index.
Identifiers: LCCN 2019004821 (print) | LCCN 2019006832 (ebook) | ISBN 9780429031403 (e-Book) | ISBN 9780367143466 (hardback : alk. paper)
Subjects: LCSH: Health services administration—Information technology. | Information storage and retrieval systems—Medical care. | Medical records—Data processing.
Classification: LCC R858 (ebook) | LCC R858 .H25 2019 (print) | DDC 362.10285—dc23
LC record available at https://lccn.loc.gov/2019004821

Visit the Taylor & Francis Web site at
http://www.taylorandfrancis.com

and the CRC Press Web site at
http://www.crcpress.com

To Emmy and Becca—keep doing good stuff … keep learning from your stumbles … and keep making it fun!

To Perri—my best friend, wife, and most important source of support. Thanks for everything, especially for your love. Much aloha.

To Emmy and Reece—keep doing good stuff, keep learning from your mistakes, and keep making it fun!

To Peri—my best friend, wife, and most important source of support. Thanks for everything, especially for your love. Much aloha.

C

Contents

Foreword

Ross Koppel, PhD, FACMI,
University of Pennsylvania and SUNY @ Buffalo

Once again, the editors and authors of *HIT or Miss* endow us with lessons on actual implementations and uses of health information technology (HIT)—electronic health records (EHRs) and other digital efforts designed to make healthcare more efficient, safe, and less costly. Although there are some wonderful exceptions, these stories illustrate how many (most?) careful plans are often shattered by the complexity of healthcare delivery. Every vignette should be required reading by every medical information technology (IT) person, every EHR vendor, every medical and IT leader (Chief Medical Information Officer/CMIO, Chief Information Officer/CIO, Chief Technology Officer/CTO, and Chief Executive Officer/CEO), and anyone with the authority to buy or install digital technology in a medical setting. Every EHR contract and every consultant agreement with healthcare providers should include this book in the document, and be required reading.

The few hours it would take these leaders to read this volume would be the best return on investment (ROI) they will ever achieve. These lessons will result in reductions of frustration, patient harm, clinician rage, organizational disharmony, and burnout. They would also save money and time. This book will not eliminate HIT's unintended consequences, but it will help readers more quickly identify them, prepare for them, reduce them, and find solutions for them.

Some of the recent offerings in this third edition highlight the difficulties of integrating HIT into medical workflows or into some of the stakeholders' workflows. Many of the vignettes illustrate the unfortunate results of communication failure—among teams, among professions, among consultants, among users and intended users, among consultants, and among IT sellers with everyone else. Moreover, even when the groups communicate and are all involved with the HIT's implementation and design, there are usually what are perceived as winners and losers—where the outcomes favor one profession or service more than others; where one group adopts the resulting products, while others ignore them; and where some functions work as desired and others do not integrate into workflows, or fail completely.

There are also new stories about old problems, for example, ongoing dissatisfaction with computerized decision support (CDS) alerts; finding them irrelevant, annoying, or downright dangerous because they interfere with thought-flow and workflow, because the pop-ups hide essential information, and because they are so often wrong. Excessive and inappropriate alerts result in override rates that remain stunningly high, often in the 95%–99% range, which exacerbates dissatisfaction.

There are new and thoughtful pieces on problems created when leaders seek to change the scope or scale of a planned project. Many of the contemplated changes initially seem wise. But these stories tell of results that are anything but wise. The changes in plans wreak havoc not only on the new or planned added efforts, but also on even the existing systems. Alas, this lesson about late modifications is a difficult one because we know that it's often impossible to predict what will emerge when envisioning or effecting HIT changes. We want to encourage—not discourage—flexible and responsive adjustments and improvements to HIT projects. The complications point to the complex and interrelatedness of HIT. EHRs are made up of thousands (hundreds of thousands) of moving parts, algorithms, expected inputs (e.g., patient weights, pharmacy data, laboratory reports), pieces of vestigial software embedded into the larger whole. When we add the myriad other interacting elements from outside laboratories, inventory systems, pharmaceutical company changes, and from the thousands of devices (e.g., smart pumps, monitors), we confront the reality that EHRs and medicine's digital landscape are moving entities, not static "things." Previously, I've suggested that an EHR is always changing—with new algorithms, new drugs, new processes, and new rules. EHRs are a river, not a lake. I'll extend that metaphor to the entirety of healthcare facilities and their network of providers: everything is always flowing. Also, as Heraclitus reminds us, it's never even the same river.

This third edition builds on the previous two editions of *HIT or Miss,* which were enclaves of honesty amid the incessant advertising by the HIT industry, its supporters in government, and the enthusiasts who were so enamored of HIT's promise that they regarded any criticism as heresy. The first two editions of *HIT or Miss* contained what few uttered but what we all knew to be essential, basic, and true: implementing HIT is difficult, often precarious, and always involves uncertain outcomes. Nevertheless, most of us felt and still feel the promise of HIT is so great that it was and is worth the effort. The earlier editions of *HIT or Miss* did not say the emperor was naked, but they exposed the threadbare reality faced by medical offices and hospitals implementing and using HIT. This third edition is even stronger. It reminds us that HIT is a magnificent idea, but its execution is generally a serious struggle—most often a struggle each hospital or office negotiates without the needed information from sharing honest stories like these. As the saying goes: "You've seen one EHR implementation, you've seen one EHR implementation." To make the systems work always requires a lot more work than imagined.

We've known for years that "IT Projects Have a 70% Failure Rate…" (Novak, 2012). HIMSS offered project management training as a solution. Ordinarily, an admission of that high a failure rate would generate condemnation from HIMSS and the Office of the National Coordinator for Health Information Technology (ONC), accusing those voicing such data of technophobia, Luddite tendencies, and worse. But the costs of digital systems in money and time are so great, and the benefits are so desired, few can admit failure. Instead, we invest millions more and usually get something to function after months or years of additional toil. What the industry promoters still fail to understand is that we often learn far more from examining our mistakes than from touting our successes—especially when those successes may obscure myriad problems that were later surmounted at great cost.

One of the joys of this third edition of *HIT or Miss* is that it continues to move us up on the learning curve from the dominant presentation of HIT as unalloyed joy and progress to the reality of what must be done to get HIT to work *in situ*. It shows us the absurdity of the continued refusal of industry and government to demand data standards and to delay or sidestep interoperability needs. It again illustrates the need for usability as a cause of patient-safety dangers and clinical inefficiencies. It reminds us of the need for constant vigilance and evaluation by clinical and IT personnel, along with cooperation from vendors and regulators. That is also why this book is so valuable. Achieving usable HIT requires that we learn from these clear and thoughtful examples. Each chapter offers invaluable lessons on HIT's implementation and use. Some focus on order entry; some on bar coding; some on EHRs; some on medication reconciliation; most on workflow; almost all on the need for planning and how planning is never enough.

Collectively, these vignettes often delineate the ongoing, Hobbesian struggles of machine vs. man vs. local organization vs. enterprise headquarters vs. professional allegiance (e.g., nurses vs. doctors vs. pharmacists) vs. vendor sales departments vs. consultants vs. IT staff vs. HIT designers vs. cybersecurity protectors vs. finance departments vs. everyone's desire to help patients and avoid errors. Happily, the providers are usually well-intentioned, good people who deliver good care. Sometimes, the struggles are overwhelming, and the care is not good. Patient safety requires resilience and the seemingly paradoxical task of seeing what falls through the cracks. Making HIT work requires similar observational skills. It requires that we recognize when the extra clicks, confusing data displays, and lousy navigation that we have learned and to which we are now accustomed are dangerous and lead to errors. Errors we sometimes don't see.

Almost all of chapters speak of the vision and synoptic understanding required for HIT to work. We learn that we are never done:

- Upgrades and patches are constant.
- Connections with the many other systems are vulnerabilities as well as opportunities.
- Our clinicians need ongoing training on changes.
- If we are a teaching hospital, we face additional challenges of HIT training while teaching patient care.
- All facilities face new users of varying skill levels.
- Almost all facilities confront users with experiences of other systems or implementations (ongoing or past) with very different interfaces and ways of finding essential data.

Many of these chapters discuss efforts to achieve regulatory compliance. While the ONC and Centers for Medicare and Medicaid Services (CMS) are currently seeking greater flexibility, we are still burdened with their original sin of requiring providers to purchase HIT rather than with first demanding HIT with the data fluidity and usability that would make users want to buy it. Many, also, are incensed at the ONC's continuing refusal to press vendors seriously to adopt data and usability standards, and to allow open discussion and presentation of faults (e.g., screenshots of dangerous data displays). Without data standards, HIT remains the "Tower of HIT Babel" these authors so well describe. Providers need to have a way not only to get *one* system to work, but also to get many IT systems to work together … while each is undergoing change from vendors, users, and the interplay with others' systems.

Before even the first edition of *HIT or Miss* existed, there were, of course, efforts to tell the real tales of HIT implementations. But unhappy reports were spurned as the ravings of malcontents and technophobes. *HIT or Miss*'s first edition was a needed guide for those seeking to implement HIT, which was of course best accomplished with the knowledge only learned from real experiences in the trenches. The first two editions provided some of that. With this third edition, we have more guidance from more examples and greater insights. The editorial comments, and the analyses accompanying each vignette, continue to be models of brevity and clear thinking.

The argument about whether or not HIT is better than paper is silly. HIT is better than paper. It is also better than wet clay slabs with cuneiform styluses, pigeons, or smoke signals. The task we face is to implement HIT in ways that work reasonably well, and then use HIT to better serve patients and clinicians. *HIT or Miss, Third Edition* is just what the doctor needs, and should order stat.

Acknowledgments

The *HIT or Miss* books have always been a team effort. Thanks to American Medical Informatics Association (AMIA) for providing us with the forum to create the idea and the support for this third edition; the AMIA Clinical Information Systems Working Group (CIS-WG) and the Ethics, Legal and Social Issues Working Group for promoting the concept and helping to lead the process; the Health Information and Management Systems Society (HIMSS) and CRC Press for helping to prepare the manuscript and marketing our product; our colleagues for sharing many failed—and successful—health information technology (HIT) initiatives; and the editorial team for their support, ideas, and terrific writing, recruiting, and editing.

Introduction and Methodology

Introduction

(J. Leviss and L. Ozeran)

On February 24, 2009, President Barack Obama pledged to the entire US Congress, "Our... plan will invest in electronic health records and new technology that will reduce errors, bring down costs, ensure privacy, and save lives."

President Obama declared that digitizing healthcare would be a critical success factor in improving healthcare in the United States and the overall US economy. Through the American Recovery and Reinvestment Act of 2009 (ARRA), the federal government offered large-scale funding to create a technology foundation for the US healthcare delivery system. The ARRA's EHR "Meaningful Use" program awarded tens of billions of dollars to physicians and hospitals which was spent on HIT software, hardware, and consulting services, all with the goal of improving the quality and efficiency of healthcare. Building on that approach, the US federal government's CMS continues to require EHRs as a central part of pay for performance and quality incentive programs.

But what has occurred so far? Many large and small healthcare organizations successfully leveraged the ARRA funding opportunity to advance into the digital age, but many others faltered. Innumerous anecdotes report the high frequency with which large and small healthcare provider organizations and vendors fail to follow recognized best practices for HIT implementation, even those with extensive HIT experience. Originally, the shared struggles to achieve Meaningful Use accreditation by many hospitals and physician practices raised concerns about our readiness to advance to Stages 2 and 3 on a national scale in the time frame allotted by the Meaningful Use program. Now, as organizations have pushed forward, many have created new problems and exacerbated existing ones, including physician burnout, patient safety risks, privacy and security breaches, and major cost overruns. Healthcare academic and trade journals, plus the lay press, are filled with well-documented shortfalls of HIT. Why are these problems still occurring? How can we learn from these failures to successfully implement HIT and advance our healthcare delivery systems into the modern digital age of other industries?

In the United States, sequential EHR Meaningful Use stages corresponded to advancing criteria of functionality and adoption. Meaningful Use Stage 1 focused on data capturing and sharing, but most requirements had low thresholds of adoption and did not require broad impact on the practices of most healthcare professionals within any one healthcare organization. The successful attestation for Stage 1 did not mean that a hospital or physician practice was ready to expand similar or new functionality across its entire organization. Stage 2 expanded upon the accomplishments of Stage 1 with requirements for advanced clinical processes, but still with low adoption thresholds (such as EHR reminders for preventive care for 10% of patients). Stage 2 accreditation, therefore, got more complex and involved broader aspects of a healthcare organization, but again did not require a full commitment to digitize care within a physician practice or across a major medical center. As a result, hospitals and practices could and did develop strategies to digitize parts of their organizations in order to achieve accreditation and receive the ARRA payments, without needing to support full-scale transformation to digital healthcare.

Meaningful Use Stage 3 required measuring the clinical care and results, addressing shortcomings, and improving clinical outcomes, but now this has been supplanted by new CMS payment programs, and, more importantly, the anticipated realization that large-scale quality and transformative programs require digital data, including EHRs and other advanced HIT systems. Therefore, the ROI for the federal government's HIT investment first requires large-scale successful and sustainable rollouts of technologies that had only been "piloted" for Stages 1 and 2; this means that achieving success in Stages 1 and 2 did not necessarily prepare us for our current state. And, in many cases, the early successes created the false assumption in organizations that they were prepared for vastly more complex and larger HIT-based initiatives.

Some cases to consider:

A multisite fifty-provider ambulatory care organization is live on an EHR for 2 years—all demographic and clinical processes are completely dependent on the EHR and its practice management system, including patient registration, test results review, CPOE, and clinical documentation. One day, the EHR develops slow response times and in a few hours becomes unusable (Chapter 28).

A hospital system plans a simultaneous EHR transition and an upgrade to the Obstetric Department's fetal monitoring system. Detailed plans, implementation meetings, and technical checklists help keep the project on target … until go-live day when fetal monitoring tracing do not correlate with the paper backups being used in the transition of systems (Chapter 19).

A hospital's implementation of voice-recognition software stalls with very limited adoption by physicians, who prefer the legacy dictation system…until a malware attack disables the entire dictation system (Chapter 34).

A medical center recruits and hires a physician at 80% time to be the CPOE go-live leader—chair the governance committees, spearhead communications about CPOE, and oversee the design, build, and rollout of CPOE. Without sufficient support for a full CMIO role, the physician becomes overwhelmed and leaves. Without formal leadership, the initiative has significant delays and fails to deliver the original functionality of the CPOE system (Chapter 21).

What defines failure? For the purposes of discussion, we, the editorial team of *HIT or Miss, Third Edition*, define a HIT failure as "a case in which an unintended negative consequence occurred, such as a project delay, a substantial cost overrun, a failure to meet an intended goal or objective, or complete abandonment of the project."

HIT projects fail at a rate up to 70% of the time (Kaplan, 2009). What happens when HIT projects fail? What will happen when the same hospitals or physician practices that struggled to meet Meaningful Use Stage 1 are unable to meet the level of HIT performance required by CMS or commercial payers? What will happen when scarce healthcare dollars are spent on projects that do not meet the intended goals? Or when patients are harmed as a result of failed HIT projects? How do health systems and individual providers analyze the costs, challenges, and patient safety problems from such failed initiatives?

The editors of this book have led successful EHR and HIT projects that brought readily available patient and health information to all points of healthcare delivery and offered the types of quality and efficiency benefits that typically are targeted with digital transformation. As a group, we are both excited and concerned by the potential outcomes of the ARRA funding and the US implementations of EHRs. Although ARRA addressed the financial burden of initial HIT investments, many other challenges remain for HIT projects to be successful, and for the success of the US government's massive investment.

The content and human factor challenges associated with implementing technology have proven to be formidable barriers impeding the widely available transformation that HIT could bring. Moreover, the same lessons or "best practices" required for successful HIT projects are being repeatedly learned through trial and error, over and over again, in large and small health systems without successful dissemination of the knowledge across organizations and at great financial cost and social cost. Professional conferences routinely share experiences from successful HIT initiatives, but the lessons do not appear to follow the new technologies to other organizations or update over time—the common errors remain common.

Sharing success stories does not work, or as William Soroyan wrote, "Good people are good because they've come to wisdom through failure. We get very little wisdom from success, you know" (Saroyan, 1971). Apparently in the field of HIT, we still, even after two editions of *HIT or Miss*, do "not know." As a result, the adoption of effective HIT remains at a fairly primitive stage compared with IT adoption in every other major industry.

This third collection of HIT case studies offers a continued approach to change the HIT knowledge paradigm. The third edition contains expert insight into key remaining obstacles that must be overcome to leverage IT in order to modernize and transform healthcare. The purpose of reporting HIT case studies that failed is to document, catalogue, and share key lessons that all project managers of HIT, health system leaders in informatics and technology, hospital executives, policy makers, and service and technology providers must know in order to succeed with HIT, a critical step for the transformation of all health systems.

HIT or Miss, Third Edition presents a model to discuss HIT failures in a safe and protected manner, providing an opportunity to focus on the lessons offered by a failed initiative as opposed to worrying about potential retribution for exposing a project as having failed. Learning from failures is what every major industry regularly does. Air travel safety is enabled by organizations like the Commercial Aviation Safety Team (CAST), a multidisciplinary coalition of government and industry experts that analyzes accidents and safety incidents for continued safety improvements; mountaineers famously read the journal *Accidents in North American Mountaineering* to learn about the devastating errors of their peers and avoid repeating them; and business developers scrutinize failed efforts, from outages of airline booking systems and online banking to failed market launches of new technologies. And back in healthcare, clinical departments around the world learn from clinical failures in regularly scheduled "morbidity and mortality" rounds.

At the AMIA 2006 Fall Conference, the CIS-WG hosted an "open-microphone" event called "Tales from the Trenches" where members shared HIT failures from their own institutions. The "Tales from the Trenches" event, created for professional development and entertainment purposes, quickly proved the value of sharing failure cases and lessons learned in a safe and protected environment. A group of us committed to publishing a collection of brief vignettes that documented situations that did not go quite right, but could be generalized so a larger audience would learn from the collective wisdom of these stories rather than repeat the same (often costly) mistakes. We committed to deidentifying all aspects of the submissions prior to publication and all submitting authors agreed to have their names appear in the book, separate, and not linked to their case submissions. The unanimous agreement among all contributing authors to have their names listed in all three editions of *HIT or Miss* reinforces the message that reviewing failed initiatives offers valuable knowledge and insight, rather than an opportunity for casting blame and defensive posturing.

You will find these case studies catalogued by HIT project (such as CPOE and ambulatory EHR), but the index will also allow you to search based upon types of lessons learned (such as project management and technology failure). The catalogue and index should enable you, the reader, to find the right anecdote that best applies to your specific circumstance and to share with others in your organization. The storytelling format is intended to make it easier for you to reach out to peers, superiors, and staff to say "this could be us" and then to proactively address problems before they spiral out of control.

Learning from failures is an iterative process. Do not permit all of the cost of failure to be borne by your organization. Instead, reflect on these failures as if they occurred in your circumstance so that you can improve your organization's chances of success and reduce your risk of financial and social loss. Some have called for national and international reporting databases of HIT failure—we ask that at the very least, let's start in our own organizations. We trust that you will find this collection to be a useful guide in your efforts. With effective knowledge sharing, we can successfully lead healthcare into the digital age.

Methodology

All cases published in *HIT or Miss, Third Edition*, were voluntarily submitted by authors who were directly involved in the projects themselves; all contributing authors to all three editions deserve credit in this effort and are therefore listed as authors, even if their case appeared in an earlier edition and not the third edition. This was also done to maintain anonymity by not removing authors' names for cases that were not reprinted. Prior to the first edition of *HIT or Miss*, the editorial team agreed upon the definition of HIT failure:

> An HIT project failure is one in which an unintended negative consequence occurred such as a project delay, a substantial cost overrun, failure to meet an intended goal or objective, or abandonment of the project.

Requests for deidentified cases that met the definition were solicited from various professional society listservs and other professional networking. All submissions were carefully reviewed by the editorial team for publication. The editorial team assumed ultimate responsibility for reviewing, organizing, editing, and deidentifying the case material, and for providing additional expert commentary. All submitting authors of cases attested to participation in the described HIT project and the originality of the work. All cases were deidentified, removing all names of locations, organizations, and vendors, as well as identifying descriptions that were not essential to the lessons offered by the case. All opinions and analyses of the authors and editors are purely their own and do not necessarily reflect the opinions of the other authors or editors of *HIT or Miss*, AMIA, or HIMSS.

Editor

Dr. Jonathan Leviss, MD FACP, has championed technology-enabled transformation in healthcare for over 20 years, including serving as: the first CMIO at New York City Health + Hospitals, a decade before Meaningful Use; CMO at Sentillion, making single sign-on a standard in healthcare; and a physician leader creating value across large and small health systems, health plans, and for profit and not for profit companies. Dr. Leviss is the Medical Director for Adult Medicine at the Greater New Bedford Community Health Center in Massachusetts and faculty at the Brown University School of Public Health. He is board-certified in internal medicine by the American Board of Internal Medicine (ABIM) and in the subspecialty of clinical informatics by the American Board of Preventive Medicine (ABPM).

Associate Editors

Dr. Melissa Baysari, PhD, is Associate Professor in Digital Health at the University of Sydney, Australia. Her research interests include human factors and computerized decision support, with a focus on digital solutions to support medication management. Prior to focusing on medication safety since 2009, Dr. Baysari studied railway safety and train driver errors.

Dr. Christopher Corbit, MD, is the Medical Informatics Director for SC TeamHealth and the Facility Medical Director for Colleton Medical Center. He previously served as the Chief Medical Informatics Officer for Emergency Medicine Physicians/US Acute Care Solutions for over 8 years. He is a practicing emergency medicine physician and also a Principal at the HealthLytix Consulting Group.

Dr. Catherine Craven, PhD, is a Senior Clinical Informaticist at the Institute of Healthcare Delivery Science and the IT Department of the Mt. Sinai Health System in New York. She has worked in industry, provider healthcare, and library sciences. She received her PhD in clinical informatics as a National Institutes of Health (NIH)/National Library of Medicine Health Informatics Research Fellow at the University of Missouri.

Mr. David Leander is an MD-MBA candidate at Dartmouth University, class of 2020. He worked on EHR projects at many health systems before medical school as a project manager at Epic Systems and continues as a consultant since entering medical school. Mr. Leander hopes to continue his formal informatics training in residency.

Dr. Karl Poterack, MD, is board-certified in clinical informatics as well as anesthesiology. He serves as the Medical Director for Applied Clinical Informatics for Mayo Clinic; he practices anesthesiology at the Mayo Clinic Hospital in Phoenix, Arizona.

Dr. Eric Rose, MD, is the Vice President of Terminology Management at Intelligent Medical Objects (IMO), responsible for managing terminology content creation operations as well as contributing to company-wide product, go-to-market, and partner engagement strategy. Dr. Rose has held numerous health informatics leadership positions in health systems and industry; he is also a family physician and clinical faculty at the University of Washington School of Medicine.

Dr. Richard Schreiber, MD, is an Associate CMIO for the Geisinger Health System at Geisinger Holy Spirit Hospital; the Regional Assistant Dean of the Geisinger Commonwealth School of Medicine; a practicing hospitalist; and an informatics researcher focusing on clinical decision support, documentation, and venous thromboembolic disease. He is board-certified in clinical informatics.

Dr. Christina Stephan, MD, PhD, has over 15 years of experience in advancing innovative health technology and EHR solutions for clinical and population health systems through strategic planning, education, and research and development, including the Director of Medical Informatics at Health Book, an Associate Director of Health Management and Informatics at the University of Missouri School of Medicine, and the Co-chair of the AMIA Public Health Informatics Working Group.

Dr. Kai Zheng, PhD, focuses on consumer-facing technologies and design; he is an Associate Professor of Informatics at the Donald Bren School of Information and Computer Sciences and the Director of the Center for Biomedical informatics at the Institute for Clinical and Translational Science, both at the University of California—Irvine. He is the Chair of the AMIA CIS-WG.

Contributing Experts, Authors, and Author Teams

Jeffrey Adams, PhD, RN; Audrey Parks, MBA; and Virginia Williams, MSN, RN
Lawrence B. Afrin, MD; Frank Clark, PhD; John Waller, MD; Patrick Cawley, MD; Timothy Hartzog, MD; Mark Daniels, MS; and Deborah Campbell, RN
Melissa Baysari, PhD
Pam Charney, PhD, RD
Christopher Corbit, MD
Catherine Craven, PhD
Chris Doyle, MD
Wen Dombrowski, MD
Michael Gallagher, MD, MPH
Nicholas Genes MD, PhD, and Romona Tulloch, MS, RN
Justin Graham, MD, MS
Julie Gregoire, RPh
Brian Gugerty, DNS, RN
Christopher Harle, PhD; Marvin Dewar, MD, JD; and Laura Gruber, MBA, MHS
Jacqueline Henriquez, RNC, MSN
Melinda Jenkins, PhD, FNP
Henry W. Jones III
Bonnie Kaplan, PhD
Gail Keenan, PhD, RN
David Leander
Christoph Lehmann, MD; Roberto A. Romero, BS; and George R. Kim, MD
Jonathan Leviss, MD
Steven Magid, MD, Richard Benigno, and Jessica Kovac
George McAlpine, MBA RN and Aditi Vakil, MBBS, MHA
Sandi Mitchell, BS Pharm, MSIS
Ilene Moore, MD
Kenneth Ong, MD, MPH
Paul Oppenheimer, MD
Larry Ozeran, MD
Patrick A. Palmieri, EdS, RN
Liron Pantanowitz, MD and Anil V. Parwani, MD, PhD
Eric Poon, MD, MPH
Brad Rognrud, MS, RPh

Eric Rose, MD
Karl Poterac, MD
Richard Schreiber, MD, and John Knapp, MSISEM
Robert Schwartz, MD
Scot Silverstein, MD
Christina Stephan, MD, PhD
Diane Stevens, RN
Walton Sumner, MD and Phil Asaro, MD
Aditi Vakil, MBBS, MHA and Ken Koppenhaver, BSN, PhD
Vivian Vimarlund, Bahlol Rahimi, and Toomas Timpka
Riikka Vuokko, Anne Forsell, and Helena Karsten
Edward Wu, MD
Kai Zheng, PhD

HOSPITAL CARE FOCUS I

Six Blind Sages and the Electronic Health Record

If six blind sages approached an electronic health record (EHR), like the elephant, the observations would vary greatly. An EHR could be observed to enhance communications, improve efficiency, standardize practices, or improve health care quality and safety. Each observation would be valid. However, each serves different masters (or end-users) whose needs must be understood and respected. Failure to agree on an overall goal for an EHR, to recognize the "animal" in its entirety, prevents problems from being managed or conflicts from being overcome.

Chapter 1

Build It with Them, Make It Mandatory, and They Will Come: Implementing CPOE

Editor: Bonnie Kaplan
Yale University

Contents

Project Categories: computerized provider order entry (CPOE), inpatient electronic health record (EHR)

Lessons Learned Categories: implementation approaches, leadership/governance

Case Study

Middle Health System (Middle) has a 650-bed "downtown" hospital, a 350-bed suburban hospital, a 160-bed rehabilitation hospital, and two rural hospitals with 75–100 beds. They have 20 other divisions, including a 100-provider medical practice and a visiting nurse business.

Over 15 years, Middle had steady improvements in automation of many business and clinical processes, and then entered another phase, the "clinician high impact" phase of health information technology (HIT). They would acquire and implement new modules of their main vendor's electronic health record (EHR) in their inpatient settings: computerized provider order entry (CPOE), bar code medication administration (BCMA), advanced nursing documentation, and then physician clinical documentation. This would take physicians from occasional users of HIT to dependence on HIT to plan, order, document, and make clinical decisions. The new system would take nurses from moderate users of HIT to heavy users.

CPOE was the first module in the "clinician high impact" phase to be implemented. Middle's chief medical informatics officer position was vacant, so the HIT project came under the direction of the chief information officer (CIO). He was aware of two common recommendations of those who have implemented CPOE:

- "Make CPOE use mandatory."
- "Implement CPOE throughout the enterprise."

However, the CIO thought that mandating the use of CPOE was "all well and good for university medical centers," where the ratio of residents to physicians is high. Residents are younger and thus more comfortable with computers; in addition, they are under the direction of their superiors and can be ordered to perform certain tasks. His organization had 50 residents and 1,000 hospitalists, surgeons, midlevel providers, and community doctors. It was unrealistic, he thought, to mandate CPOE. His thinking was, "Build it right, and they will come."

The CPOE planning team also decided on a pilot approach. To mitigate the risk of confusion with a combination of paper and electronic orders, the two nursing units in the suburban hospital that had the fewest transfers from or into other units were chosen as the pilot units.

Despite adequate training of providers and more than adequate support during go-live, several physicians avoided using CPOE on the pilot units from the start. These physicians phoned in their orders so as not to be "harassed" by the bevy of CPOE go-live support staff. Most providers at least tolerated the system, but many of those complained of the increased time it took to write orders. Several physicians on the pilot units confided to project team members that they were just "playing along" with the CPOE and were not truly supportive of the change. "If it fails, it will go away, so I don't need to learn it," said one physician who continued to write orders with a pen.

At day 16, 66% of the orders were created via CPOE. A successful pilot was declared. Several of the key players on the CPOE team took vacations. The project manager took 2 weeks off. Upon her return, she discovered that only 15% of the orders were being placed by CPOE. Out of concern for patient safety issues in a mixed CPOE and paper order environment, CPOE was discontinued on the pilot units 2 weeks later.

Author's Analysis

Following are the key lessons learned from the Middle Health System case.

- *Change management is at least as important as technical management, process transformation, and other critical aspects of a CPOE project.* Many people resist change in general. Most clinicians really resist change to their core processes to plan, order, and document care, which a CPOE implementation directly affects. A strong change management plan should be created and executed for a CPOE project.
- *Make CPOE use mandatory for all providers who write orders.* To keep providers from getting around this requirement, have all orders that are not entered directly by CPOE go through a predetermined process, such as the Joint Commission telephone order read-back procedure: a nurse logs onto the system, retrieves information for the patient in question, enters the

order the provider wants, and reads it back to the provider. Because this process takes at least twice as long as the provider ordering directly into the computer via CPOE, providers quickly learn to enter their own orders.

- *Don't call it a "pilot." Consider using a rapid multiphase implementation of CPOE.* Many of the physicians involved regarded the pilot as a tryout of CPOE rather than the beginning of CPOE. You want to give the strong message that phase 1 of implementation is where users learn and then apply the lessons to other units, after a period of consolidation. Through dialogue with clinicians throughout the planning and implementation phases, a clear understanding of the benefits and costs of CPOE not only to the organization but also to individual organizational members should develop so that people are thinking and saying, "It's here to stay, so I'd better learn it."
- *Don't withdraw* CPOE *go-live support too quickly.* Users typically become comfortable with CPOE after entering orders on approximately 30 patients. A high-volume order writer might write orders on 15 patients per week and thus will have reached the first plateau of competent use of CPOE in about 2 weeks. A low-volume order writer might write orders on one or two patients a week. You may have to keep some scaled-down go-live support for up to 6 months for low-volume order writers.

Editor's Commentary

It is not unusual for initial enthusiasm or usage to taper off. Two weeks is too short a time for a change to become institutionalized. Many problems can occur in the first few weeks without warranting discontinuing an implementation, and apparent successes can occur without warranting that all is well. Sustained support, reinforcement, and evaluating what is happening are needed to maintain a desired trajectory.

Attention should have been paid to early indicators that there could be problems. Not all providers were willing to use the system so as to avoid what they considered "harassment" by the support staff. Others "at least tolerated the system" but complained that it took longer to write orders. Some even confided that they were not supportive of the change, but were "playing along." It appears that none of these issues were addressed. If it takes longer to enter orders, physicians need to understand the benefits of CPOE that justify that extra time. Perhaps the time it takes to enter orders would decrease as staff learned better how to use the system, in which case they should have been helped both to understand the learning curve and to grasp concepts more quickly. Training, however, was described as "at least adequate" when it could have been better than minimally sufficient.

Different user communities, such as nurses and physicians, will have different incentives, training and support needs, attitudes, and aptitudes that need addressing. The benefits of using the system, or at least reasons why it should be used even if there are no obvious benefits to the users, also need to be highlighted and reinforced.

The pilot units were chosen because they had a low volume of transfers. The case study does not indicate how these units were viewed by the rest of the organization or whether there were other characteristics that could have affected what developed. A positive experience with the first units where change is implemented will serve as a good example to other units. In addition to selecting a test bed that is not too challenging, as was done here, other considerations include whether people on the unit might be respected project champions and whether there is strong leadership support in the unit for the project.

Another issue is that several key players took vacation at the same time, very early in the implementation. Although the vacation time was likely well deserved, having several key players gone at the same time meant there were not enough people available to notice and address the developing problem of nonuse of CPOE. Mechanisms to assess progress and take steps to alleviate problematic developments before they got out of hand should have been in place. Especially in the early days of implementation, it can be quite helpful to continue with training efforts as unfamiliar situations are encountered, and also to monitor where things do not go smoothly, where workarounds are occurring, and where complaints are developing. It appears there was no such plan in place, and without key people on site, there was no ad hoc means of addressing emerging issues. As a result, an early success quickly turned into an early failure.

Lessons Learned

- Change management is critical for CPOE projects.
- Make CPOE mandatory.
- Do not call it a "pilot."
- Do not withdraw CPOE go-live support too quickly.

Chapter 2

One Size Does Not Fit All: Multihospital EHR Implementation

Editor: Pam Charney
University of North Georgia

Contents

Project Categories: inpatient electronic health record (EHR), computerized provider order entry (CPOE)

Lessons Learned Categories: implementation approaches, staffing resources, training, workflow

Case Study

A multihospital health system opened a brand new hospital (Hospital A) with a strong focus on paperless records and use of cutting-edge technology and innovation. An electronic health record (EHR) vendor was selected to assist with this goal. While a few minor issues were identified, Hospital A went into operation fairly smoothly. The emergency department (ED) at Hospital A used a tracking board, computerized provider order entry (CPOE), and documentation in the EHR by both nurses and physicians. Daily census in Hospital A's ED was low, and the system was used for all patients presenting to the ED. Based on this success, the health system decided to implement the system at its other hospitals.

The next hospital (Hospital B) to implement the enterprise EHR hospital-wide was very different from Hospital A. Hospital A was brand new and had been specifically designed for heavy use of technology in patient care. In contrast, Hospital B was over 50 years old and was not designed for workflows involving an EHR. Also, when compared to Hospital A, the daily census and acuity for Hospital B's ED was much higher. While Hospital A went live from the start with the new EHR, Hospital B had preexisting workflows that covered nursing documentation, physician ordering via paper templates, and the dictation of physician notes.

There was also a difference in the information technology infrastructure and training capacity between the two sites. Staff at Hospital A were given 2 weeks of EHR training before the hospital began admitting patients. Staff at Hospital B had full-time patient responsibilities, so training was scheduled during off-duty hours. Despite this, the vendor noted that the ED nursing and physician staff of Hospital B were very engaged in the training.

Unfortunately, the EHR go-live at Hospital B had an enormously negative impact on ED workflow. Staffing had been increased for both nurses and physicians for go-live, but the time required for both nursing and physician documentation, along with additional time needed for CPOE, exceeded expectations. The percentage of patients who left without being seen increased from 2% to 12%, resulting in loss of hospital revenue. It took 6 months to return to baseline for this metric. Additional nursing and physician hours were still required with an even greater increase in hours than initially planned during go-live. Patient satisfaction, which had been steady for the previous year at the 70th percentile, dropped to the 5th percentile in the first 3 months following go-live before beginning to trend upward again.

Some of the issues that accounted for this included:

- A steep learning curve for documentation
- Staff documenting by typing rather than using templates due to missing options and fields on the templates
- Difficulty in finding common items and areas for documentation in the system.

These issues resulted in increased time spent on documentation and less time on patient care. System inefficiency in the higher-volume ED at Hospital B required additional nursing and physician staffing, leading to increased costs for the hospital and physician group.

Some of the unintended consequences also included the need for the nursing and medical directors to spend significant time documenting system issues and engaging in rework and redesign. There were ongoing biweekly team meetings with the ED leadership, health information management, accounting, and the coding teams to improve documentation issues. Nurses and physicians were also required to complete addenda to correct charting issues identified after charts had been created. This created additional non-patient work time for the staff.

Based on their experience at Hospital B, the health system administration decided to hold the implementation at the other system hospitals. They are reevaluating their choice of EHR vendor due to the issues inherent in the design of the current system.

Author's Analysis

Hospital A was able to successfully adopt an EHR system due to several factors, including lower patient volume, lack of legacy paper records, and a physical plant designed to accommodate information technology hardware. Even though some of the issues with the documentation were consistent between the two sites, staff had significantly different availability to work on the issues. Staff at Hospital A had sufficient time to find items in the EHR and create needed workarounds, while staff at Hospital B did not have this luxury.

There are several recommendations that can be made to help correct some of the issues seen in Hospital B's implementation.

1. *Nurses and physicians from each care setting need to be involved in the build and testing prior to go-live in.*

   Since the system was already being used at Hospital A, there was very limited involvement of the clinical staff in the application build for Hospital B. As a result, required documentation fields were missing, resulting in significant workarounds and workflow inefficiencies. Also, since there were no Hospital B clinicians involved in the build and testing, there were fewer superusers available for support during the Hospital B implementation phase.
2. *Leverage system expertise; rotate clinical users from other go-live sites to Hospital B to experience the system in a high-volume ED.*

   Having nursing and physician staff rotate from Hospital A to Hospital B during go-live would add experienced users in the ED. Not only would this have benefited the go-live site at Hospital B, but it would also have given additional experience and learning to the staff of Hospital A related to issues that might arise when Hospital A's census increased in the future.
3. *Anticipate at least a 6-month impact in productivity, and the need for additional nursing and physician staffing.*

   Depending on the workflow and capacity of the ED and on the EHR vendor, there might be a significant impact on not only productivity, but also patient satisfaction. Plans and budgets might need to be adjusted to keep additional staff in order to deal with the increased demands on clinical staff by the EHR.
4. *Provide 30- and 90-day reeducation sessions.*

   During the post-op live meetings to address issues, a recurrent theme of lack of follow-up vendor-sponsored training sessions was identified. Not only would additional training allow for additional interaction with the vendor, but it would also foster feedback discussions about issues with current EHR workflow.

Editor's Commentary

Administrators at multi-facility healthcare systems are often able to take advantage of cost savings due to their large-volume purchasing habits. It is not uncommon for large healthcare systems to require that all facilities utilize the same vendors for medications, supplies, and equipment. Requests for supplies not included on the formulary frequently necessitate detailed paperwork, several layers of approval, and other tactics. Thus, it is not surprising that administrators at the hospital system described here felt that the same EHR would be appropriate for each hospital in the system.

In this case study, decision makers for the healthcare system felt they were achieving economy of scale by using the same EHR for Hospital B. Using the same system would save enormous amounts of time and money if it were successful. However, implementation of an EHR is certainly not as simple as deciding which medications and supplies to stock. Therefore, the key points that could have prevented this failure were missed.

It is not clear what (if any) discussions were had with the EHR vendor concerning differences in size and focus of the hospitals in the system. Even if the software was designed to function well regardless of facility size and patient mix, the patient care environment and staff were significantly different between the two facilities, which most likely played a significant role in the failure of the EHR implementation at Hospital B.

Training is a key component in EHR implementation. Given that Hospital A had a successful implementation following 2 weeks of training with no patient care responsibilities, staff at Hospital B should have received even more intensive training. While clinician resistance to the use of EHRs is often cited as a roadblock to implementation, it appears that physicians and nurses at Hospital B were not resisting and were engaged and willing. However, it would be difficult at best to achieve the same level of training as that achieved by Hospital A. Given this reality, it is surprising that leadership in the system did not think to rotate some staff from Hospital A to Hospital B to provide additional support "on the ground."

Hospital A had infrastructure to support use of the EHR, while Hospital B did not. Thus, successes that were achieved at Hospital A in a short period of time could not be expected to occur at Hospital B because Hospital B's environment of care was not designed for EHR use. Chances are that simple ergonomic principles such as workstation placement, number of available computers, lighting, and room design were significantly different, leading to additional stress placed on providers at Hospital B.

It is noteworthy that a major pain point at Hospital B was the time required to document patient care, and that the pre-built documentation tools in the system were deemed unusable because they lacked options for recording certain pieces of data. In most EHR systems, such functionality is highly configurable, and it is possible that there was a missed opportunity at Hospital B to tailor the documentation tools to the local needs of the providers and their patient population.

Therefore, what was initially touted as a wildly successful EHR implementation at one hospital in a multisite system rapidly turned into an EHR failure when well-meaning administrators attempted to install the same system into a significantly different environment of care. EHR success depends on many factors; people, software, local configuration, and infrastructure are key. Neglecting to address one of these factors can have significant adverse consequences.

Lessons Learned

- Local nursing and physician involvement in EHR build and testing prior to go-live is essential.
- Anticipate clinician productivity losses and plan accordingly.
- Leverage internal expertise—rotate clinician users from one go-live site to another.
- Provide follow-up training after go-live.

Chapter 3

Putting the Cart before the Horse: IDN Integration

Editor: Christina Stephan

University of Missouri

Contents

Project Categories: inpatient electronic health record

Lessons Learned Categories: implementation approaches, project management, system configuration, system design, workflow

Big complexacademic medical center is an integrated delivery network in a highly competitive urban center. With a strategic vision for growth, mergers and acquisitions are a regular part of the business plan. The combination of two large health systems resulted in a seven-hospital system and a vast ambulatory network of practices. This combination into a new even larger and more complex organization also came with a variety of disparate electronic health record (EHR) systems, and registration, scheduling, and hospital admission, discharge, and transfer (ADT) systems. To leverage the full assets of the organization, the ability to have a single patient record across the health system was a critical goal. After an initial project to align enterprise master patient indices was completed, the next step was to replace legacy EHR systems with one enterprise EHR system.

As the scope of the project to replace the inpatient EHR at two of the hospitals in the newly combined organization took shape, all of the clinical areas were assessed including the emergency department, pharmacy, operating rooms (ORs), and inpatient units. Much of the work of the design of these areas came from the previous implementations at the hospitals prior to the merger. The one area that had not been implemented previously included the ORs and other procedural areas due to their legacy systems in place (e.g., interventional radiology, preadmission testing, cardiac catheterization laboratory, electrophysiology laboratory, endoscopy laboratory). However, partway through the design and build of the 18-month project, information technology (IT) leadership made the decision to also include the replacement of registration and scheduling systems in the procedural areas outside of the ORs. The goal was to get one step ahead of a future EHR integration by replacing the legacy scheduling system used in the procedural areas, which was separate from the hospital ADT system.

In theory, this seemed like a laudable goal to further the vision of standardization of systems. However, many unexpected consequences resulted. With an integrated EHR system tightly linked to the enterprise master patient index and a separate hospital ADT system, the work of booking an OR case became a multiple-step process of adding a patient to the hospital ADT system first and then booking a case in the EHR system. This was a major change in process from the previous system, which was separate from the hospital ADT system. The implementation of the registration and scheduling system changed the workflow of scheduling cases in procedural areas from a centralized process in the admitting office using the hospital ADT system to a decentralized process in the local clinical settings. As a result, staff members had to cross-train in registration functions who had never had this as part of their job responsibilities while also learning to use the new registration and scheduling system.

The impact of these changes became obvious on the first days of the go-live when preregistrations for patients were not completed properly. In many of the procedural areas, staff had to revert to paper even for clinical documentation. For several weeks in the procedural areas, IT staff and vendor resources shadowed clinicians and other staff and provided intensive support to allow for proper functioning. This had a cascading effect on many downstream processes: a patient arrived for a procedure in the OR and did not have the preadmission testing documentation; basic patient billing processes were interrupted; and patient movement throughout the hospital was even impeded. Some of these problems were so severe that dozens of patient procedures were canceled and rescheduled even after the patient had already arrived.

Author's Analysis

Combining the objectives of EHR replacement and scheduling systems replacement, while maintaining a legacy ADT system, was problematic and should not have been done without a thorough understanding of all of the operational and system impacts across the organization. The health system did not address the multilevel change from the clinical frontline, departmental management or administrative roles, or leadership levels across multiple functional areas systems, such as OR scheduling, ADT, and EHR. The integrated system was expected to scale across multiple hospitals, each with a unique organizational culture, as the project goals were ambitiously expanded without concomitant changes in the project management plan or timeline.

Overall, the ADT project created a significant risk to the overall success of the systems integration project, impacting patient care and the stress level of all of the clinicians and staff who had to live through the painful transition process. As a result, the perception of the new IT system was marred by the transition experience, even though the new system was more advanced than the legacy systems being replaced.

Expert Commentary

This case describes mid-implementation scope change to include substantive system integration, which fundamentally changed the nature and complexity of the project. With such a far-reaching shift in project plans and goals, a new or expanded "readiness assessment," implementation plan, and evaluation should have been conducted. HIT implementations in a complex dynamic health care setting are widely accepted as challenging and disruptive to established business processes and clinical workflows (Abbot) with well-documented failures. The health care delivery setting, clinic, or hospital environment can be dynamic and unpredictable, as Abbot and colleagues described "a complex and adaptive system" (CAS). Complex and adaptive settings present unique and ever-changing challenges and require similar features in implementation planning execution and evaluation methods (Leykum).

If the implementation team had undertaken a more detailed initial assessment, possibly using a framework such as with an adaptive plan which accounted for setting context and processes, costly delays may have been reduced or avoided. The optimization of this implementation requires a more comprehensive and multilayered implementation plan with an adaptive deployment process fitted to the situational context while maintaining adherence to the system integration requirements and specifications. While there are many such models and frameworks (Damschroeder, 2009), one planning and evaluation framework that provides a good fit for the system and organization in this case study is known as Practical, Robust Implementation, and Sustainability Model (PRISM) (Feldstein, 2008). The PRISM framework can serve as systematic checklist aiding the implementation team when considering contextual influences in system interactions—adoption, implementation, maintenance, reach, and effectiveness (Feldstein, 2008).

This practical model builds on several others with a focus on key factors for successful implementation, diffusion, maintenance, and outcome measures and encompasses prior models including diffusion of innovations (Rogers, 1995; Ellis, 2008; Bradley, 2004), social ecology (Green, 1996), the PRECEDE/PROCEED model (Green, 1999), as well as quality improvement elements (Chapman, 2012; Berwick, 2003; Sperl-Hillen, 2004; Nolan, 2005).

Lessons Learned

- Scope change is dangerous.
- Integration of disparate systems is subject to contextual and technical barriers.
- A proof of concept and demonstration of the feasibility of a planned system integration can uncover technology, data, and organizational "readiness gaps."

Chapter 4

Hospital Objectives versus Project Timelines: An Electronic Medication Administration Record

Editor: Brian Gugerty
United States Centers for Disease Control and Prevention

Contents

Project Categories: electronic medication administration record (eMAR), inpatient electronic health record (EHR)

Lessons Learned Categories: communication, leadership, staffing resources, technology problems

Case Study

The chief information officer (CIO) at a large teaching hospital, with support from executive management at the hospital, committed to implementing an electronic medication administration record (eMAR) with bedside documentation. The project was to be featured in the hospital's Joint Commission accreditation inspection during the next year. The CIO highlighted the risks inherent in paper MARs including the limited ability for a nurse to have up-to-date information from a patient's paper medication list. A medicine teaching service was selected for the pilot. The hospital had already implemented broad functionality with a robust clinical information system, but the eMAR represented the first initiative that required 100% compliance by clinicians for clinical data entry, rather than the optional computerized provider order entry (CPOE) and clinical documentation modules, diagnostic test results system, and picture archiving communication system (PACS) implemented previously. Several dependencies were identified during the early planning stages for the project:

- Extensive development of an integrated medication management system by the core healthcare information system (HIS) vendor, including new functionality for CPOE, pharmacy medication management, and the eMAR
- Workflow transformation for nurses, pharmacists, and physicians in the medication management process (from order entry by physicians, through order verification and medication preparation by pharmacists, to medication administration and patient assessment by nurses)
- New hardware procurement and installation to support the new eMAR, including a wireless network in the pilot inpatient unit
- Software configuration by the hospital information technology (IT) team and the vendor
- Implementation of the new software
- Training of all involved staff.

The vendor worked with an interdisciplinary team of IT staff, nurses, pharmacists, and physicians to develop the functionality necessary to support best practices for medication management, from ordering to administration. Various committees met monthly, weekly, and even daily, with participants numbering from 2 to 40 depending on the topic addressed. The collective input and collaboration enabled the group to explore new concepts of interdisciplinary medication management, including pharmacy–physician communication for medication dose adjustment and confidential reporting of adverse drug events and medication errors.

Vendors demonstrated workstations on wheels (WOWs) of different sizes, weights, and with varying degrees of mobility, to the nursing and IT groups. The interdisciplinary group evaluated different laptops, recognizing that size, weight, ease of use, and even battery life would be important to the success of the eMAR. Best practices in system design and implementation appeared to be in place for the important patient safety initiative; the hospital continually stressed the importance of the project for the Joint Commission visit.

Project timelines began to slip. With only a few months before the scheduled go-live, the vendor delayed the delivery of the software. Additionally, the hospital's help desk became overburdened with support issues for existing systems, including problems of access to clinical systems; certain functions of the HIS; and properly functioning printers, computers, and monitors. In the final month before go-live, the mobile computer vendor announced a delay in the delivery of the WOWs for the pilot.

Several clinician leaders requested that the project wait until all systems could be fully tested and until the hospital refocused on routine operations after the scheduled Joint Commission visit, but the CIO remained committed to completing the initiative because it was to be a highlight in the Joint Commission visit. Ultimately, all devices arrived on the eMAR pilot medicine inpatient unit, the IT team implemented the software, and the nursing unit went live. For several days, the IT team staffed the pilot unit around the clock with nurses trained in the new eMAR to assist physicians, pharmacists, and nurses with the rollout. Clinical and administrative staff reacted well to the rollout, and the Joint Commission inspection team noted the achievement as evidence of leadership in the field of healthcare technology. Then, the focus on the pilot unit faded.

Over the next few weeks, several changes occurred in the pilot unit. The nurses who regularly staffed the unit, and whose average age was about 10 years older than those who selected the WOWs for the eMAR, complained of difficulty reading the small fonts on the screens of the WOWs. Nurses who rotated to the medicine unit after the heavily staffed rollout said they received inadequate training on the eMAR and preferred the previous paper MAR. The WOWs began crashing and freezing during regular use, requiring frequent reboots; nurses found that leaving the devices standing in the nursing station prevented such dysfunction but also prevented bedside use of the technology. Calls to the IT help desk for support went unanswered for up to 72 h. Meanwhile, the CIO continued to discuss the successful pilot, unaware that nurses on the pilot unit had begun to print out a paper MAR for use on each shift; the paper MAR could be brought to the patient's bedside. The nurses relied on the paper MAR for patient care, updating changes in the patient's record at the end of the shift, just as they did prior to the rollout of the eMAR. During follow-up interviews at the pilot site, the nurses on the unit were surprised to learn that corporate management at the health system celebrated the achievement of the hospital's pilot eMAR; the nurses described the implementation as a disaster and a waste of resources. They had reverted to their original paper-based practices.

Author's Analysis

This failed implementation highlights many lessons about HIT initiatives, including failed project planning, failed technology configuration and testing, and failed leadership. Most importantly, clinical IT initiatives require the leadership of the clinician end-users. If the nursing department had led or co-led the eMAR initiative, the ensuing problems would have been less likely to develop unmonitored. As the nurses discovered problems with software, hardware, or training, the nursing department would have had the authority to slow, modify, or halt the initiative, instead of remaining unaware of the issue. If the project team had not faced an arbitrary deadline, such as a Joint Commission visit, but rather focused on completing the implementation successfully, adequate time might have allowed the discovery of the inadequate wireless network and staff training. Also, the experience underscores the role of the IT help desk during implementation and support of information systems. Help desks and IT support must create support processes sufficient for the applications and environments in hospitals, which include immediate response to problems in acute care areas. Often, the cost and staff of an enlarged help desk are not included as part of a system rollout, which can lead to support shortfalls after go-live. As a tool, IT offers opportunities to transform healthcare in an unprecedented manner; however, a CIO must strategize to work within the given resources of a health system or to expand those resources as required for expanding initiatives. In the case of the failed eMAR, a technology strategy outpaced the operating plan of a hospital as well as the capacity of an IT department. The resulting failure cost money and staff efficiency, and possibly compromised clinical care.

Editor's Commentary

The eMAR pilot project described in this case study was ambitious from the outset. Its success depended on software to be developed by the software vendor, workflow changes across clinical departments, and a host of new hardware from WOWs to wireless networks. Also, there was a lot riding on the success of the pilot because it was a showcase for the medical center for the Joint

Commission visit. An experienced project manager would have sized up this project from the very beginning as one with an inordinately high degree of risk of failure emanating from multiple sources. Hindsight is, relatively speaking, easy, however.

Yet despite the "could have been predicted" software and hardware delays and the "should have been anticipated" help desk degradation all occurring prior to go-live (go-live is usually defined as the 1- to 4-week period after the system is turned on), they pulled it off! The pilot go-live was a success. Then, a classic occurrence happened. The powers that be declared victory, moved on to other things, and withdrew resources. Research has demonstrated three phases of healthcare IT projects: pre-implementation, go-live, and post-implementation. All three phases should be optimally managed for the projects' objectives to stand a chance of being achieved and the gains from the new processes and technology to solidify, thus becoming the new norm for the clinical environment. Then and only then can closure truly occur.

It appears that this project had some serious faults in the pre-implementation period, including poor project planning, failed technical configuration, and near absence of testing, as the author pointed out in the discussion on lessons learned. Despite these shortcomings, the pilot could have been salvaged if the focus and resources showered on the project during go-live remained, even in an attenuated form, during the post-implementation period. All the issues mentioned as real problems appeared after the system was turned on and especially after the extra support during go-live was withdrawn: small font sizes, inadequate training of nurses floating to the pilot unit, crashing WOWs, and near total collapse of the help desk. Taken individually with merely adequate resources and proper management focus, these issues could have been easily resolved. Adequate and proper attention during the post-implementation period would likely have resulted in the new workflows, which the author did not state were problematic and therefore were presumably acceptable, solidifying the patient safety improvements being truly actualized. Some project managers and IT/clinical informatics staff treat such a new application in just this way for a pilot, providing adequate or even light pre-implementation planning, showering the go-live phase with support, and addressing problems in the post-implementation period. When most of the issues are resolved on the pilot unit, where they should be expected to occur, then and only then is the application rolled out to other units.

I could not agree more with the author's statement that "most importantly, clinical IT initiatives require the leadership of the clinician end-users" if by leadership it is not understood that the clinician end-user literally has to be leading the project. Perhaps the widely used (outside of the U.S., anyway) PRINCE2 project management methodology (www.axelos.com/best-practice-solutions/prince2), where the project manager reports to a project board composed of an executive sponsor from the organization, a senior representative of the end-user community, and a senior technical representative throughout the entire project, could allow effective clinical end-user leadership. The glaring leadership failure in this case study, in my mind at least, was with the CIO focusing on the achievement of his or her apparent real goal of creating "evidence of leadership in the field of healthcare technology" at the expense of solidifying carefully crafted new processes that improved patient safety.

Lessons Learned

- Clinician leadership is critical to HIT initiatives.
- IT support is critical during, and just after, a go-live.
- Effective project planning includes proper resource management.

Chapter 5

Clinical Quality Improvement or Administrative Oversight: Clinical Decision Support Systems

Editor: Jonathan Leviss
Greater New Bedford Community Health Center

Contents

Project Categories: computerized provider order entry (CPOE), inpatient electronic health record (EHR)

Lessons Learned Categories: communication, workflow

Case Study

Hospital administration was proud because clinicians at their small hospital were using a new clinical decision support system that alerted them when standard clinical practices were not followed. The system checked laboratory and medication orders against diagnoses in one specialty area, matched those diagnoses with symptoms for conditions, and also issued alerts when various data indicated abnormalities. The new system, the administration was convinced, was improving quality. It worked so well that they wanted to extend its use from inpatient to ambulatory care.

Direct observations and questions of end-users raised additional questions, however. Some attending physicians said the system was good, but was mainly for less-skilled clinicians or for residents who still needed to learn. Those residents and clinicians said it was good for reviewing diagnostic criteria and guidelines, but the alerts did not really provide new information or result in changed orders or practice. Further, in order to get past the requirement that all required symptoms had to be entered before the diagnosis would be accepted by the software, residents entered the symptoms they knew to be required, not necessarily the symptoms the patient had. The head of resident training knew there were problems, but also wanted to support administration.

Administration had tried to do everything right. They used a participatory design approach, and the head of quality assurance, himself a physician, was a key figure in the project. A local computer scientist had produced the system in close consultation with clinical and quality assurance staff. All clinicians were trained to use the system, as were residents when they began their rotations at this hospital.

Clinical staff, however, did not feel involved in creating the system or in determining when and how it was used. Clinicians saw the system as the administration's reporting tool, whereas the administration described the system as benefiting clinicians and improving clinical care. Further, the clinical staff felt pressured, recently having gone through a merger with a nearby larger hospital and having to adjust to new ways of doing things. For them, the clinical decision support system was yet another burden.

Even with the problems, the system did report mismatches between symptoms and diagnosis, diagnosis and orders for medications or laboratory work, and alerts for abnormalities. The use of this system was well in advance of other hospitals, and the administration was proud of the progress made. They did not know about the underlying issues, but had wisely brought in others to investigate before rolling out the system for outpatient care. Administration and the clinicians had different notions of success.

Author's Analysis

Lesson 1: Watch what people do rather than depend only on what they say. The ways residents were gaming the system were not apparent until outside consultants observed residents showing each other how to enter data from a new patient into the system, explaining ways to circumvent some of the system's controls. Of course, it was not presented quite that starkly, but almost.

Lesson 2: Pay attention to data quality and to the influencing factors. Quality assurance was based on the data entered by the clinicians. Quality assurance staff thought that data entered by clinicians improved care, as documented by reports derived from these data. Clinicians, though, were sometimes entering data that reflected their understanding of system requirements rather than their examination of the patient, even when they knew the two might be in conflict. Consider trustworthiness of data in light of system requirements and reward structures.

Lesson 3: Incorporation of practice guidelines into clinical decision support systems does not necessarily result in increased compliance with the guidelines if workarounds and "system gaming" occur.

Lesson 4: There always will be problems. The trick is to identify the problems before they cause harm. Evaluation is necessary and should be done in skillful and nonthreatening ways that can uncover what is happening on the floors, in treatment areas, in residents' rooms—anywhere health information technology (HIT) is used, or supposed to be used. Often, evaluation needs to be independent—either independent from the project team or independent from the health system.

Editor's Commentary

The case study highlights three key lessons: integrating effective clinical decision support is challenging; clinicians are peoplewho work in health systems, and they are affected by the current issues and culture of their organization; and projects require effective ongoing evaluation.

The wealth of literature on failed and successful computerized decision support documents the difficulties in introducing the right knowledge to physicians at the right point in care delivery without creating burdensome work or providing information that is already known or irrelevant to a particular patient. Additional references discussing this topic are included at the end of this case discussion.

Introducing information systems to clinical care requires changing the way clinicians interact with patients and gather and process information *and* challenges their decision-making at the point of care in front of both colleagues and patients. These changes can be stressful for clinicians; if other major stressors already exist, such as a recent hospital merger, new programs to measure clinicians' quality performance, or decreased physician income, then the stress of a new HIT system may be impossible to bear. Organizations need to recognize the stress level and tolerance for change of their own staffs and plan accordingly so that successful initiatives can be introduced at appropriate times. A delayed project that succeeds is more valuable, and less expensive, than a project started on time that fails.

Objective evaluation is critical to determine what aspects of a project should be continued, or expanded, and what aspects should be modified. Depending on the size of the project, scope, and complexity, an evaluation could be extensive or brief. Part of ongoing evaluation also requires regular, open communication between the end-user community, the health system management, and the information technology (IT) project team. Most health systems that succeed in creating the open dialogue between these groups have a system of interdisciplinary informatics governance—models range from interdisciplinary committees to role-based committees with committee chairs joining together in interdisciplinary forums to foster open communication. Both approaches typically involve quality management. The essential component is the opportunity for hospital management, IT, and the clinicians to express their views, concerns, and experiences, while also listening to those of the other groups. Transparent discussions about positive and negative aspects of HIT initiatives help reveal problems early for effective resolution. Sometimes, outside expertise is required to objectively evaluate a project and to remove any positive or negative bias; "outside" could mean simply someone other than the project team members or a contracted consultant with expertise in the area of the project for evaluation. Large health systems could even rotate individuals to facilities other than their primary site of work to serve as evaluators. Evaluation should be part of the improvement cycle of an HIT project, if not throughout the entire project life cycle, providing insight to further improve the initiative.

Lessons Learned

- Expect problems; the key is evaluating projects to identify problems and address them early.
- IT quality assurance requires some in-depth review of data, clinician workflow, and other details of a new process and/or technology.
- Organizational culture and current circumstances may limit the ability for members to change processes. A culture that inhibits direct and open communication leads to diminished stakeholder input in favor of conflict avoidance behaviors that often defeat the intent of HIT systems.

Additional Reading

Kuperman, G.J., A. Bobb, T.H. Payne, A.J. Avery, T.K. Gandhi, G. Burns, D.C. Classen, D.W. Bates. 2007. Medication-related clinical decision support in computerized provider order entry systems: A review. *Journal of the American Medical Informatics Association* 14 (1):29–40.

Kuperman, G.J., R.M. Reichley, T.C. Bailey. 2006. Using commercial knowledge bases for clinical decision support: Opportunities, hurdles, and recommendations. *Journal of the American Medical Informatics Association* 13 (4):369–71.

Killelea, B.K., R. Kaushal, M. Cooper, G.J. Kuperman. 2007. To what extent do pediatricians accept computer-based dosing suggestions? *Pediatrics* 119 (1):e69–75.

Chapter 6

A Legacy Shortfall Reinforces a New Endeavor: Business Intelligence

Editor: Jonathan Leviss

Greater New Bedford Community Health Center

Contents

Project Categories: inpatient electronic health record (EHR), population health and analytics

Lessons Learned Categories: communication, data model, staffing resources, system configuration

The board of directors for a hospital system made a significant investment in a medical quality initiative. The medical executive committee recognized the need for a business intelligence (BI) platform for outcomes analytics as an absolute requirement to maintain top performance in mandatory reporting and to support a culture that managed on metrics. The result was a multimillion-dollar, 3-year project to create an enterprise-wide data system to provide traditional and predictive analytics for three major clinical quality initiatives.

Like many initiatives, the project had its share of scope creep and cost overruns, resulting in management criticism and project team concern. In advance of the go-live for the BI platform, the lead analyst and an integration expert were collaborating on the cornerstone project for quality. This was a BI subsystem which would provide the main medical group physicians with insight to their quality performance and overhead burden. The information to fulfill this need was complex and broadly represented core transactional systems. The physicians helped create a list of process indicators for delivery of care, performance on reported metrics, use of evidence-based medicine, and patient's costs and satisfaction from treatment.

As the quality project was progressing, a new ambulatory surgery center launched in outlying communities. The center was planned to be a major source of revenue for the growing health system. The case mix for this facility was very favorable with projections to keep operating rooms (ORs) fully booked. The OR turnover processes were lean, and schedulers were very keen on maintaining high access for all surgeons. Soon after the opening of the new ambulatory surgery center, there was an unacceptable dip in revenue due to idle time in the major ORs. Initial evaluations could not explain the problem as the surgery scheduling system showed consistently booked schedules, with a favorable amount of high-margin surgeries in the mix.

The data quality processes for the new surgery scorecard, however, showed an imbalance in admissions data in the new analytics system. When the lead analyst reported to the steering committee, he noted that total admissions and total admitting messages did not balance. Since the surgery metrics were only reporting on contribution margin, all cancelation messages were being omitted from the analytics platform; additionally, the scheduling system itself did not show cancelations in its standard reports. The coincidence of cancelations, and the gap in the scheduling system to identify causes for idle OR time, was perfectly timed to create a great save.

When the cancelation messages were installed in the new analytic system, it was painfully obvious that a limited number of surgeons were associated with same-day cancelations on booked OR cases. The types of cases, and the specific surgeons, allowed the health system to make inquiries directly with the surgeons and schedulers involved. The same-day cancelations fell into two types: patient cancelations and no-shows. With these new insights, the OR administration investigated further.

To address the patient-initiated cancelations, perioperative nurses were interviewed as well as staff at two surgeon's offices. A team reviewed the cases to date and discovered that the canceled patients were actually arriving for their surgeries, but were sent home due to poor preparation (most commonly due to having eaten earlier that day or not stopping anticoagulants). Education, and providing better patient preparation, quickly closed that gap. The remaining physician associated with idle OR times had a scheduler who was booking patients before preauthorization was complete. The health system reworked the processes with input from the community physician's offices, and ultimately provided streamlined OR access for fully authorized and confirmed patients. The immediate result was an ambulatory surgery program that had stellar utilization, quality and physician satisfaction, plus health system-wide support for the expanded BI team and the new platform it was implementing.

Author's Analysis

The case above served as an object lesson for the data analytics team; the very data which had no value to one specific use case was crucial to revealing an operational gap.

Like many health IT specialists, the lead analyst and integration expert had come from other industries. One was from the pharmaceutical industry and the other from a medical supply company. While both of those industries are broadly considered 'healthcare industry', they operate, respectively, more like a process manufacturing company and a packaged goods distributor than like a clinical provider. As such, the systems, process, and metrics developed by these two specialists were all aligned to producing intentional, transactional, and rational products and services. The systems in which the data was generated were designed to capture facts related to processes which themselves were optimized for producing specific results. Typically, the analysis is partitioned to analyses organizationally 'close' to the transactional sources.

Some healthcare processes lend themselves to conventional measurement. These processes are reasonably repeatable and standard. Preauthorization, admission data entry, and cycle time for a laboratory test machine are examples of processes that have a limited number of workflows and deviations. They are less sensitive to patient behavior, misadventure, and knowledge work by clinical providers. Data cubes and routine reporting are sufficient for daily operations and continuous improvement.

However, other healthcare processes are unlike most other systems. In many of these cases, patient behavior and provider behavior drive a bulk of transactions along with chance and misadventure.

Digging deep for cause and effect, or identifying hidden patterns of variability requires more sophisticated analysis and more granular data. In order to find the root cause, the BI team actually had to look at the unscrubbed data and recognize that the pattern of data 'failures' was itself pointing to the root cause. This would not have been possible without the skilled BI team nor the new BI platform being developed and implemented. Also, without the standard management reports' failure to highlight the cause of OR revenue shortfall, the value of the BI platform might have been continually questioned and the project ultimately might have been shut down.

Since this one application yielded a $300,000 save to revenue, the BI team began a program to identify unusual patterns in staged data. Over the course of 6 months, the BI platform cost overruns were offset by around $500,000 in other cost savings.

Editor's Commentary

From the author's case report and analysis, one has to wonder if the BI platform would have been supported if the team had not happened upon the early success with uncovering the ambulatory surgery center's revenue shortfall. This early unplanned success well illustrates why the project's technology (i.e., data feeds) and expertise were different from, and superior to prior quality improvement efforts. As the author states, with the solid support to continue, other similar scenarios appeared that further proved the value of the new BI approach. Otherwise, this case might have been written about the failure of a new BI platform initiative, rather than its success due to the failure of the preexisting program.

Lessons Learned

- The skill set of the informatics team working on a project is at least as important asthe technology itself, and sometimes more important.
- A project's return on investment (ROI) is dependent on specific metrics, which can change during a project due to many reasons (e.g., market forces, new problems within an organization, or even organizational political change).
- Complex and expensive projects best maintain support when predefined short-term objectives are recognized and valued by administrative leadership and other opinion leaders.
- Communication about progress and early achievements in a long and expensive project is critical to maintaining organizational support (including resources and leadership commitment).

Chapter 7

When Value Endures: Legacy Data Viewer

Editor: Melissa Baysari
University of Sydney

Contents

Project Categories: inpatient electronic health record (EHR)

Lessons Learned Categories: communication, implementation approaches, system design, training

A large hospital replaced its in-house developed system of electronic clinical records with a new commercial integrated electronic health record (EHR) called "Humongous". The legacy system consisted of several different programs each covering different specialties or areas of the hospital, e.g., laboratory, anesthesia, radiology, and emergency department (ED) as well as two physician order entry systems. Because of these multiple legacy programs, the hospital information technology (IT) department had also developed an integrated viewer ("UniView") to provide a single point of access to clinical notes, reports, and laboratory results that were available in its various clinical programs. After the new integrated system "Humongous" was implemented, the majority of the legacy systems were retired; however, "UniView" was continued in operation to provide access to legacy data more than 3 years old which had not been loaded into "Humongous". However, since no major changes in the configuration of "UniView" were made, it also continued to provide access to new data that was entered into "Humongous". The implementation of "Humongous" proceeded smoothly overall, with no more problems than to be expected in a new implementation. In fact, post-implementation user surveys showed a high degree of physician satisfaction with "Humongous", with many of them commenting that they saw little to no impact on their daily workflows.

Three years after the conversion, it was recognized that the security features of "UniView" were no longer in line with current best practices, and that these deficits could not be remediated because of "UniView's" architecture. To provide continued access to legacy data not in "Humongous", a new viewer was designed and implemented by the IT department ("BaseView"). This implementation of "BaseView" was only designed to provide access to legacy data; new data would not be viewable. Part of the process of training users to use the new viewer involved informing them that new data would not be entered into "BaseView"; at this point, it was discovered that approximately 40% of the physician staff had been using "UniView" routinely to access clinical notes and laboratory results rather than using "Humongous". In fact, many of these users did not know how to find information they used on a daily basis in "Humongous", which had now been implemented over 3 years ago. These users' dependence on "UniView" resulted in additional training having to be provided to use "Humongous". As these "UniView-dependent" users, many of whom were concentrated in surgical specialties, received this further remedial training in "Humongous", acceptance of many of its screen views was so poor that the decision was made by clinical leadership to create new screen views that were more like the corresponding views in "UniView" that had previously been well accepted by the physician users. These training and reconfiguration efforts consumed a lot of significant amount of IT resources to in effect partially re-implement a 3-year-old system.

Author's Analysis

Most users of electronic clinical systems typically view them simply as tools to get their daily work done, much in the way they would view a telephone or pager. Once they find a way to get the information that they need, they will usually continue to use that method unless shown a better way or are forced to change. In this case, a viewer that was intended to provide access to legacy data only continued to provide access to new data; the significance of this was underappreciated by informatics and IT personnel, as well as by clinical leadership. Because users were still able to access the data and information they needed in the way they always had accessed it, they had no reason to change. In fact, once forced to change, they found the new system to be significantly less "user friendly" than the old system. In this case, not taking into account human nature, clinical workflows and basic principles of user experience led to a costly rework several years after an apparently successful implementation. This situation could have been mitigated prior to implementation by the use of stimulations and user experience testing to identify the workflows that clinicians actually used to access information, rather than an idealized workflow that might have been desired by IT and clinical leadership. It is worthwhile to remember that in the real world, users will always find a way that is quickest and easiest for them to get their tasks accomplished.

Editor's Commentary

This is a very interesting case study that demonstrates the importance of monitoring system use and seeking feedback from users post-implementation of a new system. These methods would have identified much earlier on that 40% of physicians were using the integrated viewer "UniView", instead of the new "Humongous" system to access patient information. Modifications could then have been made to training and/or the new system to improve uptake of the new EHR.

A question that immediately springs to mind is, why did users continue to use "UniView"? We all prefer technology that is familiar, that we know how to use well and are comfortable with. In their analysis, the author highlights that users saw no reason to change, because they were able to access information via "UniView" in the same way they always had. This suggests that the benefits of the new EHR were perhaps not effectively communicated to users. We all require strong motivation to change the way we work and to learn a new system. What provided the motivation here? Were users aware of the limitations of the legacy systems? "UniView" appeared to address the main problem (i.e., poor integration)—so what was the rationale for switching to the new EHR? And were users on board with the transition?

The author suggests that the organization did not take into account human nature, clinical workflows, and basic principles of user experience. Perhaps an in-depth exploration of the way physicians practiced their work to identify what worked well with the legacy systems and what users liked about "UniView", and then incorporating knowledge gained into design of the new EHR would have resulted in a more useful, usable, and therefore used system. Complementing pre-implementation usability testing with some post-implementation observations of how the systems are actually used in practice is extremely valuable. This would allow implementers to determine the "fit" between systems and users in their context of use.

Lessons Learned

- New system use should be monitored post-implementation.
- Understanding clinician workflow is critical to supporting or changing the workflow with new systems.

Chapter 8

Usability Reigns Supreme: Medication Alerts

Editor: Christina Stephan

University of Missouri

Contents

Project Categories: inpatient electronic health record (EHR), computerized physician order entry (CPOE)

Lessons Learned Categories: system configuration, system design

A 600-bed hospital implemented a new vendor electronic health record (EHR). The EHR utilized a third-party medication database to provide alerts on drug-drug interactions. The alerting system recognized three classes of interactions: (1) drug allergy, (2) drug-drug interaction "severe", and (3) drug-drug interaction "major". Clinical leadership, because of a desire to utilize the electronic system to reduce the number of critical incidents due to drug-drug interactions, made a decision to configure the system to provide alerts to ordering clinicians when any of these interactions occurred. The "major" drug-drug interaction category included very rare and unusual reported interactions, many of them between drugs that were commonly used together. There were thousands of such interactions in this so-called major category.

For example, the intravenous analgesic fentanyl and the intravenous antiemetic ondansetron were categorized in the database as a "major" interaction and thus triggered an alert in the system. The alert was included because possible interactions between the two had been reported to the FDA approximately eight times over a 15-year period. However, at this hospital which performed nearly 30,000 surgical procedures per year, these two medications were ordered together on over for at least 90% of all surgical patients. During this time, the drug-drug interaction had never been identified as the focus of a suspected critical incident.

Like many medication alert systems, the alert was configured as a "pop-up" window with a hard stop. This prevented the ordering clinician from continuing with entering orders until he or she had taken an action to address the alert pop-up. The alert occurred every time the two medications were ordered. Subsequently, routine order sets generated several drug-drug interaction alerts. As commonly happens with pop-up windows that are encountered repeatedly, the clinicians often quickly clicked through the alerts and the vast majority of these alerts were overridden.

Clinicians often encountered another usability issue. The visual appearance of the drug-drug interaction alert and the allergy alert was almost identical unless they were examined very closely. Due to the visual similarity, many of the allergy alerts were overridden as well because clinicians did not recognize them as allergy per se, but instead thought they were the most commonly encountered (and thus believed to be most clinically insignificant) "major" drug-drug interaction alerts. In fact, several medication allergy incidents were reported to the hospital pharmacy. The ordering clinician overrode an allergy alert believing it to be a routinely encountered "major" drug-drug interaction alert.

After 5 years of use, an audit of the system showed that over 95% of all drug-drug interaction alerts were overridden; over 87% of drug allergy alerts were overridden as well. Based on the volume of alerts that were generated, it was estimated that across the entire hospital, between 12 and 18 h of clinician time was being spent every day to address drug-drug interaction alerts. After this audit was performed, clinical leadership reevaluated the alert settings. A decision was made to change the alerts so that the "major" drug-drug interactions no longer produced an alert. After this change, the percentage of allergy alerts that were overridden dropped, there was actually a decrease in the number of medication incidents reported to the pharmacy, and it was estimated that the time spent dealing with drug-drug interaction alerts was reduced to approximately 2–3 h every day across the hospital. A conservative estimate is that over the preceding 5 years, an estimated 13,000 h of clinician time (or greater than 1 FTE) had been spent dealing with EHR alerts that were likely of little or no real clinical value.

Author's Analysis

Medication alerting to avoid errors and interaction problems is viewed as a significant potential benefit of electronic health records. However, to be of value, the systems must be designed to fit clinical workflow efficiently. Pop-up windows with hard stops are commonly seen by users in their non-healthcare online experience and are associated with a highly negative connotation. In general, clinicians will find the easiest way possible to get past the pop-up window to complete the medication ordering task Additionally, the visual similarity of the allergy alert pop-up to the "major" drug-drug interaction alert pop-up was a poor choice from a usability standpoint. In the mental model of most clinical users, the allergy alert could be described as a significant alert, while the "major" drug-drug interactions that are of rare clinical significance could be considered more of a nuisance alert. In this way, the alerting situation was very similar to the well-described phenomenon of alarm fatigue that occurs when clinical alarms are set with too high of a sensitivity. Better examination and understanding of clinical workflows, standardized practice patterns, and usability testing could have mitigated this issue and saved valuable clinician time that is better spent caring for patients than dealing with the electronic record.

Expert Commentary

This case study illustrates how the usability of an EHR can become an underappreciated feature of the health record interface screens associated with costly unexpectedly negative impact in clinical operations. Furthermore, potentially unsafe use of specific time-saving EHR tools can introduce medical errors. In addition to the widespread belief that computerized physician order entry (CPOE), coupled with medication safety alerts, improves patient care safety and quality, these tools save clinician time and clinical operating costs. However, when poorly designed and executed, as described in this case, the medication alerts, a critical safety feature was ignored, and likely an annoyance to those who would have benefitted from its use. Worse, the design and implementation choices, such as the lack of a distinctive appearance and tailored alert triggers, caused apparent difficulty in discernment between a medication and a patient allergy alert with important patient safety concerns. The underlying usability design flaws may have been detected prior to implementation if the implementation team discussed usability during planning sessions or detected the issue in early testing or trials in a limited clinical setting.

From the case write-up, it appears that the planning process was adequate, which leads one to question whether clinical stakeholders were fully engaged in planning and testing new system features.

Succinctly stated by Ratwani and colleagues,

> EHR usability can dramatically affect clinicians' satisfaction with the system and the system's ability to enable consistently safe and high-quality care. Decisions made during EHR implementation can have a profound impact on the usability and safety of the system; improving implementation processes to optimize EHR usability and safety can help EHRs reach their full potential.
>
> *Ratwani (2017)*

While multiple factors can impact optimization of EHR investment, implementation, and adoption, usability issues are a key determining factor. Published studies and accounts in the medical literature that address usability factors continue to increase. However, this continues to be a major implementation challenge. Many approaches to improve usability have been described, such as the use of a subject matter expert, EHR user simulation laboratory, and learning directly from other healthcare organizations, as well as other methods. A key lesson learned in this case study would be to test and review use trials while involving a wide range of stakeholders and experts with maintenance of an ongoing dialogue of potential causes of EHR usability pitfalls.

Lessons Learned

- Minimize interruption alerts to avoid alert fatigue.
- Test all new features with real end-users for usability issues.
- Regularly review metrics to assess value and impact of alerts.

Additional Reading

Dexheimer JW, Kirkendall ES, Kouril M, Hagedorn PA, Duan LL, Mahdi M, Szczesniak R, Spooner A. The effects of medication alerts on prescriber response in a pediatric hospital. *Appl Clin Inform*. April 2017; 8(2): 491–501. doi:10.4338/ACI-2016-10-RA-0168.

Wright A, Ai A, Ash J, Wiesel JF, Hickman TT, Aaron S, McEvoy D, Borkowski S, Pavithra I Dissanayake, Embi P, Galanter W, Harper J, Kassakian SZ, Ramoni R, Schreiber R, Sirajuddin A, Bates DW, Sittig DF. Clinical decision support alert malfunctions: analysis and empirically derived taxonomy. *J Am Med Inform Assoc*. May 2018; 25(5): 496–506. doi:10.1093/jamia/ocx106.

Chapter 9

A Mobile App That Didn't: Antibiotic Approvals

Editor: David Leander
Dartmouth

Contents

Project Categories: Inpatient electronic health record (EHR), computerized provider order entry (CPOE)

Lessons Learned Categories: communication, leadership/governance, workflow

Our tertiary teaching hospital, like many institutions, adopts a traffic light system for its antimicrobial restrictions. Green antimicrobials (e.g. cefazolin) can be used anytime, while red antimicrobials (e.g. tigecycline) are always restricted, and prescribers are required to obtain approval from an infectious disease (ID) physician, typically via phone, before being allowed to prescribe. Orange antimicrobials (e.g. ciprofloxacin) are tricky. These can be used for some indications without approval, and for other indications, approval is needed. Once approved, the ID physician issues the prescriber with an approval number and the prescriber should document this approval number in the computerized provider order entry (CPOE) system.

Audits at the hospital have shown that compliance with the hospital's antimicrobial policy is poor. Antimicrobial stewardship (AMS) functionality within the CPOE is limited, making it difficult to identify restricted antimicrobials, to document approvals, and to review expired approvals. Prior investigation showed that prescribers do not typically seek approval from ID physicians for restricted antimicrobials, that the indications documented are sometimes inaccurate, and that approval numbers were not consistently documented in the CPOE. In an attempt to streamline the antimicrobial approval process, the AMS team, in collaboration with pharmacy, the IT department, and a human factors expert, designed a mobile application to facilitate AMS.

The purpose-built app extracted Orange and Red antimicrobial prescription information from the CPOE system and displayed this in an easy-to-read list. Prescriptions could be sorted and filtered, allowing for users to quickly identify which antimicrobials had been ordered, which needed approval, and which had been approved already. AMS team members could approve the use of restricted antimicrobials from within the app, providing these staff with a means of undertaking *antimicrobial reviews on the go*. For example, while rounding in the intensive care unit (ICU), the ID physician could filter patients in the app to see only those in the ICU, and review and approve prescriptions as they navigated through the ward round.

In principle, the app met a need for access to antimicrobial information, intelligently filtered, and easily sorted. But in reality, the app was not used as intended. Brief education sessions were delivered to prospective users, particularly the AMS team and pharmacists, and this resulted in an initial burst of activity in the app. But this was followed by a gradual decline in use over several months until 1 year post-implementation, and the app was no longer utilized by any provider group. The app's full benefit would only have been realized if adopted by all relevant parties: by the AMS team to approve, pharmacists to review or escalate, and by prescribers to review. In the absence of an agreed-upon workflow, the app became less valuable for providers. When not used by providers, there was little incentive for the AMS team to take the time to document their approval into the app. When not used by the AMS team, there was limited information for others to review.

Although intended to meet a need for mobile reviews on the go, in the end the app did not quite get there.

Author's Analysis

There were a number of factors that likely contributed to the mobile app not being utilized and so not achieving its desired benefits.

- Awareness of the app was poor among some staff groups. More targeted education, especially of prescribers, was needed.
- Roles and responsibilities surrounding the app's use were not clearly defined. Interdependencies between staff were also not highlighted. That is, all provider groups needed to use the app for it to be effective.
- Information inputted into the app could not be sent back to the CPOE. If an antimicrobial was approved from within the app, users were required to log into the app to review the approval status.

Overall, the key barriers to adoption are related to awareness and workflow. All stakeholders needed to be aware of how the app would fit with current workflows, its limitations, and roles and responsibilities of staff with respect to workflow. Experience has taught us that understanding how work is done and how an intervention is likely to support or disrupt that work is critical prior to a system's implementation. What this case highlights is that communicating that information to all provider groups to ensure a shared understanding of interdependencies among teams is also essential for uptake and optimal use of an IT intervention.

Editor's Commentary

The author makes sound observations and assessments. One element missing from this discussion is the "why" behind the antibiotic approval policies and "why" implementing a mobile app for antimicrobial approval could achieve an important goal for the organization. Perhaps more description and an education effort for the prescribers about the clinical importance of antimicrobial resistance with particular bacteria strains could have encouraged more use of this app. The implementation of the app also seemed unilateral, in that the ID physicians were pushing for its adoption; however, other prescribers were not necessarily supportive. This app's failed implementation highlights the divide in priorities that can occur across any hospital; in this case, the ID physicians were concerned about antibiotic stewardship, whereas other clinicians were focused on ordering their preferred medication for the patient quickly and easily. Lastly, perhaps what was needed was simply a more effective communication effort to address the differing perceptions of both the AMS problem and the mobile app solution, which might have more effectively supported the adoption of the app.

Lessons Learned

- All users must see the value in new technology, or they will not adopt it.
- Different user groups have different unique workflows and workflow needs.
- Always try to overcommunicate to all involved.

Chapter 10

Disruptive Workflow Disrupts the Rollout: Electronic Medication Reconciliation

Editor: Gail Keenan
University of Florida

Contents

Project Categories: inpatient electronic health record (EHR), computerized provider order entry (CPOE), electronic medication administration record (eMAR), pharmacy information system (IS)

Lessons Learned Categories: implementation approaches, leadership/governance, system design, workflow

Case Study

After several years of a poorly focused information technology (IT) effort, a four-hospital health system created a new health informatics department and hired a chief medical information officer (CMIO) in 2006. The IT direction changed dramatically thereafter, as the organization entered into partnership with a single electronic health record (EHR) vendor. Between 2006 and 2011, the health system implemented nursing documentation, electronic medication administration record (eMAR), bar code medication administration (BCMA), longitudinal allergies and medication histories, and computerized provider order entry CPOE) at all four hospitals. After having received system-wide approval in 2010, the health system moved quickly in 2011 to add a fully electronic medication reconciliation program into its EHR as a means of meeting American Recovery and Reinvestment Act (ARRA) of 2009 Meaningful Use requirements.

The new medication reconciliation program was quite different from the existing system in that it was fully electronic, required a pharmacist to interview each patient on admission, and generated a new discharge report. In the existing medication reconciliation system, a clinician (nurse, physician, or pharmacist) entered all patient allergies and home medications into a longitudinal component of the EHR. Once gathered in the EHR, this data supported the generation of a paper report that was used to complete the medication reconciliation process. Providers liked the process because it was easy to complete, often taking as little as 5 s for reconciling a complex patient medication list. Clinicians also acknowledged its value and ease of use in making decisions about which medications to continue and discontinue at each transition of care (such as admission, transfer level of care, and discharge). The use of pharmacists to carry out the major portion of the medication reconciliation in the new system would involve a major workflow change necessitating hiring of additional pharmacists.

The leaders of the organization were nonetheless very supportive of the new system, believing that assigning the pharmacist a primary role in medication reconciliation was an excellent strategy for improving medication outcome. In fact, the enthusiasm for the new system was so high that the purchasing committee and hospital executive were willing to waive a small pilot because of the need to turn on the system in all four hospitals at the same time. As a result, the impact onworkflow was never fully assessed prior to purchase and implementation of the new system. Go-live thus commenced without a clear understanding of how the system would affect workflow. Once live, however, it was quickly learned that the entry and reconciliation of complex medication lists was taking most pharmacists more than 30 min. Even the most savvy EHR pharmacists required at least 20 min to complete complex reconciliations. Two weeks after go-live at all hospitals, workflow delays and provider dissatisfaction became problematic and the CMIO and hospital executives made a decision to discontinue the use of the new medication reconciliation program.

Author's Analysis

There were a number of points of failure that resulted from the lack of attention to important details. The health system did not consider and should have considered the following prior to implementation:

- Set an acceptable time for completing electronic medication reconciliation for each transition of care (such as admit, transfer, and discharge) and validate that the time frame is achievable in the new system.
- Determine which tasks could be done simultaneously and which tasks should be supported by the new electronic system (such as discontinuing meds when transferring level of care, or continuing a number of medications upon discharge).
- Identify provider "mindsets" that could not be corrected by electronic medication reconciliation systems (such as providers who refused to take more than 5 s in the process and instead placed a vertical line through the continue columns for all medications (an unsafe practice).

- Assess vendor standard reports for relevance to one's own organization; anticipate the need for customization, including the impact of customization on the project resources and timeline.
- Provide critical and concrete evidence that the new system will work as expected before full implementation (such as bypassing a pilot because of the requirement that the system be "turned on" everywhere all at once to later learn that it was possible to hide the new system while piloting it).

Editor's Commentary

EHRs and their components are extremely complex and require systematic and careful evaluation before purchase and implementation in practice. There are countless examples of very expensive systems being bought and implemented and failing miserably due to poor evaluation up front. As a result, not only are the initial expenses of the system lost (in those situations where the system is scrapped) but also additional expenses are incurred, frequently much higher than the original costs, to reconcile problems that result. As such, there is no better strategy for containing the cost of EHRs than doing one's homework ahead of purchase and implementation. The interesting aspect of this case is that there were knowledgeable people involved in the decisions but they clearly did not do their homework and suffered "expensive" consequences.

One wonders why organizations fail to do their homework when making expensive decisions given the devastating financial outcomes that can occur. In some instances, the parties to the decision do not have sufficient knowledge to make the right decision, while in others wishful thinking seems to be the culprit. Either way, there should be no excuse allowed for failure to systematically evaluate the impact of a costly product given the potential negative financial and other outcomes that can occur for the organization and healthcare in general. The fact of the matter is that it is sometimes hard to measure the impact of EHR-related decisions and accountability for them. When accountability is not clearly specified, there is no incentive to ensure the best decisions are made. In this case, one could blame the purchasing committee, the CMIO, or the key administrators involved in the decision. In the end, however, when the accountability is diffused, there is no real accountability.

To limit or avoid negative outcomes for major EHR-related purchases, it is absolutely essential that there be a process that is routinely followed and a mechanism of accountability. In rushing to implement an EHR system or feature to meet regulatory requirements, or take advantage of financial incentives from private or public payors, implementers may be tempted to make decisions without appropriate analysis of their consequences, necessitating costly remediation efforts. Had the organization in this case used a systematic process in its evaluation of the new medication reconciliation system, they would likely have uncovered many of the problems that were discovered after implementation. If an organization requires the use of a standard policy for evaluating major EHR procurements, wishful thinking decisions can be avoided. Such a policy would include both the steps for systematic evaluation of EHR products and a clear mechanism of accountability. The mechanism for accountability, for example, might be to have all members of the purchasing committee sign a letter indicating that the evaluation process produced clear and compelling evidence that the product will work as intended in the organization with no additional costs.

Lessons Learned

- The impact of new electronic systems on provider workflow must be assessed prior to full implementation in order to avoid unintended consequences.
- Standard features of proposed products must be evaluated in order to ensure that the new features work within an organization.
- A standard evaluation process and lines of accountability must be created for decisions related to major EHR products in order to eliminate “wishful decision-making.”
- Never assume anything about an EHR product and application of it to an organization in the absence of convincing evidence.

Chapter 11

Anatomy of a Preventable Mistake: Unrecognized Workflow Change in Medication Management

Editor: Jonathan Leviss

Greater New Bedford Community Health Center

Contents

Project Categories: inpatient electronic health record (EHR), computerized provider order entry (CPOE), electronic medication administration record (eMAR), pharmacy information system (IS)

Lessons Learned Categories: implementation approaches, leadership/governance, system design, workflow

Case Study

A hospital-wide electronic health record (EHR) was installed in a midsized community hospital. This was the first installation of the product within the healthcare system. There were three other systems in use in specialty areas (labor and delivery, emergency department, and operating room), in addition to the laboratory and picture archiving and communication system (PACS).

The underlying structure of this EHR was such that all work was considered an individual "action" or task. Nursing staff were told that all tasks must be completed. Completion might include a documented reason for inaction. Some tasks involved multiple parts, such as administering a medication that required more than one step.

The EHR had been live for a year, and although many issues had been addressed, some were still outstanding. Medical records remained in a hybrid format, electronic or paper. However, physician orders remained strictly on paper. Bar code medication administration (BCMA) was added 9 months after the EHR was implemented. The pharmacy created a "catch-up schedule" (or forced schedule) so that all medications would be given at standard times unless otherwise ordered.

A patient was admitted to the hospital for administration of chemotherapy. During the hospitalization, the patient complained of chest pain and was found to have a high probability of pulmonary embolism on a ventilation/perfusion (V/Q) scan. At approximately 10:00 a.m., an order was written for a dose of low-molecular-weight heparin (LMWH) to be given every 12 h. The order was processed at 1:00 p.m., and a dose was given by a nurse sometime shortly before going off shift at 3:00 p.m. The pharmacy had previously entered the order with a forced dosing schedule of 5:00 p.m. and 5:00 a.m. The next shift's nurse gave the regularly scheduled dose according to the routine schedule at 5:00 p.m. It was unclear what sign-out occurred between the nurses, though a situation-background-assessment-response (SBAR) format was standard within the organization. The subsequent dose was given at 5:00 a.m. as scheduled. At approximately 8:00 a.m., the patient complained of being weak on standing and was found to have a massive gastrointestinal (GI) bleed, which persisted over 24 h. Esophagogastroduodenoscopy (EGD) revealed much blood but no clear treatable source. Angiography showed a bleeding esophageal vessel that was successfully embolized.

The case was reviewed utilizing a root-cause analysis (RCA) methodology. Difficulty accessing the pertinent information in the EHR confounded the analysis. Key findings included the following issues:

- Inability of the nursing staff to see the entire day's medication schedule at once
- Inadequate handoff between nursing staff members
- Inclusion of high-risk/high-alert medications in the forced schedule process.

Nursing staff were never provided a computerized display equivalent to the paper medication administration record (MAR), although one had been created for physician use after complaints were received. Instead, nurses needed to check multiple screens to find when the last dose was actually administered. In fact, medications were not displayed in relation to any other medication or dosing regimen.

Actions taken after the RCA included the following steps:

- Exclusion of LMWH from forced schedule
- Creation of an alert prompt to remind nurses to check "last dose administered" for high-risk/high-alert medications
- Education of nursing staff about contacting pharmacy to reset the forced schedule if a medication was given late
- Retraining of nursing staff for SBAR use at shift change
- Addition of an alert (via BCMA) to the pharmacy
- Creation of a full MAR screen for nursing use.

Author's Analysis

The specific situation in this case is unfortunately not unusual. Workflow changes are common, and even expected, with the implementation of EHRs. Many problems occur because evaluations of the preexisting workflows are either not done at all or overlooked. At times, potential areas for new errors may not be easily identified without a skilled and thorough workflow evaluation. Assessment of the future state workflow should have identified potential risks and points of failure for the new medication system.

This error occurred 1 year after the system was fully implemented. It is unknown if there were any similar overdoses that did not lead to patient harm between the initial go-live date and the date of this event. The continuous process of monitoring and addressing problems should not have ended just because the technology was live.

Task management within this product is poorly designed, as both pharmacy and nursing staff members need to go through multiple screens to administer each medication (even with BCMA), and charting when a drug is not given (held for any reason or skipped due to timing issues) is even more difficult (five screens and an average of 5 min). What appear to be straightforward orders (such as "discontinue Foley cath") involve multiple related tasks that are not linked, thus requiring the nurse to select the task to discontinue (such as "discontinue Foley") and also the associated care task (such as "discontinue Foley care"); these two items are in totally different areas of the documentation. Care processes that involve high risk require extra attention, whether the processes are paper-based or technology-enabled; the higher the risk and the greater the workflow change, the greater the need for extra attention. This need was not addressed. If the clinician end-users had been involved in the decisions and processes to select, implement, and use the technology, these shortcomings could have been identified before the project failure.

The administration was determined to make this EHR work, having already spent a significant amount of time, effort, and money (rumored to be approximately $60 million) on implementation to date. Physicians were frequently frustrated with the apparent lack of response or slow response to their complaints. Nursing staff either loved the system or hated the system. (Of note, age is not a predictor of nursing staff acceptance of the system.)

Prior to this event, the company's chief executive officer (CEO), chief technology officer (CTO), and chief marketing officer (CMO) met with concerned physicians about the ongoing problems that had been noted. The CEO indicated that "all development stopped" in order to meet the Meaningful Use requirements and become a Certified health information technology (HIT) Product so that customers could use the software to achieve Meaningful Use accreditation from the Office of the National Coordinator for HIT (ONC).

The proposed solutions are helpful, but it is unclear how the information about the drug dosing gets into the electronic SBAR. Adding yet another alert contributes to alert fatigue. Unless the medication can be administered through the full MAR screen, it only creates another place the nurses need to look for information. Asking busy nurses to call busy pharmacists to tell them a dose was given late is unlikely to happen on a regular basis.

Editor's Commentary

The beginning of this case gives the impression that within 1 year of the implementation of the EHR and medication administration system, there was insufficient attention and effort on continued improvement of both the technology and how clinicians used the technology. What processes were in place to continually solicit feedback from providers about problems with the EHR? Who was the visible executive to lead this process? Was there a single clinician (or technology) lead for the EHR, who should have recognized that just as the physicians required a different view of the medication record, so might the nurses?

The typical HIT initiative is iterative, with continued attention required to enable continued improvement, similar to complex healthcare processes in general. Many health systems with computerized provider order entry (CPOE) and BCMA are still early in their own experiences and learning how to best use and optimize these technologies. Extra vigilance for detected and potential problems is critical, with an effective improvement cycle to address problems. Executive and project leaders need to transition the implementation charge of "let's use the system" to the optimization charge of "let's address the problems you are having with the system."

This case raises several questions: When the BCMA system introduced new workflows for nurses, including the "catch-up schedule" for medication, what workflow analysis did the clinical and IT teams perform? Did they perform formal failure mode and effects analysis (FMEA)? FMEA is a means of identifying and evaluating what can go wrong in a process, without requiring the experience of a negative occurrence, so that adverse events can be averted proactively. It can be helpful in mitigating the risks of new processes and technologies in healthcare. If an interdisciplinary team had evaluated the "catch-up schedule" for medication and the new medication user interface (UI) with an FMEA approach, overdosing of medications, specifically high-alert medications like anticoagulants, could have been identified as a risk and addressed (ISMP, 2007). Finally, the author describes several technical shortcomings of the EHR. Did the clinicians feel the benefits outweighed the problems (or vice versa)? How was this issue discussed and addressed by the health system? Often, resource constraints limit the ability to meet clinician requests for new HIT; specific technology options, vendor configuration services, or training may be determined to be too expensive or unnecessary. Why did the EHR leadership address the physicians' need for a better medication list view but not the nurses' similar need? Was the project leadership aware of the challenges for nurses reviewing a patient's medications in the new system? Was the problem identified but not addressed? Were nurses involved in system selection, workflow redesign, and implementation?

Learning from the example here, a nurse's ability to easily review patient medications is as important as a physician's, and clinicians', concerns about workflow with HIT should be evaluated carefully as part of system selection, implementation, and optimization.

Lessons Learned

- Assessing future state workflows is critical.
- High-risk care processes require extra attention.
- Targeted clinicians must be involved in decisions to select, implement, and use HIT.
- HIT projects are ongoing—once a technology is live, continuous process improvements are still needed.

Additional Reading

https://ismp.org/sites/default/files/attachments/2018-02/FMEAofAnticoagulants.pdf.

Chapter 12

Failure to Plan, Failure to Rollout: Bar Code Medication Verification Failure

Editor: Pam Charney
University of North Georgia

Contents

Project Categories: inpatient electronic health record (EHR), electronic medication administration record (eMAR), pharmacy information system (IS)

Lessons Learned Categories: implementation approaches, leadership/governance, staffing resources, technology problems, workflow

Case Study

A community hospital implemented a bar code medication verification (BMV) system to improve tracking of medications and support safe medication administration. In addition to the software for BMV, hospital administrators purchased laptop computers stationed atop wheeled carts, or workstations on wheels (WOWs), and medication bar code scanners.

Software was selected for the program because it had the same look and feel of software currently in use to enter orders, review consults, and retrieve laboratory results. Two pharmacists were trained to customize the system. Additionally, two nurse managers were assigned to assist in development and implementation. Because of staffing limitations, information technology (IT) was not involved in BMV development or implementation.

BMV went live using a stepwise plan. All end-users were required to attend one classroom session. Superusers were selected from nursing staff and received the same training as other nurses. Following completion of the classroom sessions, one nursing unit was selected each month for a 3-day go-live process. During the go-live phase, nurses on each unit were paired one-to-one with a superuser of the BMV system for 6 h. There was no training or help desk assistance provided for use of the WOWs.

Shortly after implementation, many of the laptops began to crash when the BMV system was opened. Because IT was not involved in the BMV program implementation, users were told to contact the pharmacy for assistance. Superusers were also tasked with troubleshooting hardware problems, which left little time for assisting with BMV implementation or their own nursing duties.

Facilities engineering was not involved in the program and had not been assigned to maintain or repair the laptop carts. Lacking proper authorization, they refused to assist in repairs until documentation was prepared and approved. It was not unusual to see one of the BMV pharmacist programmers roaming the floors, screwdriver in hand, repairing laptop carts.

At the end of the first year, expensive external extra-long-lasting laptop batteries with wall-mounted chargers stopped recharging so more had to be purchased. Other hardware problems were encountered. Scanner cords broke because they were not long enough and busy nursing staff had stretched them past their limit. Batteries on cordless scanners would not recharge and had to be replaced. At this point, IT took on responsibility for hardware issues and during the second year of the program was able to purchase enough spare laptop batteries and scanners to service the hospital.

The IT department was able to hire more staff and was finally able to provide help desk services for the BMV program. Because of the huge backlog of work, WOWs with repair tickets would sit in unit storage rooms for days to weeks. Unit nurses felt that little or no importance was placed on how the nurses would function when the WOWs were not functional. Lacking support, nurses felt that it was assumed they would share the remaining WOWs. Former superuser nurses were occasionally able to solve some of the problems and created workarounds to keep the WOWs functional as much as possible.

When computer-savvy nurses were able to take on some repairs without authorization from IT, conflicts developed between nursing and IT. Nursing's requirements for functional WOWs for the BMV system needed to take precedence over IT support for other hospital functions, creating stress on IT staff.

As hardware and software failures increased, nurses stopped scanning medication because there were not enough scanners, laptops, or WOWs available. Workarounds were created by carrying extra identification bracelets to scan and by hand-typing drug numbers into documentation fields, which initially was only to be done for the rare case when the bar code would not scan. In this manner, nurses could sign out their medications while still sitting at the nurses' station. Medication errors were made, the same medication errors the BMV system was supposed to correct.

Medications were kept in a med room that housed a dispensing machine. Nurses had to enter their username and personal identification number (PIN) (or fingerprint), choose the patient, choose the medication, remove it, and sign out. Only a brief orientation session to this system was provided including the safety and security features of medication dispensing systems. It was not uncommon for a nurse to remove second doses of meds from the dispenser and place them in their pocket so they would not have to return to the machine for a drug they knew they would be given in 3–4 h. Although against policy, nurses routinely did this with controlled medications because in the paper system if a nurse forgot to sign off the medicine, someone could sign and cosign it so the record was kept properly. However, the signature omission would be maintained in the new BMV system and the pharmacy department would note the discrepancies in the count of the meds: two doses removed from the dispenser and only one dose recorded. Medications went missing. Lastly, password sharing was not uncommon as most nurses failed to realize the implications and gravity of this practice.

Author's Analysis

Within 2 years of go-live, the system was considered a failure; the lack of support from IT and facilities engineering was seen as the primary cause of the failure. Ultimately, the entire electronic health record (EHR) system was abandoned for a newer platform that integrated CPOE, test results, and all clinical notes including physician and ancillary departments. Several wrong strategies led to this failed effort. The project lacked a clear collaborative partnership between nursing and IT. While clinical leadership is critical to a health IT initiative, so is IT leadership. The clinical leadership contributed content and strategic leadership, but that is not sufficient for success. The lack of involvement of the hospital's IT department meant that critical project resources were absent from the planning stages through implementation and into the support stage. Engineering's input into device selection might have averted the hardware complications that occurred, such as the problems with batteries, computer carts, and scanners. A knowledgeable help desk would have been able to support the clinician users who struggled with a technology that was critical to patient care.

The hospital ultimately developed a different approach to EHR adoption. Computer training courses are available for all employees as one step in preparing staff. In general, the hospital leadership has higher hopes that the new federal and state regulations and incentives as well as a more integrated approach will ease the burden for all staff.

Editor's Commentary

BMV programs are sophisticated, complex systems that are supposed to increase the safety of patients and decrease errors in medication administration. It is imperative that all departments of a healthcare organization be involved from the planning stage and that they are adequately prepared to meet the inevitable challenges. Failure to properly plan, design, and implement such complex systems is quite often a guarantee that the system will fail. In this case, it is not surprising that the system failed. Rather, it is surprising that it was kept in place for 2 years before finally being discontinued.

Although not specifically stated, it appears individuals with IT project management expertise were not involved with this project. The first step towards system failure appears to be that system users were not included in system selection. Instead, a system was chosen primarily because it had the same "look and feel" of software currently in use. What is not known is how well that system was meeting user needs for medication administration. Individuals selected to lead the project were most likely not aware of end-user needs and expectations and certainly did not have the knowledge and skill needed to implement an IT project of this magnitude. A cascade of poor communication, lack of understanding of workflow, and insufficient training and support led to the eventual system failure.

It would be difficult to pinpoint one specific misstep that caused the BMV system to fail. The decision by hospital administrators to purchase equipment for the system apparently without involvement from nursing, IT, or pharmacy suggests a "top-down" management style, where management dictates exactly how work is to be accomplished. Chances are that administrators did not see the need to develop and implement a project plan. There was no individual assigned overall responsibility for the system. Instead, components of the system were assigned to different departments who did not communicate or collaborate with each other.

Chances are that appropriate attention to the need for strong leadership, appropriate project management, and some ability for the departments involved to collaborate and solve problems (instead of blaming each other) would have given the BMV system a fighting chance for success.

Lessons Learned

- Clinicians and IT must be included from the planning through rollout stages of complex IT projects.
- Successful implementation requires sufficient help desk staffing well beyond the go-live phase.
- Clinicians and IT need a clear understanding of each other's role and workload.
- Nursing and IT need to have a clear understanding of each other's role and workload so that conflict can be avoided.
- Qualified IT professionals must participate in the selection of equipment and support of IT hardware.
- Health IT projects require an identified leader with strong accountability.

Chapter 13

Fitting a Square Peg into a Round Hole: Enterprise EHR for Obstetrics

Editor: Christopher Corbit
TeamHealth

Contents

Project Categories: inpatient electronic health record (EHR)

Lessons Learned Categories: leadership/governance, project management, system design

This project was part of a broader implementation of an enterprise electronic medical record (EMR) at a multihospital, community healthcare system. A maternity admissions unit served as the "emergency department" for patients who were pregnant and needed to be seen immediately. The department had previously used an emergency department software, as it operated like an emergency department, which was equipped to handle the occasional male patient who presented with urgent chest pain. The enterprise implementation moved forward with this transition from legacy emergency department system to the new enterprise emergency department product, as was intuitive to the customer and the software team.

However, as the implementation moved forward, it was clear that this department needed obstetrics (OB) specific tools that were not standardly a part of the emergency department product. For example, clinicians needed access to document pregnancy status and access to document a delivery, which sometimes happened in the department. These issues created multiple issues for the software team in terms of creating new workflows for deliveries in an emergency room product and the ADT issues associated with creating baby patient records. The implementation project team developed custom ways to meet these OB-specific needs of the department. A large part of this problem-solving work came from merging both the emergency department and obstetrics software modules. The ability to utilize both department functionalities was an unexpected discovery in the code that allowed for both aspects of emergency department and obstetrics department to be respected based on hidden fields in the record that were shown or hidden based on the type of department. This discovery was made by a new project manager at the software company, eager to impress his client and superiors. Despite not being the intended design, the workflows functioned as expected. The client was pleased with this careful, step-by-step process of getting the exact access to tools the clinicians were looking for. This analysis and design developed trust with the client.

Unfortunately, the project team went about this implementation without consulting the software developers. After all of the build and the subsequent workflows were validated, which took several weeks of work, the project lead thought this should be brought to developers to assess feasibility before moving forward. The rookie project manager had only been at the company for a matter of months and did not understand the corporate culture of developers and had heard stories from mentors about blazing their own path within the company by "owning" new aspects of the charting functionality. Upon meeting with developers, they immediately rejected the idea and demanded that the customer be told that both emergency and OB modules could not be combined. The way that the system was able to operate as both an emergency department and obstetrics unit was unprecedented, and something that the developer team did not know what effects could be for future development. Despite urging developers that there were no existing issues, and offering them to explore through testing, they declined to investigate further and demanded that this implementation be overhauled. The customer was blind-sighted by this news and begrudgingly began to install the obstetrics project, missing out on all of the emergency department functionalities that they had come to expect.

Author's Analysis

Unfortunately, the project team underestimated their dependence on the electronic health record (EHR) vendor's development team and the authority the vendor's development team had over product development. The development team had the ultimate power to halt what the customer-facing team saw as innovative ideas. Basically, the project team manager, with good intentions, was caught in between trying to be innovative and being unaware of the need to work more closely with product development when trying to address a customer's unmet need.

After further work on this project, it became clear that there were hard-coded divisions between the EHR modules based on clinical specialty and any requests to blend modules were heavily rejected by the EHR vendor's development team. The project team and customer had to accept that sometimes there is an inflexibility of enterprise software to take on areas of care that differ significantly from mainstream organizational needs.

Expert Commentary

This case is a clear example of end users and departments having to change their workflow to accommodate the EMR's capabilities versus adopting the EMR's capabilities to support the department's need. As this case illustrates, and seen in many EMR implementations, keeping development easier for the vendor creates a workflow that is more difficult for the client. Unfortunately, in today's environment, clients have little recourse when dealing with a previously selected enterprise vendor, especially when the lack of workflow flexibility effects just one department. The cost and challenge of changing vendors far outweighs the issues with a single department's need.

While not specifically discussed in this, moving from one electronic system to another electronic system (especially best of breed [BoB] to enterprise systems) is often more difficult than moving from a nonelectronic/paper-based system. The first system used at this healthcare system was a BoB system that, although not perfect, was able to be optimized to their unique departmental needs. The enterprise system, although technically able to reproduce most of this functionality to the client's agreement, was triumphed by the vendors wanting to minimize development time. Survey after survey highlights many of the essential issues clinicians and hospitals have with their EMRs and the ways in which they often block innovation and their ability to deliver quality patient care.

Looking at the history of EMRs in healthcare, along with other industries that have gone through a similar process, we are at the far swing of the pendulum towards enterprise systems. Initially, BoB systems started to fill the areas of specific departmental needs. As these systems grew in popularity and numbers, issues arose due to the number of technical interfaces needed to connect them and the silos of patient data created by them. Enterprise systems started to develop or buy these systems and interfaced them internally to decrease the amount of resources needed by a hospital/health system to maintain them. In addition, governmental incentives have significantly pushed the pendulum to the enterprise side. As illustrated by this case, this can lead to difficulty with specific departments where the enterprise system doesn't meet their needs and there is no recourse in that situation. However, I do feel the pendulum will swing back as it becomes easier to interface enterprise systems with third-party systems. Integration Substitutable Medical Applications and Reusable Technology (SMART), Fast Healthcare Interoperability Resources (FHIR) and better standards for sharing data among different systems will accelerate this pendulum reversal. EMRs are becoming commodity platforms. The most successful one will be the EMR vendor that provides the best platform for innovation—the most open and most extensible platform.

Lessons Learned

- Developers rule: always go to developers if an idea of using the software is unprecedented, as the hierarchy calls the shots.
- Despite being "integrated", enterprise software is still extremely siloed. In this example, merging the obstetrics tools within an emergency department module would seem relatively low effort assuming that the chart itself is integrated.

Chapter 14

Basic Math: HL7 Interfaces from CPOE to Pharmacy to eMAR

Editors: Larry Ozeran
Clinical Informatics, Inc.

Jonathan Leviss
Greater New Bedford Community Health Center

Contents

Project Categories: inpatient electronic health record (EHR), computerized provider order entry (CPOE), electronic medication administration record (eMAR), pharmacy information system (IS)

Lessons Learned Categories: system configuration, technology problems

Case Study

In our computerized provider order entry (CPOE) system, a medication order was generated for warfarin 7 mg daily. Using an HL7 interface message, the medication order was communicated to an external pharmacy system. Because there was no dispensable product of warfarin 7 mg, the pharmacist converted the order into dispensable products, a 5 mg tablet and a 2 mg tablet.

Several days later, clinicians observed that the patient's anticoagulation laboratory results or international normalized ratios (INRswere at panic levels, but there had been no easily identified originating event. The anticoagulation medications were reviewed, and the clinicians were surprised at the warfarin dosing—it was much higher than originally ordered. The clinicians ordered a dose of warfarin 7 mg daily, yet the order and the electronic medication administration record (eMAR) both indicated a dose of warfarin 14 mg. Upon review of the audit trail, the provider had entered warfarin 7 mg, but after the pharmacy verification, the order was modified to warfarin 14 mg.

The first step was to implement an immediate workaround, which was to discontinue the order and reenter the medication order differently. Because the medication dose required two separate products to be dispensed (warfarin 2 and 5 mg), the order was reentered successfully as two separate medication orders.

Authors' Analysis

The complexities of an interfaced medication order between two disparate vendor applications cannot be overestimated. Iatrogenic events can change the data outcome and affect clinical outcomes.

The complexities of HL7 include both the technology standards and the semantic standards. Events like a medication order generate an HL7 message that is communicated through an interface engine and then to the receiving system. As the message travels, each computer has the ability to interpret and even modify the content of the data based on defined algorithms.

During evaluation, the situation was replicated in our test system. The troubleshooting efforts were focused on the multiple product situation. Because the medication dose required two separate products be dispensed, the successful workaround was to enter two separate orders while the troubleshooting continued. In the CPOE system, the medication is ordered as a generic name and a dose, without product-level considerations.

Appropriately, within a pharmacy application, the medication order was interpreted into the dispensing product level. Within this pharmacy system, there was functionality for a multiproduct medication order being represented as a single medication order. If the generic formulary item is the same, the medication dose requiring two products can be combined in a single order. The warfarin 7 mg order included two dispensing products: warfarin 2 mg and warfarin 5 mg.

Upon review, the original CPOE HL7 message that was sent to the pharmacy system was passed through an enterprise interface engine and then a CPOE interface engine before being received by the external pharmacy application and used the same route upon return to the CPOE system. The CPOE system identified the generic product and dose, while the pharmacy system identified the generic and dispensing products required to provide the dose.

In HL7, the "RXE" segment represents the pharmacy encoded order data (Hann's On Software, 2008). The "Give amount" and "Give units" values are updated during the "perfection process" (pharmacy verification). With a multiproduct order, two separate RXE segments are defined. In this case, there were two RXE segments: one for warfarin 2 mg and the other for warfarin 5 mg. As the pharmacy application had a process to manage multiple RXE segments, an unexpected data transformation occurred. The result was that instead of adding the amounts to a total dose, it multiplied the subcomponents, thus generating 14 mg instead of the expected 7 mg. So the calculation was

$$2\text{ RXE components} \times (2\text{ mg}) + 2\text{ RXE components} \times (5\text{ mg}) = 14\text{ mg}$$

The CPOE application accepted the verification with the dose modification from the pharmacy system and changed the order view and the eMAR view of the order to a dose of 14 mg. There was no alert, only an overwriting of the original order; the modification went unnoticed until a clinical situation arose.

Once the issue was identified, additional testing confirmed the situation, and the vendor was contacted. The vendor assigned the issue its highest priority, and a fix was available the next day. On site, reports were generated to check for any other instances of the situation, one additional patient was identified, and the clinicians were immediately involved. There were no adverse long-term impacts on either of the patients.

Editors' Commentary

This scenario reminds us of some very important lessons.

1. *The source of an aberrant event may not be immediately evident.*

   This is why it is critical to check all of your assumptions when something goes wrong. The authors and their institution must be commended for taking a clear and meticulous approach in investigating this issue.
2. *Computers* DO *make mistakes, when we provide the wrong information or the wrong instructions.*

   There is a tendency to think that the data we get from the computer must be right, simply because it came from the computer. This expectation and the resultant complacency can blind us to embedded errors.
3. *Testing is critical to mitigate health information technology (HIT)-related risk.*

   Rigorous testing is critical prior to implementing new technologies and even upgrades to existing systems. While comprehensive testing of every possible permutation of system inputs is rarely practical, it is advisable to perform testing of focused high-risk processes, such as the one described in this case, which automatically updates the content of a physician order in a CPOE system.

   Anecdotal evidence indicates that many hospitals do not have appropriately replicated environments in which to thoroughly test systems prior to rollout; test environments may not include the full array of clinical information systems or a sufficiently large test database, or involve clinicians who understand the more sophisticated data flows that are generated during clinical care.
4. *Whenever we computerize a medical process to reduce errors, there is always a risk that new errors will be introduced.*

   Unreasonably positive expectations for HIT are not uncommon; automation of clinical processes entails risk as well. The issue described in this case was fortuitously caught before severe patient harm could result. Had the specifics been only slightly different, however, the results could have been very serious *and* harder to detect. For instance, if the drug in question had been digoxin, it might have been very difficult to identify, because digoxin toxicity develops more slowly than warfarin toxicity. We must remember that every change that can bring an improvement to our provision of healthcare can also bring new problems, and we must be diligent about finding those problems. That means that managers, executives, regulators, legislators, and every other leader who plays a role in our healthcare system must be aware that technology brings costs beyond the financial, and they must support implementing technology safely. We must properly balance accuracy with rapid change.

Lessons Learned

- Perform extensive testing with a large number of scenarios involving different product-level data.
- Involve clinicians who are technology savvy to participate in testing of scenarios.
- Empower all clinicians to question medication doses and other aspects of clinical care processes, even if they involve information systems.

Chapter 15

In with the New Does Not Mean *Out with the Old*: Mobile Devices

Editor: Richard Schreiber
Geisinger Health System

Contents

Project Categories: inpatient electronic health record (EHR), infrastructure and technology

Lessons Learned Categories: staffing resources, technology problems

A large academic medical center used a legacy application on mobile devices for specimen collection and documentation of vital signs in the inpatient setting. The legacy application and the mobile hardware had reached end-of-life, with a hard end-date at which time both the application and hardware required replacement. Device, connectivity, and system-stability issues plagued the old system.

The electronic health record (EHR) that had been implemented after the legacy application provided replacement functionality, running on new mobile devices. Information technology (IT) established a plan for rollout throughout the hospital. The new application supported the preexisting, or legacy, mobile printers used for printing of specimen labels. All of these mobile printers were the same model although of varying ages. IT made the decision not to replace the existing printers.

The project team made the following assumptions:

- The legacy printers would seamlessly transition to the new system.
- Testing a couple of printers in the test environment would identify any issues.
- Because the handheld devices and the workflows were very similar between the old and new systems, a brief, 2 h training with hands-on practice would be sufficient for assistive staff.
- And because nurses (RN) would be using workstation on wheels (WOWs) and desktop-based workflows—and not using the handhelds—tip sheets would suffice for their training instead of classroom training.

These assumptions proved wrong.

Legacy Printer Issues

Close to go-live during testing, it was discovered by chance that all printers needed a configuration update but the organization did not own the software to manage all the printers remotely. The organization either had to purchase licenses and install them immediately, or each printer would require manual updating. IT made the decision to purchase central management software. At go-live, a configuration update was pushed out to multiple devices. The configuration update worked, but it was lost when each device was rebooted. After extensive troubleshooting with the printer vendor, an issue with some printers' firmware version was identified as the root cause.

IT identified multiple firmware versions. Firmware updates were required for all devices. Even using batched central management, this took many hours.

Once the overarching printing configuration issues were resolved, hardware issues related to the age of the older printers recurred sporadically. Only replacing the older printers resolved the hardware issues.

Training Issues

Since nursing thought the distribution of a tip sheet would be enough preparation, RNs did not have classroom training. In addition, nursing had made assumptions about the support level that would be available for nurses during go-live, based on similar earlier go-lives, and that super-users without patient assignments would be available for 3 days during go-live. The IT department's go-live plan, however, was to provide minimal floor support. Somehow the messages were crossed, and the gap was discovered only a few weeks before go-live. The organization had to find money to pay RNs for overtime to provide super-user support for the rest of the nursing staff. Even with that super-user support at the time of go-live, most RNs were not aware of the tip sheets. Nursing leadership had distributed go-live information through their usual communication channels, but some RNs were not even aware of the go-live.

Nursing education delivered 2 h of classroom training for support staff, who were the primary users of the mobile devices. This training included return demonstration to confirm the support staff were able to use the devices and understood the workflows. However, despite this training, and the similarity of the devices and workflows, support staff members struggled to make the transition and often defaulted to downtime procedures due to time pressures and their own lack of knowledge. These problems persisted for approximately 2 weeks, and required frequent rounding by managers and staff education to resolve. Laboratory accessioning experienced the most significant impact of excessive use of downtime procedures.

System Issues

Technical and user issues, including printer interface difficulties with the laboratory system, noncompleted print queue configurations, and dropped print queues, persisted beyond the 3 days of budgeted super-user support. The technical instability of the printer hardware during go-live continued for almost 2 weeks. Out of frustration, and due to the time pressures of patient care, many units remained on downtime procedures (the manual completion of a paper laboratory requisition form for each specimen), even after the technical issues were resolved. This resulted in 2 weeks of daily leadership calls including nursing, laboratory, and IT, to manage the crisis operationally and return to normal operations. The volume of downtime requisitions required the laboratory to increase staffing. The additional staffmitigated potential impacts on turnaround time and patient care and throughput levels; however, it put extreme staffing and financial pressure on the laboratory.

IT Security Process and Mobile Device Management

IT security introduced a new process for device management during the implementation, but it was not applied to the in-progress project. IT security failed to evaluate in-flight projects, and the new process was not applied. The mobile devices were not consistently configured to support the security requirements, and as a result, not all nonclinical applications were locked. This allowed some users to use the devices for unapproved functions such as taking pictures.

Author's Analysis

The project was seen as quick and simple, but was neither in the end. Each of the issues with printers, training, systems, and security created new problems and expense for the organization and its ability to care for patients. Extra staff had to be brought in and paid for; delays in laboratories created delays in patient care, which led to further delays in throughput. Some areas like emergency departments were disproportionately impacted, and such areas needed to be clearly identified in advance. Without some basic flawed assumptions in the beginning, this could have been a smooth project.

Editor's Commentary

Shortcutting workflow assessment invariably leads to disruptions during go-lives. Failure to understand fully the current workflow creates inherent assumptions that will thwart a go-live. Analyzing the current workflow and how the future workflow will occur leads naturally to a test plan for the new hardware and software. Even if current workflow appears to work smoothly, it is unwise to assume that new hardware will function similarly in the future workflow. The assumptions made during this installation should have been red flags for go-live failure, especially if these assumptions were explicit during the project.

It is also unwise to assume that new workflows are "easy", "simple", or that "just" a tip sheet suffices for training. Only end users can make those judgments, as those involved in the update are so immersed in the upgrade, devices, and hardware that it is too easy to miss significant changes in workflow. Nontechnical personnel should participate in the current-to-future workflow analyses to identify training issues early, and later to review the go-live plan to advise on a training program.

The flexibility of the nursing education department, and its ability to provide hands-on education and support, likely saved the day for this project. IT departments and administrators cannot rely on such last-minute deployment.

Lessons Learned

- A thorough current state assessment includes
  - evaluating legacy systems (hardware and software) including life of hardware, firmware versions, software versions, and hardware compatibility
  - a full security evaluation of devices, including mobile devices and native apps.
- Train everyone even if you think the change will not be huge.
- Perform a complete organizational impact assessment.
- Create a contingency plan based on the worst-case scenario.

Chapter 16

First-Time Failures Ensured Later Success: Pharmacy System Upgrade

Editor: Eric Rose
Intelligent Medical Objects

Contents

Project Categories: inpatient electronic health record (EHR), computerized provider order entry (CPOE), pharmacy information system (IS)

Lessons Learned Categories: implementation approaches, staffing resources, system design, training, workflow

This case history describes the highly problematic introduction of the computerized provider order entry (CPOE) module of an electronic health record (EHR) system at a community hospital, and the successful application of lessons learned to a subsequent implementation at the same hospital.

At this hospital, before CPOE was introduced, providers wrote medication orders on paper. These were manually transcribed by pharmacy staff into a pharmacy information system (PIS), which had a unidirectional outbound interface to the hospital's EHR. Clinicians were able to view patients' medication lists in the EHR, and nurses used the EHR's medication administration record capability. During this time, providers had access to paper medication order set forms which had been built by pharmacy staff, and for which the pharmacy maintained corresponding electronic order sets in the PIS. These included so-called convenience order sets, such as one for electrolyte replacement, which included detailed dosing, as needed (or PRN) reasons, and administration instructions.

In the mid-2000s, the hospital incrementally implemented a new EHR system. Phase 1 did not involve any changes to physician or pharmacy workflows: the pharmacy continued to use the original PIS and physicians continued to write orders on paper, which pharmacy staff transcribed into the PIS.

Phase 2 implementation included a pharmacy module which supported CPOE and which replaced the legacy PIS. During this phase, pharmacist and physician informaticists focused their attention on optimizing electronic order sets to achieve standardization and provide tools to support physician adoption. CPOE was never mandatory. The expectation was that clinicians would adopt CPOE readily, making it easier for the pharmacists to focus on clinical review of the medication orders, rather than manual transcription of written orders. Consequently, the informatics team focused less attention on pharmacy workflows. The paper "convenience order sets" continued to be available to providers. However, since the informatics staff did not build these order sets within the new pharmacy module, pharmacy staff had to transcribe each component of the order set individually, which was much more laborious than the workflow in the legacy PIS. In addition, the convenience order sets were not built into the CPOE system.

Upon the initiation of phase 2, two impacts became immediately apparent. First, physicians who were attempting to use the CPOE module for situations covered by the convenience order sets were frustrated that the CPOE system did not provide a means to enter all those details "in one place". In some cases, they omitted important details, requiring that pharmacists enter them. In addition, the lack of build-out of the convenience order sets in the pharmacy module caused delays in order entry, pharmacy verification, medication dispensing, and medication administration.

For several days after go-live, all technical, informatics, and volunteer staff assisted in working through these tasks to address the backlog. Fortunately, no adverse patient events were detected. An after-action review of the implementation revealed that budgetary and personnel constraints led to an incomplete understanding of the impact on pharmacy workflows of not building the variety of medication details and administration instructions. To ensure the hospital "got it right" for patients, it was crucial to rebuild the trust of the clinicians and nurses in pharmacy capabilities, as well as in information technology. This took considerable time and effort.

Ten years later, the hospital transitioned to another EHR vendor product. The informatics staff remembered well the lessons learned and worked hard to ensure that the transition would be smoother. Factors that favorably aided in the success of the transition included that CPOE was to be mandatory. Also, there was a much larger physician and pharmacy informatics staff, more analysts, and more experience on the part of the acquiring hospital in making such transitions. This allowed the local hospital's informatics personnel time to focus on gaps between existing and future workflows.

For the transition to the new EHR, there was an intentional and substantial focus on pharmacy as well as clinician workflows. The new EHR already contained numerous order sets and convenience panels. The physician informaticist ensured that order sets would reflect current local physician workflows, and the pharmacy informaticist ensured that convenience order sets would facilitate pharmacy workflow including validation and clinical review of the medication orders. Both teams worked via a formal process to identify gaps in the new vendor product that needed to be filled, and gaps in current workflows for which the new product could provide a solution. This process began as soon as the system announced a change in EHR vendor and continued until go-live 2½ years later. This is in stark contrast to the initial EHR installation for which order set and pharmacy build occurred over a period of 17 months with a much smaller staff.

The prior experiences led to several other changes in approach. The first EHR installation used a "train-the-trainer" model to onboard clinicians and pharmacists. Those who served as trainers were not veteran users of the system, which probably introduced inefficient workflows and workarounds.

For the EHR transition, training was far more intensive. For the pharmacists, the vendor recommended 2-month training; the hospital expanded this to 4 months. Key components in this transition included a full understanding of the vocabulary and terminology of each vendor's product, basic login processes, side-by-side screenshots comparing the legacy and new systems, study guides, and assigned, extensive practice problems with practice patients in a comprehensive training environment. In-house pharmacists and consulting professional trainers long-experienced in the use of the new EHR led the training. Each pharmacist had to complete a competency program.

The pharmacy department allotted 20 h of training time for each pharmacist incorporated as part of their routine daily workflow. Pharmacists and pharmacy department leadership invested over 400 h of training and over 60 h of technician training within normal working hours, without scheduled overtime. Normal pharmacy departmental operations continued without interruptions or reductions in services.

Prior to installation of the new EHR, the chief medical informatics officer gave numerous presentations about expectations, especially for mandatory CPOE. A slow cultural shift did seem to occur, perhaps aided by the time that elapsed between the merger of the two organizations and the new EHR go-live.

After installation of the new product, there were no delays in validation, clinical review, or dispensing of pharmacy products. Clinicians expressed satisfaction that many order sets were available in the new system, and that even ones that the larger institution had built reflected the workflow nuances of the local hospital. Convenience sets were present; pharmacists did not have to manually enter orders. Although many clinicians grumbled about the CPOE requirement, there was 100% electronic compliance within a few days for inpatient orders.

Author's Analysis

For the first EHR go-live, the informaticists correctly focused on CPOE adoption and physician workflow but neglected adequate attention to the downstream impact on the pharmacy. The lack of resources to build both the clinician order sets with full details and the corresponding pharmacy build for those clinicians still using paper contributed to the extensive backlogs.

Although the budgetary and personnel constraints were real hindrances, the lack of fully analyzed electronic workflows in retrospect should have signaled a reconsideration of the go-live timeline. There was an overly optimistic expectation of the clinician culture that they would adopt CPOE quickly, which would obviate the obstacles. This optimism obscured planning for the larger-than-expected amount of paper orders.

With the transition to the new EHR, CPOE became mandatory. Written orders (with a few well-defined exceptions) were not allowed. This cultural shift contributed to success.

Recognizing the naiveté of the informaticists' first attempts led to clear and honest after-action analysis and conclusions. Although it is true that the second transition involved a larger, more experienced staff, the informaticists at the community hospital were keenly aware of local requirements and were able to work with the incoming EHR team to assure a smooth and successful transition.

Editor's Commentary

The basic structure of the modern hospital and its various departments, including medical, nursing, laboratory, imaging, and others, has been in place for over a century. Systematizing the flow of information and work across these departments—which is part of what is entailed by the implementation of a comprehensive EHR system—is an enormously complex and truly revolutionary undertaking. Unlike most of the cases in this book, this one contrasts two projects that occurred several years apart: the first of them highly troubled and the second remarkably successful. In doing so, it provides a helpful reminder of the challenges of this grand undertaking, and the rapid progress that has been made in recent years along a very steep "learning curve".

The most obvious flaw in the approach taken with the first implementation was the failure to recognize the degree to which an existing system (the convenience order sets) was contributing to efficiency and patient safety on a day-to-day basis. While it may seem obvious, it is absolutely critical, with every implementation, to make a list of the things that are working well and make sure that they aren't unintentionally disrupted. This may be particularly difficult when those systems include nonelectronic processes, like paper forms. Also, if these systems have been in place for a long time and are highly ingrained in day-to-day work, the individuals who use them might not even think to mention them when they are asked "what are the tools that you use to help you get your work done?" However, simple methods, like shadowing individuals as they work, can uncover them.

From another perspective, this story also speaks to the fact that some departments or professional roles within a health delivery system may receive less consideration than others in the implementation of health IT systems. This may reflect an intentional strategy informed by concern for maximizing the efficiency of the highest-paid staff members as well as political factors. However, as the case illustrates, interdependencies exist among all hospital personnel, not unlike species in an ecosystem. A software problem that reduces the efficiency of a pharmacist may affect the workflows of nursing and medical staff, as well as the outcome of greatest concern to the overall organization—the outcome of the patient.

The authors point out that the second implementation included a larger staff and more time for analysis, system configuration, and user training. These were undoubtedly important success factors, but I suspect that staff composition and methodology were at least as important. Including a broader representation of the end-user community sharply reduces the risk of overlooking the systems that work correctly, or missing some important implication of a software configuration or workflow design decision. In addition, it seems that in the second project, the team systematically looked for gaps (e.g. gaps in order set coverage) between current and future states to avoid repeating the initial experience. This is particularly critical in projects where users will be required to utilize a particular technology, as occurred in the second project.

Lastly, this case illustrates the vital importance of experience in an informatics team. As noted above, the application of informatics to health care is a revolutionary undertaking, which, while perhaps not in its infancy, is at most in its adolescence. Just as every patient is different and a clinician's skill grows with everyone they treat, every informatics project is different, and informaticist who is willing to confront mistakes and learn from them will find that with each successive project, their insights and judgment continually evolve.

Lessons Learned

- Close cooperation between physician, pharmacy, and nursing informaticists can avert unexpected breakdowns of medication processes.
- End-to-end analysis of workflows is crucial to ensure smooth new or transitioning EHR installations.

- Thorough functional testing and gap analysis is mandatory, with participation from each department impacted by workflow changes, including testing of unusual workflows and workflow variations.
- The cost-savings of a train-the-trainer model may be lost if inexperienced staff cannot be trained effectively to address expected and unexpected events.

Chapter 17

Device Selection: No Other Phase Is More Important: Mobile Nursing Devices

Editor: Gail Keenan

University of Florida

Contents

Project Categories: infrastructure and technology

Lessons Learned Categories: leadership, project management, workflow

Case Study

Several years ago, the author participated as a consultant in a device needs assessment for point-of-care documentation devices for Big Healthcare System (BHS). Our consultant team was engaged because of an unsatisfactory response from an employee to a member of the facility's board of directors. The question was "How did we arrive at the decision to select these certain machines that you are asking $1.7 million to purchase?"

Our team defined the following metrics for device selection:

Device form factor analysis (workstations on wheels, or WOWs), tablets, other handheld devices)
Space availability within patient rooms during use and storage

Provisions for spare machines
Downtime strategies
Analysis of various clinician usage and preferences
Wireless networking capacity and coverage
Integration with bar coding and scanning technologies
Electrical outlet availability (location and quantity)
Reallocation of existing desktop machines for physician usage.

In total, this process was completed over the course of 8 weeks, and upon presentation to the board of directors, our team received a standing ovation. Upon completion of our work, we presented our strategy and success around device selection, and the abstract of this write-up received a national award.

Based on this success, there was great confidence in our processes. In a new opportunity for a similar device selection process as part of a larger project at a Regional Community Hospital (RCH) in the West, we expected to repeat our success. The project was initiated, and RCH built a team of invested, skilled, and knowledgeable clinical and information technology staff. However, the device selection team was scheduled to meet weekly, as opposed to the concentrated "all hands on deck" efforts experienced at BHS. Thus, from the project design stage, the process was changed to be longer in duration at RCH than our process of 8 weeks at BHS. Almost 2 years later, point-of-care devices were only just being purchased for use by nursing assistants, respiratory care therapists, and some sporadic use in the intensive care unit.

As a result of the slower, comprehensive, and methodical process for device selection, we identified opportunities that would not have been possible in a quicker, more concentrated project. Some of our notable findings are the following:

The emergence of newer point-of-care technologies (tablets with scanners)
Postponement of capital expenditures
Reconciling specific challenges with wireless network coverage and capacity constraints
Resolution of infection control issues related to device cleaning and storage
Planning for medication administration and pharmacy delivery process changes
Configuration of WOWs.

This methodical approach created a new challenge to our credibility, especially among the nursing staff. Because significant aspects of point-of-care device selection require participation from front-line nursing staff, we engaged the nursing staff early in the selection approval process. Although early involvement provided education and buy-in, it also led to significant delays in acquisition and deployment, which caused frustration among the nursing staff.

Author's Analysis

The single most important lesson learned is that the desired outcomes should dictate the duration and method of the decision-making process that is needed when selecting point-of-care devices. Both short and prolonged decision-making processes bring benefits and challenges. For example, the singular decisions and delays that occurred at RCH actually translated into a number of benefits. The selection team was able to develop a better understanding of the nurses' needs and to value their input, which resulted in greater buy-in among the nurses. On the other hand, the cumulative nature of the delays was a source of frustration, causing the team to appear inept and adversely influencing the senior management's perceptions of the validity of the team's recommendations. While this manuscript was being written, we neared what we hoped would be the end of the device selection and acquisition cycle. We designed a phased purchase and implementation planned to occur over the course of the next 6 months. This should allow for device storage, power management, and configuration as well as education, training, and workflow redesign for pharmacy and nursing staff.

Should this author participate in a similar project in the future, the experiences at both organizations will serve well. Point-of-care device selection timelines can and should be set by the interdisciplinary device selection team. While this team adhered to their mission, the practical objectives were missed because of a strict interpretation.

Editor's Commentary

This case illustrates one of the central tensions of planning for any type of change in a healthcare environment: that between taking sufficient time for meticulous planning and execution, and going so slowly that the benefits of the effort are delayed, the community of users gets discouraged, and the internal sponsors of the effort may suffer political damage or loss of credibility. The author wisely suggests that neither approach is always appropriate. Rather, a conscious decision should be made based on the trade-offs involved and how they relate to the organization's priorities.

Because conventional wisdom extols the merits of "decisiveness," it is no surprise that most would favor the short process of BHS in device selection if given the choice between it and the longer RCH process. Certainly, the extra costs of a longer process alone provide "immediate" and powerful evidence that when presented will quickly squelch any interest in engaging in a more involved and longer selection process. Most would agree, however, that our health technology decisions have a dramatic impact on the delivery of care and once made cannot be easily reversed. It thus is absolutely essential that the very best decisions be made in the selection phase because this is the only phase in which the purchase of a bad system can be prevented and the associated costs abated.

The piece most frequently given the least attention in the selection phase is the expected impact of technology on the user, whose work should be made easier, safer, more efficient, and effective. In this scenario, RCH was more cognizant of the people issues than BCH. Nonetheless, the case study did indicate that RCH lacked a strategy for how to efficiently incorporate the "people side" into the selection. RCH focused on learning the nurses' opinions about and getting buy-in for a system that the user had not tested under real-time conditions. Clinicians' opinions of systems that have not been fully tested under real-time conditions should not be treated as conclusive evidence of the benefits and value of the system. To remedy this repeating problem, I recommend that all organizations engage in a process by which the products being reviewed are tested under simulated conditions in a clinical setting. In this way, organizations will discover the overt and covert impact of these devices on the users and the system at large.

Lessons Learned

- Structure a decision-making process to achieve the desired outcomes and communicate this to participants.
- The "selection" phase is the critical phase to prevent the purchase of bad technology; invest time and money to be very thoughtful about HIT selection.
- The opinions of users about products they have never used under real-time conditions are not solid evidence of the value of an information technology device.
- Simulate the impact of devices during evaluation under real-time conditions to better understand the effect on users and the care delivery system as a whole.

Chapter 18

How Many Is Too Many: ICU Data Capture

Editor: Kai Zheng
University of California-Irvine

Contents

Project Categories: inpatient electronic health record (EHR), infrastructure and technology

Lessons Learned Categories: data model, leadership/governance, training, workflow

There is no question that technology capable of capturing critical data into electronic health records (EHRs) offers significant advantages to nurses and other clinicians. Various vendor products can capture all vital signs; some also capture cardiac rhythm, patient activity and movement, or data from indwelling devices. The nurse or physician must review the data either on device screen or in the EHR, and accept, decline, or edit the information before it becomes part of the final record.

A community hospital was using data capture technology to pull vital sign data into its EHR. One critical care unit used one vendor product, while another used a different product. This was due to gradual introduction of the technology over time as different units were refurbished. Analysts, nurses, and physicians knew that the two products analyzed trend data differently. In one case, the product reported the geometrical mean data of the recorded values over a designated interval (generally 15 min, but this was adjusted according to physician orders), while the other transmitted to the data capture interface the most recent values within the 30 s prior to transmission.

Nurses in the respective units received orientation to these differences as they rotated through the units. All nurses were aware of the need to validate the readings irrespective of the technology, and adjust therapy with the technical differences in mind.

Much later, the community hospital merged with a large integrated delivery network. This included a decided transformation to the larger hospital's EHR. The larger institution questioned the differences in the output of the two vital sign vendor products and raised concerns about continuing with either product. There was immediate concern from the nursing and physician staff about removal of a technology with which everyone was familiar.

The plan to change EHRs was already in the works, and the transition was imminent. The hospital was faced with a dilemma: continuing with a two-product solution, with which staff were well acquainted or abandoning one product. However, for the latter solution, there was no assurance if and when the monitoring equipment could be replaced and it was known that the cost would be extraordinary—at least $1 million. Staff expressed considerable concern regarding potential reduction in their efficiency and disruption to their workflow that might be associated with either proposed change.

The experts in the technology of these products, with vendor support, gave several educational sessions to the larger institution's information technology (IT) and information security teams, as well as to the medical executive committee and the nursing staff. It was concluded that the differences in reporting were relatively minor, especially for short time interval data. Since both products are commonly used in many hospitals across the country, and were fully licensed and approved, there were no legal issues identified. Further, staff already using these devices were well acquainted with the details of the equipment. The community hospital personnel reassured the larger system, which allowed continuation of data capture from both devices into the EHR despite the differences between the various units.

For the hospital, it came down to a managerial decision: using a single vendor solution which could be disruptive to the workflow of many clinicians and incur a considerable cost to correct? Or accept the relatively minor technical differences and mitigate any risks by careful orientation and instruction to staff? Rather than interfering with workflows during the looming EHR transition, the hospital and governing institution decided to continue with both products.

Author's Analysis

Some have called for more post-marketing surveillance of medical devices to understand performance differences and any possible consequences of differences in the real world.[1] The Food and Drug Administration (FDA) currently has no guidelines requiring medical device vendors to have a standard testing environment.[2] It is difficult to predict the behavior of such devices without real-time data. At the very least, there are several scenarios that might assist implementers to develop, test, upgrade, and apply patches for such devices:

1. Take down interfaces and use a "dummy" to produce vital signs and connect to the EHR.
2. Register a test patient in a production environment and have the dummy module feed vital signs.
3. Temporarily repoint production interfaces to a test environment for each vendor product to test safely. This would necessitate a downtime to those who use the functionality in production.

---

[1] Reynolds IS, Rising JP, Coukell AJ, Paulson KH, Redberg RF. Assessing the safety and effectiveness of devices after US Food and Drug Administration Approval. *JAMA Int Med.* 2014;174(11):1773–1779.

[2] https://www.fda.gov/medicaldevices/deviceregulationandguidance/overview/ucm134499.htm accessed August 16, 2018.

Editor's Commentary

While poor data interoperability remains a key barrier to effective health information exchange, in recent years, significant progress has been made in developing interoperability standards and enforcing their use among EHR vendors. By contrast, how to reliably and consistently move data between medical devices and health IT systems has received far less attention. There seems to be a presumption that, because physiological data such as vital signs are highly structured and relatively less complex, incorporating such data into the EHR should be problem-free.

However, as this case amply demonstrates, different medical device vendors may decide to develop their own way of reporting data to the EHR; this variation could be multifaceted, from the frequency of data reporting to how data are summarized and presented. In clinical environments that have to use a mixture of products from different device vendors, this could result in confusions, higher cognitive load exerted upon clinicians who need to constantly remember and reconcile the differences, and thus a greater patient safety risk.

Adopting products from the same vendor may appear to be a plausible solution. However, because of a large number of legacy systems that are still in use, making such investments is unrealistic for many clinical settings. Thus, dealing with multiple vendor products, each having a different way of handling data, will be a long-lasting task. How to keep the balance between tolerating imperfect data due to vendor variation and eliminating this patient safety hazard with a high cost is a difficult managerial decision for healthcare administrators.

As this case summarizes, there are multiple remedies to the problem ranging from enhancing staff training to thorough testing of medical devices prior to acquisition and upgrading, with special attention paid to how well their data can be integrated into the existing data and IT environment. However, to reach a longer-term solution, it requires the industry to come together to develop data exchange standards for reporting the data captured by their devices to the EHR. Otherwise, we will be having this same discussion over and over again.

In the end, it is impossible to fully address all of the system support and end-user training issues when multiple complex systems are used as described in this case. The challenge for any organization is to know whether enough of the potential issues are being addressed to avoid an adverse medical event, which can only be fully assessed in hindsight. This case should be viewed as a "failure waiting to happen" as opposed to one that has already occurred.

Lessons Learned

- A full understanding of the output of any data-generating devices and the data-normalizing process in the middleware is essential for proper interpretation of the data captured.
- Develop a testing plan prior to implementation of medical devices and middleware, including upgrades or interfacing to EHRs, or other information systems.
- Users of the technology must receive adequate education about the data tools to fully understand what the information means for their patients.
- Caution must be taken when proposing to remove technology that has proven to be in safe use.

Chapter 19

Simultaneous Systems Migration: Fetal Monitoring

Editor: Christina Stephan
University of Missouri

Contents

Project Categories: inpatient electronic health record (EHR)

Lessons Learned Categories: systems configuration, technology problems

At one of the system's hospitals, a hospital-wide implementation was planned to transition to a new electronic health record (EHR) system for both the inpatient and outpatient facilities. Prior to the EHR system migration, the documentation was highly fragmented because various systems were used for admitting, discharging, billing, and documenting patient care. For the Labor and Delivery (L&D) department, this entailed the implementation of two additional modules. The new EHR included a new fetal monitoring system and a new operating room (OR) module for surgical patients. Prior to the system migration, documentation for mothers in the L&D department took place in EHR A, and the documentation for the baby was done in EHR B. There was no interfacing between the two systems, and much of the information had to be transcribed from one electronic record to the next. A significant amount of documentation was still occurring on paper.

Prior to the system migration go-live, the L&D department used System W for the surveillance and archiving of the fetal tracing. There was central fetal monitoring surveillance at various locations throughout the unit as well as in each birthing room. Although System W had the capability to support full documentation, a different system was being used for documentation during L&D phase. A new fetal monitoring system was selected because of its capability to interface with the new EHR. Documentation and vital signs from the fetal monitoring system would flow directly into the

EHR, and information entered in the EHR would flow back to the fetal monitoring system. The goal for this implementation was to consolidate the various systems into one in order to achieve one comprehensive record and for authorized access to patient information at the bedside.

Much planning took place in anticipation of the new EHR and new fetal monitoring system. Normally, L&D was a very busy unit, and unexpected arrivals might show up at any time. For the go-live, however, an effort was made not to schedule any elective procedures or inductions in order to maintain a low census. In addition, more staff and super-users were hired in order to facilitate a smoother transition.

On the day of go-live, the plan was to go live with the new fetal monitoring system first, and a few hours later with the new EHR. On Saturday at 11:00 p.m., the current fetal monitoring system was deactivated, and the staff was instructed to switch to downtime procedures. This meant that for that during the specified period, all fetal monitoring tracings were not going to be saved electronically, and the paper tracings were going to be appropriately labeled and archived to in the Health Information Management (HIM) department.

Switching from the current fetal monitoring system to the new fetal monitoring system entailed switching to new Moxa network cables because the old cables were not compatible with the new fetal monitoring system. The switching out of the cables began at 11:00 p.m. and was expected to be completed by 1:00 a.m., by which time the new Moxa network cables were to be plugged into their respective ports. At approximately 1:00 a.m., the switch to the new fetal monitoring system was completed and the tracings began to be saved electronically. The fetal tracings were viewable on the central surveillance screens as well in each of the birthing rooms. As a safety measure, the nurse manager and the obstetrics director made the decision to continue archive paper fetal tracings from the fetal monitors. During this time, the current EHR was deactivated, and the staff switched to downtime documentation procedures for the EHR. There was a lot of chaos because the staff was adapting to a new EHR and a new fetal monitoring system simultaneously.

At approximately 5:30 a.m., the L&D nurse educator, who was working in the capacity of a super-user, became aware that a paper fetal tracing did not match the fetal surveillance screen. Upon closer inspection, the charge nurse and the nurse educator discovered that none of the fetal tracings matched to the correct patient. There were a total of 11 fetal tracings affected. The onsite implementation team supporting the fetal monitoring system, as well as the hospital's IT team, were immediately notified. At this point, the fetal monitoring system was shut down in order to determine what had transpired. The L&D nurses were informed to disregard the electronic fetal tracings and to use the paper fetal strips in making any clinical decisions.

Upon further investigation, the IT clinical application analyst and the project manager determined that when plugging the Moxa cable into the ports, the team assumed that the corresponding ports were directly aligned when in fact, the correct port was the one immediately below it. In addition, the cables had been labeled erroneously in the old fetal monitoring system all along.

Once it was discovered that the Moxa cables had been transposed, an action plan was quickly put in place. A team consisting of the fetal monitor implementation team, the IT application analyst, and nursing staff assembled to correctly plug the cables to the appropriate ports, and to properly label the cables. Once each connection was made, the fetal tracing was relaunched, and the team asked each nurse individually to verify that the fetal tracing matched the patient. Nursing staff noted in each patient record that the electronic fetal tracings should be disregarded and saved on paper for the specified time period. Nursing staff conducted a reconciliation to ensure that all affected patients were captured, that an event note was documented, and that the paper fetal tracings were archived by HIM.

Author's Analysis

This purely mechanical set of errors could have been prevented by establishing an orderly approach to the connections of the fetal monitoring system. Testing should have involved both IT and the clinical team, to more easily review and confirm that the tracing corresponded to the correct patients. Combining this system replacement with the go-live for a new EHR may have led to this error due to the sheer volume of activity at the health system and involving IT.

However, a simple review of the connection setup followed by testing should have been required prior to go-live with clinical monitoring data as important as fetal tracings.

- First go live with the fetal monitoring system and do a separate go-live for the EHR.
- Have each nurse verify that the fetal tracings correspond to the correct patient.
- Test, label, and diagram existing connections prior to installations of new cables accordingly.
- Have checklist in place to ensure no steps are missed.

Expert Commentary

EHR system migration is increasingly common as is the addition of more advanced EHR tools to existing systems. Much of this process is like the initial implementation of a new EHR system; however, there are additional considerations and decisions to be addressed during planning and implementation phases.

In this case study, the health care organization has planned an EHR system enterprise migration and concurrent addition of the L&D departments. Either endeavor is a complex undertaking alone, while the simultaneous system migration combined with the addition of a new clinical department taxed the implementation team and stakeholders. This approach also introduced patient safety concerns with the discovery of a misconfigured monitoring system in the L&D department.

Frameworks and/or checklists are frequently used in the planning and implementation process, and there are many to choose from. One framework, the sociotechnical framework (Sittig and Singh, 2010), describes eight elements. The eight elements include the hardware and software; clinical content; the user interface; people/system users; clinical workflow and communication processes; internal organizational policies, procedures, organizational culture, external rules, and regulations; the measurement; and monitoring (For further descriptions and examples, see citation below.) Hardware and infrastructure considerations, especially inspection and validation, could have identified and averted the connection errors among monitoring equipment. While this was a critical patient safety issue in this case study, discovery of the misconnections required correction and testing and validation, introduced additional unexpected time and effort, consumed unbudgeted resources, and caused unnecessary implementation delays.

Each of the eight elements described in the socio-technical framework should be carefully considered by a fully engaged group of stakeholders. Separately identified implementation stages should be planned in detail and might include the transition process, data migration, validation and retention, implementation staffing, and expected outcomes. Use of frameworks or checklists has become a necessary task in implementation and system migration. This case, which describes a planning process, illustrates the consequences of the lack of use of a safety checklist or framework to inform a comprehensive systematic implementation plan.

Lessons Learned

- Multisystem implementations are significantly more complex than single-system implementations.
- Detailed project management must include software and hardware across all systems involved.
- Thorough planning and testing must be developed across each new or modified information system.
- End-users, especially clinicians, must be involved in the testing prior to go-live.

Additional Reading

Dhillon-Chattha P, McCorkle R, Borycki E. An evidence-based tool for safe configuration of electronic health records: The eSafety checklist. *Appl Clin Inform*. October 2018;9(4):817–830. doi:10.1055/s-0038-1675210. Epub November 14, 2018. www.ncbi.nlm.nih.gov/pubmed/30428487.

Pageler NM, Grazier G'Sell MJ, Chandler W, Mailes E, Yang C, Longhurst CA. A rational approach to legacy data validation when transitioning between electronic health record systems. *J Am Med Inform Assoc*. September 2016;23(5):991–994. doi:10.1093/jamia/ocv173. Epub March 14, 2016. www.ncbi.nlm.nih.gov/pubmed/26977100.

Engelmann C, Ametowobla D. Advancing the integration of hospital IT: Pitfalls and perspectives when replacing specialized software for high-risk environments with enterprise system extensions. *Appl Clin Inform*. April 2017;8(2): 515–528. doi:10.4338/ACI-2016-06-RA-0100.

Chapter 20

Notification Failure: Critical Laboratory Result

Editor: Karl Poterack
Mayo Clinic

Contents

Project Categories: inpatient electronic health record (EHR)

Lessons Learned Categories: system configuration, system design

Emergency department (ED) physicians like to stay on top of laboratory results. Our electronic health record (EHR) system has several signals to notify us of new laboratory results, such as on trackboards and within patient charts. These signals can further stratify whether the results are normal, abnormal, or markedly abnormal—also called "critical" results, which were formerly called "panic" values in the literature.

However, it's possible to miss critical results because the trackboard is full of other patients and other signals, or the patient with a critical result went home, and their name has come off the board already. Because of this, we also rely on a telephone backup system, to ensure that ED physicians do not miss a critical laboratory result.

Whenever a laboratory assay produces a critical value, the laboratory software sends a message to a technician at the laboratory call center regarding the value, as well as information on the patient and where the order came from. For example, the technician may receive a message about an elevated troponin signifying cardiac damage from a myocardial infarction, or a positive blood culture suggesting sepsis, as well as the ordering provider name, the date and time, and the patient's last reported location.

Every department in our hospital has a numeric code, based on our decades-old registration system. Therefore, if a critical value came from a test ordered by the ED, the laboratory technician would see “Ordering Department: 491” in the laboratory system. For years, this was the laboratory call center’s signal to pick up the phone, call the ED charge nurse, and relay the laboratory value and patient name. The ED charge nurse, in turn, would find ED providers taking care of the patient to let them know about the critical value. A simpler process where the laboratory technician just paged the ordering provider was rejected because too many ED providers were unreachable after their shift ended.

The patient registration system, however, eventually received an upgrade. Upon the upgrade, departments would be identified with words rather than their old numeric codes. For example, “491” would now be denoted as “ED,” which sounds like progress.

There was extensive testing of the interfaces between the registration system, clinical ordering and documentation systems, and the laboratory systems to make sure that patient movements and orders and results were all properly routed. The interface between the laboratory system and the laboratory’s call center, however, was not specifically tested.

On the day the new registration upgrade was implemented, the system appeared to be running smoothly. Soon, a patient in the ED generated a critical laboratory value. The patient was a middle-aged man with a history of diabetes, smoking, and hypertension. He complained of chest pain and palpitations. On a recent prior ED visit, he had been worked up for heart disease—but the testing at that time was negative.

The ED doctors on this new encounter focused on the potential for a pulmonary embolism (PE), but they also tested his troponin level and performed an electrocardiogram (EKG) to assess for cardiac risk.

These doctors handed off the patient to the evening team. The testing for a PE came back negative, and as for cardiac issues, the EKG was unchanged from prior. The evening ED team made a plan to discharge the patient. However, the troponin result was markedly elevated. This was apparent on the patient’s chart, and on the EHR trackboard, but the providers who received sign-out for this patient simply didn’t check these laboratory results; everyone had been focused on the PE workup.

Prior to this upgrade, the laboratory call center would normally act as a failsafe and call the ED charge nurse to notify the ED care team about the critical value. However, that call never came because the laboratory call center never received the alert for the elevated troponin value.

The call center software was configured to receive critical laboratories for specific departments—departments denoted by numeric codes. If the message had said: “Elevated troponin on Patient X, from 491” it would have gone through, and the call center system would have gotten the message. However, because of the registration system upgrade, the message said: “Elevated troponin on Patient X, from ED,” and the call center system rejected the message. The call center technician never saw it. As a result, the patient was discharged, despite having an acute myocardial infarction.

When the patient returned to the ED a few days later, with ongoing chest pain, and now, some permanent damage to his heart, the ED team finally noticed the elevated troponin from the prior visit, and an inquiry was begun as to why it went unremarked upon.

Author’s Analysis

The inquiry into this event led to the discovery that the call laboratory center system was not configured to receive messages from laboratory with the new department codes. The initial medical error report was filed by the hospital’s Risk Management team immediately. Corrections to the laboratory call center system were implemented within a little over 2 weeks. A root-cause analysis (RCA) was performed about 2 months later.

The RCA revealed that a change to the registration system meant the laboratory system was sending new messages to the laboratory's call center system, which was not properly configured to receive them. The call center system, although tasked to act as an important backup for critical laboratory-value notifications, had not received much attention in this upgrade. The IT department and vendor staff implementing the registration system upgrade communicated with their counterparts for other major systems, but they never considered testing the call center system, which was two steps downstream.

Also, the laboratory call center's system failure was that it was silent immediately after go-live. Because the system received only several messages per day, the decrease was too few to be noticed by end-users right after the registration system upgrade occurred. As a result, the notification system failure was not reported until this case was investigated.

Although it may have been tedious, these infrequently used downstream systems should have been mapped and tested with routine and outlying edge cases, prior to upgrades, to prevent patient harm.

Editor's Commentary

This case is a striking reminder of the multiple interdependencies that exist in the modern hospital; many of these interactions and interdependencies may not be appreciated without a very thorough analysis. Without bringing together stakeholders in multiple areas, all with a deep working knowledge of daily operations, and running step by step thru detailed scenarios, the situation described above would likely not have been identified in advance. Many basic quality improvement techniques recommend just this sort of process: bringing together stakeholders and process owners, not just "nominal" owners (e.g., department chairs and unit managers) but those with actual deep knowledge of the processes involved, to walk thru step by step and in detail, various scenarios, especially including those that are critical but perhaps less common, like the one detailed above (www.asq.org, Hughes, 2008).

Additionally, cases like this illustrate that it is easier to detect system malfunctions when an undesired result occurs rather than when a desired result fails to occur. Wright et al. showed that "users were much more likely to notice and report false positive alerts (ie, incorrect alerts) rather than false negatives, where an alert should have fired but did not" (Wright, 2018).

Ultimately, even with careful planning and testing in advance, there will be some scenarios such as the above that will only be detected once the "failure" occurs in the live environment. Thus, after any upgrade or system change, users need to be extra vigilant and always on the alert for potential issue. Additionally, infrastructure should be in place that is specifically looking for potential problems and that is empowered to address them when identified.

Lessons Learned

- Interdisciplinary stakeholder teams are essential to identify and evaluate existing workflows and the impact of technology driven change
- Workflow analysis should identify and review critical processes for potential impacts prior to go-live with new technology, systems, and processes
- Downstream systems should be tested as part of the workflow and system analysis of new solutions

Chapter 21

Collaboration Is Essential: Care Planning and Documentation

Editor: Jonathan Leviss
Greater New Bedford Community Health Center

Contents

Project Categories: inpatient electronic health record (EHR)

Lessons Learned Categories: leadership/governance, system design, workflow

Case Study

Several years ago, a group of researchers conducted a 2-year test of an electronic care planning and documentation tool under real-time conditions in four different hospitals. The application was web-deployed and, though not directly connected to each organization's electronic health record (EHR) during the study, it appeared seamless to users. Links to the patient's EHR and the care plan application were readily accessible through tabs located on the central computer screen, enabling the effective workflow. Moreover, since the care plan information was not redundant to or directly dependent on items in the EHR, it was not necessary to build a complicated interface between the two. Patient demographic information was the only redundancy and was entered separately into the care planning system on the first admission to avoid needing to create separate HL7 admission/discharge/transfer (ADT) feeds from each test site's EHR before full testing was completed. Prior to using the application, each staff nurse at the pilot sites was trained to represent patient problems, outcomes, and interventions with standardized terms and measures and to keep the patient's plans of care current. Once competency in the application was established, the nurse was required to enter an initial care plan or update at handoff on every patient cared for by the nurse during the previous shift.

Compliance for updating care plans at handoffs was astonishingly high (80%–90%) across all participant units in comparison to the less than 50% rate that others have found when care plan updating requirements are less stringent (such as every 24 h) (Keenen et al., 2012). The simplicity of the system and requirement for regular updating at handoff helped ensure care plans were current and in turn supported nurses in maintaining a shared understanding of the overall care and progress toward desired outcomes, a feature lacking in contemporary EHRs. At the end of the study, the nurses in all units were significantly more satisfied with the new tool than with the previous care planning systems and advocated strongly for retention of the tool. The data collected with the system provided a rich source for examining the impact of nursing care on patient outcomes because the data were coded with standardized terminologies and stored in a carefully designed relational database. Since the typical formats of nursing documentation do not allow for meaningful evaluation of the impact of nursing care, the ability to conduct such evaluation was considered a truly transformational benefit. Finally, word about the care planning system spread to nurses in other health systems; they became interested in adopting the care planning system as well.

Unfortunately, intense advocacy by managerial and staff nurses for adopting the care planning system after the study was met with opposition from central decision makers responsible for the information technology (IT) decisions at the same hospitals. The nurses consistently were told that it was necessary to adopt a single fully integrated EHR and were assured that the EHR (either in place or to be implemented) would provide functionality similar to the care planning system. As a result, the fully tested care planning system was pulled from each of the four test organizations. Previously interested health systems and hospitals not in the study also decided not to adopt the new system for the same reasons. Ultimately, the nurses in both the study and non-study hospitals seeking to implement the care planning and documentation system accepted the decisions of the IT teams at their respective hospitals, trusting that the functionality would soon appear in their EHRs.

Author's Analysis

Five years later, none of the major EHR systems in the healthcare organizations described above contained the robust features of the fully tested care planning system. The care planning features of these EHR systems provide only minimal functionality that has to be tailored to meet each hospital unit's needs. As a result, the current care planning tools at these hospitals offer no improvements over the traditional systems previously in place or the proven benefits of the care planning application. Subsequent research has corroborated the power of the data collected with the care planning system by demonstrating its value in benchmarking and the identification of nursing best practices. Most disheartening is that nurses in the organizations referred to above anecdotally acknowledge that they complete care plan documentation in EHRs mainly to meet Joint Commission and other external standard requirements rather than to support quality and efficient patient care.

There were a number of failure points in the case described above, but most link directly back to the fact that the parties involved based their decisions on insufficient information and faulty assumptions. When the model system was studied, it was common knowledge that implementing care plans and their documentation was problematic and no major EHR vendor had effectively addressed this problem.

Nurses wrongly assumed that technical barriers prevented the study tool from connecting to their EHRs and ceased to advocate for its implementation or continued use. The nurses also failed by not demanding that the chief health information system decision makers provide evidence to support the assertions about the future development and functionality of the EHRs. Instead, the nurses assumed that the decision makers were operating with sufficient knowledge about workflow and care management systems; the nurses did not recognize that it was unrealistic to expect those who are not nurses to make high-quality decisions about point-of-care work without ample input from the nurses who would be affected.

The chief health information system decision makers failed to recognize the complexity of the very costly decisions with which they were charged and the limitations of their own knowledge. The IT leaders discounted the preferences of the nurses and made assurances that could not be fulfilled. Although engineering, computer, and information experts are needed to build EHRs, these experts are not clinicians and thus do not possess the clinical knowledge necessary to build or select high-quality EHRs.

In conclusion, EHRs are very complex systems and as such require the coordination of many different types of expertise to build, test, select, and implement point-of-care meaningful use. This case also provides an example of how poor outcomes can occur when stakeholders fail to take responsibility for those aspects of the EHR that are within their domains of skills and knowledge. The decision makers clearly operated outside their scope of knowledge by not seeking a better understanding of the vendor care planning systems and by discounting the vital input of the nurses. The nurses, on the other hand, failed by abdicating responsibility to decision makers without demanding that they provide convincing evidence of the espoused care planning capabilities of the vendor EHRs.

Editor's Commentary

The author correctly notes that EHR initiatives are complex and require teams of individuals with diverse expertise. Technical, clinical, and project management leaderships are all required for a successful EHR project. EHRs are first and foremost clinical initiatives, so clinical leadership must have a critical role in all decision making. However, other factors contribute to decisions about IT strategies in a health system.

Some possible causative factors in this case:

- The executive management at the involved hospitals recognized the value of the care planning and documentation application, but was concerned about deploying a research system into a production healthcare services environment without a well-resourced support team and plan.
- The executive management was concerned about how issues found in the system would be resolved, or how the product would be further developed to meet evolving needs of nursing care planning and documentation.
- There were concerns about training and implementation tools to support a large-scale rollout of the application beyond the original four research sites.
- The research application had not been sufficiently tested against security threats.

- The creators of the application were not prepared to defend themselves against potential liability claims in case of adverse events involving the software or its performance.
- The development costs of the new system were estimated to be much more than those involved in implementing a vendor-based system.

If executive or IT management decides not to deploy a system preferred or requested by clinician leaders, the decision must be carefully thought through and then communicated effectively to the clinician leaders and staff. Buy-in for decisions about which technologies *not* to implement can be as critical as buy-in for decisions about which are being implemented. Effective and open discussions about strategic health IT strategies are critical to maintaining the allegiance and commitment of all members of a hospital community. Since all health IT decisions involve trade-offs on some level, ignoring the open discussion and not reaching consensus about key strategies will create difficulties when implementing future systems. Without the adoption of information systems, meaningful use of those systems cannot be achieved. Even specific trade-offs that affect the quality of patient care may be supported by clinicians if these trade-offs contribute to a more effective, higher quality of care health system overall.

Lessons Learned

- Integrate clinicians with adequate knowledge about point-of-care processes in the governance of EHR selections and implementations.
- Validate vendors' claims about functionality.
- Determine when the integration of disparate solutions is preferable to a single integrated system.

Chapter 22

Lessons Beyond Bar Coding: Laboratory Automation and Custom Development

Editor: Edward Wu
The New Jewish Home

Contents

Project Categories: inpatient electronic health record (EHR), laboratory information systems (LISs)

Lessons Learned Categories: implementation approaches, project management, system configuration, system design, training, workflow

Case Study

In a typical pathology laboratory, there are many so-called assets that need to be identified and tracked. These include requisitions with laboratory test orders as well as patient specimens and their derivatives, such as tissue blocks and glass slides. Deploying bar code solutions to track specimens has improved automation, efficiency, traceability, and patient safety. However, the use of bar code technology in the anatomic pathology laboratory is only a recent trend. This is largely due to a lack of available vendor solutions for use in the laboratory.

As a result of increasing asset volume and growing emphasis on patient safety, several years ago the anatomic pathology laboratory at a hospital embarked on implementing a bar code solution.

As a result of this project, they were one of the first laboratories in the United States to transition from a manual, batch model operation to one that employed automated, real-time bar code tracking.

Prior to bar code implementation, tissue specimens were received in the laboratory with handwritten labels. Ideally, specimens were accompanied by paper requisitions with patient details and physician instructions. Implementing bar coding at this stage was outside the purview of the laboratory. At the receiving area, laboratory employees manually entered cases or accessioned them into the laboratory information system (LIS), after which they were assigned a unique number. Introduction of bar coding at this step helped alleviate downstream specimen and paper mismatches, as well as the need for manual key entry of the case number and other details into the LIS.

Accessioned cases were passed on to prosectors who dissected the specimens into smaller tissue pieces to be placed within plastic cassettes. Previously, the case number and tissue key code were either handwritten or printed onto the cassettes. When prosectors transitioned to bar codes, the correct patient case immediately opened up in the LIS at their workstation. By printing bar codes directly on to the tissue cassettes (as seen in Figure 22.1) only when needed, fewer mix-ups occurred.

At later stages of tissue processing, histotechnologists cut thin tissue sections for mounting on a glass slide. Bar coding these slides (as seen in Figure 22.1) not only helped avoid mismatches, but also helped drive protocols that standardized workflow (e.g., laboratory personnel determined the exact number of sections to be cut for particular biopsies). Because over one million slides are processed per year, mislabeling errors were a major concern. A labeling error could translate into a false-positive cancer diagnosis, which would have been unacceptable.

Development of a practical and scalable bar coding solution for the laboratory was challenging and took over 3 years to accomplish. This was largely due to the limited ability of vendors to integrate bar coding solutions. The current LIS vendor was interested in participating, but did not have any of the necessary hardware (such as bar code scanners). Vendors for some of the instruments were also interested, but had not yet dealt with bar code technology. The vendor selected to supply bar coding hardware did not have software that was compatible with the current LIS. As there were no off-the-shelf solutions available, it was decided to utilize an internally developed bar code solution.

Figure 22.1 Left: Plastic tissue cassettes with robust 2D bar codes embedded into the material. Right: Examples of 1D (linear) and 2D (matrix code) laser-etched bar codes used to identify and track glass slides in the laboratory.

Despite adequate planning and sound IT project management, this venture was plagued with unexpected difficulties. Much dialogue ensued around what data bar codes would contain, what they would look like, and where they would go. Prior to implementation of bar coding, case accession number and block designation were shown on the slide label. With the implementation of bar coding, laboratory personnel wanted to keep the same information on the labels and this had to be carefully balanced within the label and font-size constraints of the bar-coded labels. Several trials were required to produce the optimal label with the correct font size and an acceptable human readability component alongside the bar code. The end result was a compromise that needed to be reached between employing a robust and a scalable bar code that was still readable to the human eye. In addition to the involvement by vendors, additional consultants with the necessary technical skills had to be brought together to help integrate the information from different systems into a single bar code. This proved challenging, and a series of numerous meetings ensued with unsuccessful attempts to get the vendors to participate in an integrated single bar code. While the consultants' knowledge was helpful, the added layer of coordination added complexity that increased and compounded delays.

Overall, due to these delays and escalating costs, there was increased resistance from senior administration who wanted an explanation of ongoing expenditures to fix something they perceived was not broken. Additionally, histology laboratory staff were resistant to change and felt that bar coding was being implemented because of internal errors. They were also concerned that the new way of producing labels would require extra time and effort, which would introduce delays in their workflow.

After a pilot implementation involving one laboratory component, bar coding was rolled out to the entire laboratory in a stepwise fashion in three of the major medical centers. It soon became evident that the bar coding efforts increased efficiency and decreased labeling errors. For example, at one medical center, the number of mislabeled slides fell from 12 to 0 per month within 6 months of implementation. At another hospital, three mislabeled slide events were encountered 6 months after implementation. This was attributed to a technologist using bar code labels in batches, instead of real time. Applying this batch of labels to the various assets led to mislabeling events.

However, the histotechnologists at a separate laboratory complained that their work was now taking much longer to complete, because they were being forced to work with only one case at a time, instead of batching their tasks. Staff training and education efforts were increased, leading to increased comfort with the change, expansion of bar coding efforts, and many other laboratories around the country following suit. Adoption of specimen tracking technology has not only proved useful for asset management and error reduction, but also helped standardize workflow, supported laboratory automation, improved overall turnaround times, and driven our workflow processes in an efficient fashion.

Author's Analysis

There are no true "plug and play" implementations of technology in healthcare environments. A universal bar code that is compatiblewith all systems in use in clinical laboratories remains elusive. While the hospital was developing a customized solution for the laboratory, vendors were simultaneously developing products of their own, which caused unnecessary friction and delays to the project. To avoid such a situation, it is recommended that all parties clearly state their role, describe their current capabilities, and make sure there are no competing interests up front.

The pilot project of bar coding one component of the laboratory was a very helpful step toward a successful implementation. The staff learned that it was not necessary to bar code every single asset in the laboratory to obtain a substantial improvement in both efficiency and patient safety. To the contrary, a phased implementation often renders more favorable results, in that the reduced scope of the overall project confers greater likelihood of initial success and user acceptance.

Because this project was so novel for the laboratory, it was difficult to plan ahead and be proactive regarding some project details. Project issues would emerge and need to be resolved quickly—hence the importance of paying attention to the details of a project in uncharted territory. Additionally, with complex and protracted projects, these details had the tendency to erode morale. Sometimes it proved more important to do things quickly rather than flawlessly.

Buy-in of all stakeholders is a key component to successful IT implementation. While informatics-related technologies may offer celebrated benefits, all parties should be aware of the operational burden they may place on overall workflow. Introducing bar coding into the laboratory was initially stressful for all workers. This was not surprising as implementing new IT or systems often means significant changes to workflow, working relationships, and other aspects of employees' daily routines. The success of an organizational change requires buy-in from all stakeholders. Therefore, it is important to make sure all staff feel empowered and understand that they are part of the solution.

Human noncompliance rather than technological issues may cause IT solutions to fail. Implementation of bar coding alone without user compliance can be problematic. In order to improve the quality of the service, it became necessary to change the current operational processes. In this laboratory, that meant that some of the manual, batch-type tasks that histotechnologists performed had to be modified, even if it took them longer to complete only one task at a time.

Editor's Commentary

Bar coding has proven to be an effective way to process goods or objects through a system. In the retail sector, it has been one of the most influential technological advances, offering great gains in efficiency. However, the use of bar coding in healthcare continues to mature, as this case illustrates. The author has described three key challenges to the adoption of bar coding: a lack of integration standards, the limitations of vendor support, and the need for substantial process change.

Because of the lack of integration standards, it was extremely difficult to find anything close to a "vendor-ready" solution. Had standards for bar code integration existed, vendors could more easily work with the author in the implementation. Instead, an internally developed strategy was required, posing a situation with inherent risks. For instance, the quality and upkeep of coding are typical challenges that arise in such a development environment. Internal development here led to a protracted project and complex issues that could not be foreseen.

Vendor cooperation was limited, and there may be multiple reasons. Vendors, with their own schedules and motivations, may not have been aligned with the interests of the healthcare organization. As this case and many others have demonstrated, vendors tend to stick to what they know best. Pushing into bar code technology would throw vendors into an area of uncertainty. Even if a vendor wished to cooperate, the high degree of customization would likely not make it economically feasible, at least initially, for continued cooperation on the project. Finally, vendors typically like to limit legal liability, and venturing into bar coding may have been too risky for them.

A third hurdle that the authors faced was the need for substantial process change. As with the implementation of any technology, ensuring adherence to proper processes is essential. It was identified that technicians should be processing samples one at a time using the new system. However, after bar code implementation, technicians reverted back to the batching of samples, which introduced error into the process. Specimens may have slipped into a batch unnoticed or may have gotten mixed up after scanning. Fortunately, the authors identified these challenges quickly and emphasized the importance of retraining on this essential process change. A key lesson here is that training, monitoring of processes, and retraining are all essential components to sustaining the momentum of technology implementations.

In more general terms, this case illustrates the challenges faced by early adopters of technology. While the organization in this case did ultimately accrue benefits from the project, it is important to anticipate that using new technologies, or existing technologies in new ways, is likely to engender unanticipated difficulties.

Lessons Learned

- Internal development of software solutions is time-consuming and requires adequate development expertise.
- If there is not a vendor-ready solution, vendors may not be aligned with end-user goals.
- Process change requires monitoring, training, and retraining.
- Phased approaches to bar code solutions can minimize impacts to workflow.

Chapter 23

A Single Point of Failure: Protecting the Data Center

Editor: Bonnie Kaplan
Yale University

Contents

Project Categories: infrastructure and technology

Lessons Learned Categories: project management, technology problems

Case Study

Tertiary medical institutions typically centralize most of their mission-critical clinical data in a central data center, which is a single physical location that is closely monitored for temperature; humidity; and the presence of smoke, fire, or flooding to prevent catastrophic failures.

When sensors detect specified deviations from environmental norms, a number of protocols are initiated with the goal of minimizing data loss. These protocols include orderly shutdown of the data servers, subsequent discontinuation of electric power, proactive mitigation of environmental threats (such as the release of fire suppressants), and computer notification (via pager) to specified on-call data center personnel.

The following two examples describe incidents involving the automatic shutdown of the central data center at an urban tertiary care academic institution when sensors detected aberrant conditions. The data center contains production databases for an institution-wide intranet server and systems for institution-wide electronic medical records, computerized provider order entry (CPOE), pharmacy dispensing, admission/discharge/transfer (ADT), and intensive care unit (ICU) clinical documentation.

Example 1

In 2005, a failure of the data center fire alarm system occurred; a piece of plastic within the housing of the wall-mounted fire alarm broke. (The manufacturing cost of the failing piece was less than $1.) This resulted in the triggering of the fire alarm with a subsequent programmed, orderly shutdown of all servers, discontinuation of electric power, and release of the fire suppressant agent halon into the data center.

For several hours, all data center services were unavailable, and providers had to switch to paper-based ordering and charting until the emergent problem was handled. Once the source of the alarm was identified and the halon was cleared, the clinical data systems were restarted without data loss and with the resumption of normal function.

Example 2

Two years later, a weekend water outage in the building housing the data center was scheduled by the maintenance staff, but was not properly communicated to the engineering staff. Despite a clearly posted policy to the contrary, maintenance staff disabled a primary water pump supplying water to the building.

The water outage interrupted the chilled water supply to the data center air handlers and resulted in a malfunction, which in turn shut down the air conditioning in the building. This resulted in a rise in environmental temperature that was detected by sensors, resulting in a programmed shutdown of the clinical servers, followed by discontinuation of electric power to the data center. Because the smoke alarm was not triggered, the fire suppression agent was not released.

Data center personnel were notified immediately of the shutdown, but its cause (air conditioning failure due to the water outage) was not immediately apparent. After several hours, water services were restored, the air conditioning was restarted, and the temperature in the data center was normalized. The clinical data systems servers were restarted without data loss.

The water outage (and the resulting cascade of air conditioning failure and data center outage) forced the clinical staff to revert to paper ordering and charting. The incident resulted in no apparent patient harm, but the lack of complete and accurate data was found to be a major user concern when the incident was reviewed by an institutional committee.

Author's Analysis

Closed-loop systems (as described in the data center environmental protection system in the previous examples) automate system responses (system shutdown, threat mitigation, and staff alert) to specified rules from defined input (abnormal environmental variables). In high-risk industries such as aeronautics and nuclear power, they are used to aid human operators (who in turn override inappropriate machine responses). In clinical care, they have been used to control experimental insulin pumps, pacemakers, and anesthesia machines, but sparingly, because of inherent risks.

"Who monitors the monitors?" is an apt question regarding the design of closed-loop systems in enterprise health information systems. The increasing reliance on clinical information technology (IT) systems (since this scenario from 2007, CPOE use within the health system has increased markedly) makes even brief unanticipated outages, such as those described above, highly disruptive, and may even jeopardize patient care with errors of omission or commission and preventable delays.

Clinical data centers must ensure information (its confidentiality, integrity, and availability) with minimal unplanned downtime. With robust designs, unplanned outages are usually minimal, and closed-loop environmental monitors, as described in the examples, usually work well, thus not warranting human surveillance. However, current designs are limited to a few independent data measurements and cannot distinguish between a true threat and an internal monitoring failure. The data center monitoring system was originally implemented with the assumption that shutting down the servers in an emergency is preferable (even in error) to data loss from continued operation resulting in permanent damage. With increasing institutional reliance, the error of commission was becoming increasingly problematic and disruptive.

What can be learned from these outages?

Data centers are "single points of failure" that are protected by monitoring systems that shut down according to a predefined set of rules that have thresholds.

The acceptability of these thresholds may change over time because of changes in institutional dependence on the data center, which may require reassessment of failure modes and their acceptability.

Planning of protection responses may require consideration of unanticipated "normal" events external to the data center with override rules, workaround protocols, and timely and appropriate human interventions.

In the case of the described institution, a remote redundant secondary data center was built. Clinical systems are now configured to switch to the secondary data center automatically in a "near-real-time" fashion in the event of an outage in the primary center.

Hospital administrators, IT staff, and vendors must be aware of how defense systems for data centers function and how they fail. They also should evolve these systems from experience. The design of redundant systems (backup environmental systems and power sources, alternative short-term data storage), "smart" closed-loop systems that infer the likelihood of true threats based on multiple inputs, and critical defense protocols are key in maintaining system availability.

Editor's Commentary

Both of the examples describe unanticipated ways that system failure occurs. Each time, sensors detected abnormalities that unnecessarily led to automatic shutdown of a data center. In each example, staff reverted to manual medical record keeping with no apparent patient harm. However, out of concern about the potential implications of such outages on patient care, a remote redundant secondary data center was established, so that system functions would be switched there if an outage occurred at the primary center.

As the author points out, contingency planning and manual procedures are vital. The examples indicate how important it was to have staff able to switch to manual procedures when automated ones failed. Moreover, a wise decision was made when a secondary data center was established so that crucial system functions could be continued smoothly if the primary center fails. While this reduces risk, as the examples above amply show, all sorts of unanticipated things may happen. As the author rightly says, it is not possible to respond correctly to all situations in systems by monitoring according to predefined rules. Thresholds need to be reevaluated periodically, and processes updated based on the lessons learned with each adverse incident.

Other potential safeguards are also suggested by these examples. In the first example, a plastic part broke, and that triggered the fire alarm. Perhaps routine parts inspections or replacements would have prevented the problem. In the second example, policy violations were the triggering event for the incident. Better training of workers might be helpful, the policy could be posted more clearly, or perhaps the policy itself needs revision. If various utilities (water, electricity) are interrupted routinely, an alert system might be put in place to warn data center staff. In addition, many healthcare organizations are moving away from maintaining their own physical computing and data centers, opting instead to purchase commercial "cloud" processing and storage resources. However, these same issues apply to commercially maintained shared cloud resources, and it is incumbent on healthcare organizations to ensure that appropriate precautionary measures and fail-over capabilities are in place even if a third party is providing them.

Without more specific information about the data center environment, it is difficult to make specific recommendations with confidence, but these suggestions illustrate that there are different ways to analyze causes of failure so as to remediate them. An approach that combines multiple foci, including technical components, processes, communication, personnel, and culture, is most likely to yield successful strategies. The title of this chapter shortchanges the richness of these examples. Rather, the stories indicate multiple failure points and ways to address them.

Lessons Learned

- Downtime management requires complex planning.
- System redundancy is required across all components of health information technology (HIT).
- Automated alarms and processes must be appropriate to a specific environment.
- System interdependencies cannot be overestimated.
- Policies and procedures must include enforcement and training or retraining.
- Communication is crucial.

Chapter 24

Vendor and Customer: Single Sign-On

Editor: Justin Graham
Hearst Health

Contents

Project Categories: inpatient electronic health record (EHR), infrastructure and technology

Lessons Learned Categories: communication, implementation approaches, leadership/governance, project management

Case Study

A nationally prominent academic health system awarded a contract for single sign-on (SSO) and context management (CM). The health system was implementing new electronic health record (EHR) features including computerized provider order entry (CPOE), and the chief information officer (CIO) wanted to improve clinician workflow with SSO and CM first. The health system had conducted an extensive selection process that included an open request for proposals, vendor technology demonstrations, and reference calls to existing health systems using the technologies desired. The selection process revealed that no single vendor could provide a complete solution to the functional requirements desired by the health system, so the final contract required additional software development of the products to be implemented. A contract was signed, and the project began.

After the project kickoff, the health system and technology vendor teams reviewed project plans and set up testing and development systems. Quickly, certain conflicts emerged in the project. The health system's CIO, a clinician, delegated the project to a junior, nonclinical, information technology (IT) manager and directed the vendor team to work with the designee and the IT team. The CIO was confident in the ability of the vendor and the IT teams to develop the right solution; the vendor team did not share the same confidence. The IT manager had a background in security technology but little experience in healthcare IT and had favored a different solution during the selection process. The project team did not include clinicians from the health system as the IT manager wanted to complete the SSO and CM configuration under management of the IT department and then present a finished solution to clinicians for implementation. Despite repeated requests from the vendor, the IT manager would not allow the vendor's development or implementation teams to engage health system clinicians during implementation. Because of this, the vendor team repeatedly advised leaders within the health system that the IT manager might not be qualified to make decisions that affected clinician workflows in clinical applications. The vendor team and the health system IT team disagreed about how to implement different functions of the SSO and CM technologies and which approaches would be preferable or even acceptable to clinicians, such as the speed-performance requirements for the SSO and CM software.

It was at this point that problems started to occur. The health system requested a formal testing plan that required a model configuration to be installed in the health system's testing infrastructure. The vendor provided the software, but without the full functionality previously communicated to the health system; the vendor continued development of the anticipated functionality and planned to make available a new software release with all the necessary functionality prior to the health system's go-live date for SSO and CM. Additionally, the health system's IT team was not able to configure its IT test environment according to the vendor's recommendations for optimal software performance. In the test system as configured, the SSO and CM software did not perform as the IT manager wanted, although the vendor team was pleased with the newly developed functionality. Throughout testing, the vendor continued the development process for the new software release, modifying the software iteratively as problems were encountered. The go-live date neared, preventing a full test scenario from being performed on a single set of code. Each step in testing was applied only to the most recent software installed at the time of the test. When code changes were made, there was no time to perform regression testing.

The vendor team maintained a project plan and tracked open issues that needed to be addressed; the project manager maintained a separate list of open issues to be addressed. Most but not all issues appeared on both lists. After continued conflicts between the vendor team and the health system's IT team about software performance and functionality, the SSO and CM software implementation was stopped. The vendor's executive team and the health system's CIO agreed the project would not go live.

Author's Analysis

This biggest surprise of this project was that it proceeded as far as it did. Following the selection process, the health system should have recognized the challenges the SSO and CM project encompassed, especially because no commercially available product met the functional requirements. A reassessment of functional requirements, the desired timeline, or the dedicated project team might have mitigated sufficient risks and allowed a successful outcome. Instead, the health system forged ahead to implement "not-yet-available" software within a predefined timeframe. The health system partnered in the challenge of developing new software without recognizing it was not prepared to do so. The approach made the health system's larger health information technology (HIT) projects (including CPOE) dependent on a project that was itself precariously dependent on a vendor's ability to develop and deliver new software, the health system's ability to implement novel software, and the project supervision of a mid-level manager without appropriate healthcare workflow expertise. And, despite the admirable intent to perform adequate testing prior to implementation, the testing scenario protocols were flawed and failed to take into account the vendor's extensive ongoing software development.

The vendor, in turn, took a serious risk with a project that was likely to fail at a nationally prominent academic health system. The vendor recognized from the beginning some of the challenges resulting from the health system's approach, but did not recognize the likelihood of failure involved in developing and testing new software within the committed project timeline. The vendor appeared to be more focused on the potential benefits of successfully developing and implementing software at a prestigious health system, rather than the reality that these benefits were unlikely to be achieved with resultant negative backlash. The vendor should have said no to the unrealistic requests of the client rather than commit to deliver and then fail to do so.

Open collaborative communication to identify problems and resolve them was the missing safety net for this high-risk HIT project; the conflicts between the health system IT team and the vendor team should have been sufficient flags to both groups that the project could not succeed. Perhaps the only successful outcome of this project was that both parties ultimately agreed that the project was going to fail, and the implementation was stopped before it was rolled out and further resources (or even patient lives) were lost. Sometimes stopping a project is the best next step.

Editor's Commentary

Custom software development is a high-risk endeavor for healthcare providers. Hospitals and health systems have business goals that revolve around optimizing patient care and meeting regulatory standards, goals that are often incompatible with the iterative cycles of requirements analysis, development, testing, and documentation that good software requires. The health system described in the case doubled down on this long shot by putting the SSO and CM project in the critical path for a major EHR rollout, and compounded the risk by putting the project in the hands of someone who may not have been qualified to manage it. Fortunately, they were wise enough to recognize their overreach and pull the plug on the software before it dragged their entire EHR project (and, likely, the health system's strategic plan) down with it.

Even if the software development had gone without a hitch, the chances of project success remained slim. In all likelihood, the health system would have soon learned that an IT project intended to radically alter clinical workflow would be doomed to failure if clinicians were not involved early in the process, if only to support change management efforts.

Lessons Learned

- Sometimes the best next step in a project is to stop.
- When customers ask for what a vendor cannot deliver, or cannot deliver without unacceptable risk, vendors should not be afraid to tell their clients "no."
- Involve clinicians early and often in projects that will affect their workflow.
- Extensive testing is essential to an HIT initiative's success.
- Vendor–customer development partnerships require effective leadership for both mutual respect and frequent open communication.

Chapter 25

The Phone's On, but Nobody's Home: Communications Upgrade

Editor: Melissa Baysari
University of Sydney

Contents

Project Categories: community-facing technologies

Lessons Learned Categories: communication, staffing resources, system configuration

In 2015, our large academic medical center was not only implementing a unified electronic health record (EHR), but also implementing a state-of-the-art "call center" phone system. Both were scheduled to go live at the same time.

The impetus for the phone system change was multifactorial. The legacy phone system was not able to follow "rules" to allow forwarding phones to covering physicians, it could not provide branching message algorithms, and more importantly, it was unable to provide data metrics such as caller wait times, hold times, and dropped calls. This affected our department in many ways. Individual offices were siloed and had difficulty cross-covering each other. If, in a single secretary office, the secretary were to be out of the office, it was very difficult to provide appropriate phone coverage; there was little or no "knowledge sharing" between offices (so that even if an office could spare a secretary, he or she would have no prior experience in that office); and there was no ability to balance the load between those offices with few calls (and staff with unused capacity) and those who received very high call volumes—where patients were typically put on hold for long periods of time resulting in many dropped calls.

The new phone system addresses many of these issues: it has the ability to allow staff to answer multiple lines from any location in the department which created more flexibility in staffing; it allows for calls to be routed appropriately, for example, so that chart requests go directly to Health Information Management and billing questions go directly to Patient Accounts (without ringing in the doctor's office); and it has robust data reporting and management tools that help supervisors make near-real-time decisions. The goal was to answer phones more quickly, in a more standardized manner, to spread the load to improve patient access, and to create a backup system so that offices could continue to operate when the primary staff are out of office.

At phone go-live, offices were grouped in virtual "pods" (three doctors, each with their own secretary in general proximity to each other). In addition, go-live was intentionally scheduled for the same time as EHR go-live. This was thought to be a good idea because staff in disparate locations would be able to immediately see patients' clinical and demographic information in the unified EHR, as well as the train of prior messages (regardless of which staff member handled the call or their location). In addition, it was believed that "transformation" could be attained in a defined (and shorter) period of time, and that both phone workflows and EHR workflows would be integrated, each supporting the other.

Unfortunately, there were many unintended consequences, and widespread clinician and office dissatisfaction. A survey was distributed to all involved offices, and several themes emerged. Early on, patients had difficulty getting through to the correct offices, they complained of being disconnected. Physicians had trouble reaching their own secretaries. Messages were left and not returned. Patients claimed they called, but there was no record documented in the EHR. Secretaries in pods had to get up and go into neighboring offices to communicate—since there was no intercom available. Patients were used to having a relationship with a single secretary, and now, their issues were being handled by multiple people they didn't know. In many offices, secretaries worked for physicians for years and knew patients and office procedures and physician preferences. Early on, this knowledge was not transferred effectively between offices. A premium was placed on rapidity of answering, rather than on having the primary secretary answering. Secretaries did not have the ability to place a call on hold while answering another call (for this same reason). The answering service had a difficult time integrating with the new workflow—and many calls were not picked up in a timely manner—and because secretaries could not place calls on hold, it seemed that they were always picking up someone's phone, and many more calls went to an answering service. In the past, because there was close proximity between secretary and physician, time-sensitive messages were frequently relayed in near real time. In the new state, messages were entered in the EHR, and doctors had to constantly monitor their EHR messages. All these issues surfaced at the same time that the entire department was dealing with the implementation of a massive EHR project.

Several steps were immediately taken: additional staff was added at peak hours. The number of offices in a pod was reduced to facilitate knowledge transfer about how to collaborate as a small team—so all secretaries were familiar with all the offices they covered. Phone menus were changed to allow routine refill requests to be recorded, and greater emphasis was placed on having inbound calls sent to the primary office secretary (with routine outbound calls made by others).

Author's Analysis

Many lessons were learned. Although physicians were made aware that a new phone system was being implemented, it was not appreciated how far reaching and widespread the consequences of this would be. Physicians were not part of the selection process and did not feel ownership of the process. The system was more complex than anticipated, and training was felt to be inadequate. Although the decision to implement the phone system concurrent with a new enterprise-wide EHR was intentional, each implementation complicated the other.

Despite the difficult transition, the effort has paid off. Offices now have the ability to cross-cover each other; certain calls are shifted to appropriate work groups such as authorizations; volume of calls is more evenly distributed between practices, leading to better utilization of staff resources, and management is able to make decisions and drive improvements based on actual data.

Editor's Commentary

This case clearly demonstrates the consequences of not understanding the complexity of work prior to implementation of an intervention. Although a number of problems with the legacy phone system were identified, highlighting the need for a new system, it appears that more could have been done to appreciate the needs and preferences of users with respect to phone call management. For example, an exploration of work practices may have identified that provision of an avenue for physicians to communicate directly with their secretaries was essential. Consultation with patients may have revealed the importance of communicating, and so developing a long-standing relationship, with a single secretary.

There are often competing interests with respect to a new intervention—satisfaction is sometimes foregone, with speed and efficiency taking priority. To some extent, this tension appeared to be at play here (i.e., long-standing relationships sacrificed for faster calls).

There are pros and cons with the implementation of multiple interventions concurrently. One could argue that it is easier for users to adjust to one big change, than multiple smaller changes, but this is likely to be dependent on the changes required and on the interdependencies between the multiple interventions. In this case, simultaneous implementation of the new phone system and new EMR appeared logical, as messages from calls would be recorded in the new EMR. However, system glitches or misuse of the system by users resulted in messages not appearing in the EMR—not an ideal situation. Was more testing or training required?

Returning to the theme of understanding how work is done, a key process that appeared to have been given limited consideration is communication of time-critical messages. Consulting with users on their preferred method for doing this (perhaps a phone call followed by a reminder in the EMR?) would have likely resulted in a more streamlined and workable solution for both physicians and secretaries.

The organization should be commended for undertaking a quick evaluation following implementation and making some changes to the system and process to rectify the problems identified. In my experience, this is rarely done.

Although many of us appreciate the complexity of implementation of systems like EMRs, CPOEs, and clinical decision support systems (CDSS) this case highlights that introduction of new technology, regardless of how sophisticated or novel, is often fraught with challenges and must not be taken on lightly.

Lessons Learned

- Simultaneous system implementations require attention to interdependencies between systems in addition to the individual systems themselves.
- User communities must always be engaged in decisions about key technology changes.
- Undertraining staff usually results in greater total expense to cover both retraining and overstaffing to accommodate for undertrained staff.

Chapter 26

Ready for the Upgrade: Upgrading a Hospital EHR for Meaningful Use

Editor: Edward Wu
The New Jewish Home

Contents

Project Categories: inpatient electronic health record (EHR), infrastructure and technology

Lessons Learned Categories: communication, contracts, leadership/governance, project management

Case Study

In this case, we describe the process of upgrading a hospital electronic health record (EHR) system in order to meet the regulatory requirements of participation in the U.S. federal "Meaningful Use" (MU) program. Our hospital, "Hospital A," was live on a commercial EHR system but needed to upgrade to a newer version of the system in order to meet MU requirements. The situation was complicated by the fact that the version of the EHR that our hospital was running was two versions behind the MU-compliant version of the software. The hospital's long-standing policy was to delay software upgrades or installations until other institutions had gone through a similar implementation. However, because of time constraints, and because they had uneventfully completed full upgrades and several incremental upgrades over the last several years, they decided to proceed.

Two options were then considered. The first would be to perform two separate and consecutive upgrades to the MU-certified version of the EHR, requiring twice the time and resources. The other option was to use an untested approach: perform an upgrade directly to the certified version as part of a single effort. Despite the lack of experience with this approach, the vendor recommended it to Hospital A as well as to other clients. Given the financial and time pressures to meet MU and with the vendor's assurances, the hospital elected to pursue this option.

At the time of this decision, the EHR system's vendor had not yet made the MU-compliant version available, and the contract terms were not defined. Both were expected within "a few weeks" of selecting our upgrade strategy. Because of deadlines imposed by the MU regulations, the longer the hospital waited for the vendor to be ready, the more they needed the efficiencies of the double upgrade. They contemplated reverting to the two-stage approach, but soon learned from other sites that this approach also had significant challenges. They eventually waited several months for contract negotiations to be completed and for the offering to be made available. There was a further delay because the vendor resources were stretched very thin and could not be assigned to the hospital for several months after the execution of the contract.

Eventually, the vendor and the hospital project team co-developed the project charter and scope, as well as a work plan with milestones and dates. Three mock go-lives were planned in preparation for go-live: one in the Development domain, one in the Train domain, and the third in the Test domain.

First up was the mock go-live for Development (Mock 1). Unfortunately, the delivery of the Development environment was delayed several weeks due to issues with vendor resources, deployment methods, and various software bugs. The delays in the validation, configuration, and testing of the Development environment infringed on the Train environment (Mock 2). The experience with Mock 2 was no different. Delivery of the environment was later than planned. Issues identified during Mock 1 recurred and new ones surfaced. The sense was that the upgrade process was unpredictable. Test (Mock 3) was also delayed significantly for similar reasons.

Because of the concerns, additional mock go-lives were planned. The hospital and vendor also decided that they would not pursue a production go-live until 7 days of system stability (without any changes required), and a successful stress test was achieved.

Eventually, five mock go-lives were required before the system was stable and worthy of placing in front of end-users for stress testing. Unfortunately, the stress testing also revealed bugs and slowness that were not seen with the previous unit and integrated testing. Additional workarounds were employed, more fixes were loaded, and the stress tests were then repeated. However, system slowness in several key areas prevented the scheduling of a Production go-live.

Throughout this upgrade process, the hospital had good communication with the vendor. Individuals from vendor leadership were engaged and on site during this entire process. Despite vendor involvement, hospital executive leadership decided to halt work on the upgrade. Consequently, the Chief Executive Officers of the vendor and the hospital met to clarify the working relationship and address the upgrade problems at hand.

Taking a step back and addressing upgrade issues with the vendor was helpful. Over the next 2 months, fix after fix was successfully loaded. The vendor engaged development partners with expertise in the server and network platforms to improve critical login issues. Weeks of thorough investigation of the EHR resolved remaining functional issues with allergy documentation; resequencing table entries solved another significant patient safety issue.

At last, 7 days of complete stability without the need for any system changes was achieved. The delays and "retrenching" ultimately cost the hospital several hundred thousand dollars plus the opportunity costs of not being able to focus on other important initiatives. So, with cost overruns and delayed timelines, the hospital finally went live with the upgrade—which was completely uneventful. Any glitches that occurred were invisible to end-users and rapidly resolved by the vendor–client team.

Both the hospital and vendor put in an extraordinary number of hours to achieve this near flawless go-live. Despite the go-live success, the hospital did suffer in other areas due to this upgrade. Some system maintenance and enhancements were delayed, and regulatory updates were postponed.

In the end, we realized were it not for our extra effort, expense, and time, the end result would have been very different.

Author's Analysis

In healthcare information technology, our misses may be as important as our successes. The project management literature is littered with mantras like "if it's worth doing at all, then it is worth doing right the first time." But how much attention is given to the effort required to put a perfect process into production on the first attempt? When patient safety is at stake, not only is it worth doing right the first time, but it also is imperative.

Although eventually the go-live was nearly flawless, the events that led up to it was like a series of sports events—complete with trick plays, errors, and injuries. In fact, the hospital incurred immense cost overruns and had to delay other important projects in patient safety and regulatory initiatives. The hospital was successful only because of its own persistence and the vendor's shared commitment to the project.

Implementations are a complex undertaking for both customers and vendors. External regulatory pressures further complicate the picture for both customers and vendors, causing additional challenges. Internal pressures—in the form of capital improvements, patient safety initiatives, and personnel changes—can make an implementation extremely challenging.

In this case, we learned that multiple failures prior to go-live can provide important information that can lead to a flawless go-live. Key to this is that vendors and customers form a partnership to work through inevitable difficulties.

Editor's Commentary

This case illustrates two major implementation missteps: not pushing a vendor to adhere to contract terms and fully trusting a vendor on a complicated upgrade. Vendor resources were not delivered as promised, and it became apparent that the vendor had very little expertise with the upgrade at hand. With a "double upgrade," the degree of difficulty goes up exponentially, and generally, most vendors have limited field experience in these situations. Ultimately, the hospital regained footing after these faults were escalated to hospital leadership.

To limit risks like this during an upgrade, three main components need to be addressed: vendor communication, key stakeholder communication, and appropriate project management.

In this case, vendor communication seemed to be going well, but the project was stalled until key hospital and vendor leadership convened. While not the norm, this is sometimes required to address risks at a senior leadership level. In fact, this may be the first time vendors learn what has been escalated to hospital executives. As readers, we do not know exactly what occurred in this meeting, but it is likely that a great deal of risk mitigation and action plans were developed.

Hospital leaders likely pushed vendors for hard deadlines (something that should have happened at the outset) and may have asked for additional vendor resources to complete the upgrades.

Communication to project sponsors and stakeholders should also take place to manage expectations. All but the most minor of upgrades should be communicated to key stakeholders. Not only do clinicians and administrators need to know the benefits of an upgrade, but they also need to be aware of downtime ramifications and potential changes to workflow. Keeping all leaders and end-users informed can manage expectations, mitigate potential downstream risks, and develop champions for the process. Additionally, involving key stakeholders early and often during an upgrade can uncover specific workflow issues that would not otherwise be addressed.

Most important to a software upgrade is appropriate project management. A software upgrade should be considered a project in and of itself. Scope, time, and resources need to be integrated into the decision to upgrade. It can be extremely tempting to just run a patch with only minimal testing, communication, or resources—but that usually is a recipe for disaster. Thorough implementation, testing, and validation are necessary for the go-live of any major upgrade, much less a double upgrade performed in one step.

In this case, communication and project management were strong, but the project required escalation to hospital leadership to ensure success. Strengths of this implementation included the dedication to a "perfect go-live" with multiple mock go-lives and constant vendor communication, despite initial setbacks. Despite their success, it is likely that a "double upgrade" will be handled with even greater caution in the future.

Lessons Learned

- Communication between vendor and hospital is necessary for successful upgrade implementation.
- Upgrades rarely go without a hitch, so good planning and ample communication can mitigate risks.
- Escalation to hospital and vendor leadership may be necessary if the project is not going well.
- If timelines are critical, contracts should include date milestones.

Chapter 27

Effective Leadership Includes the Right People: Informatics Expertise

Editor: Gail Keenan
University of Florida

Contents

Project Categories: inpatient electronic health record (EHR)

Lessons Learned Categories: data model, leadership/governance, system configuration

Case Study

A long-standing medical college and hospital with a proud history of innovation, which nearly went bankrupt, was acquired and saved by a university and a national for-profit hospital chain company. The university acquiring the medical college lacked healthcare experience. The acquired hospital had been nonprofit in its century of existence, and the takeover by a for-profit chain was somewhat of a shock to its faculty and staff. The ultimate solution, however, was felt to be better than other alternatives discussed before the takeover—including turning the facility into condominiums.

Merging the cultures of the medical college and university was proving a challenge. A culture of mistrust and anxiety about cross-college collaborations with the acquiring university seemed to prevail at the medical college. It certainly did not help when a managerial and financial "firewall" was set up between the university and the healthcare campus, so that any financial trouble in the healthcare units would not cross over to the university. The acquired managed-care-owned hospital, once part of a proud and unified academic medical center, was now largely "off limits" to management of either the medical college or university. Moreover, the acquiring for-profit hospital chain owner was losing money and divesting itself of some of the chain's local hospitals.

A medical informatics specialist with significant experience in design and implementation of clinical information technology (IT) in nearby large medical centers was hired by the main university, but with a primary appointment in a computer and information-related college and not the medical college. The informaticist was to develop an educational program in medical informatics to help set up cross-college collaborations in informatics research, and assist in other areas as needed.

The College of Medicine did not leverage the informaticist in the implementation of an electronic health record (EHR) for its for-profit faculty practice plan. The informaticist offered her services and the medical college's and faculty practice plan's dean, chief information officer (CIO), chief operations officer (COO), and other top executives were well aware of her background. Because of existing sociocultural issues that divided the acquired medical campus and the acquiring university (mostly in the domain of distrust—and perhaps disdain), the informaticist's services or advice were not utilized.

Here is a summarized report from a health information technology (HIT) blog:

> A posted record of lawsuit was filed against the EHR vendor by the University's College of Medicine's for-profit practice group, claiming that the EHR "does not function per the specifications provided." The lawsuit accused the vendor of breach of contract, fraud, and other contractual shortcomings. Over $1 million was paid for the system, and problems with claims billing cost the practice group twice that amount. The university filed an injunction requiring the EHR vendor to provide a system that performs evaluation and management (E/M or billing) coding or pay professional coders to do the job. One example they cited: no Review of Systems template existed for the E/M coder that handles allergy/immunologic or hematologic/lymphatic organ systems. They provided confirmation from the EHR vendor that certain aspects of the EHR did not function properly.

The informaticist had direct and relevant experience in EHR implementation and would have recommended extensive testing of the financial components before go-live. She had observed similar happenings at a different university, where a different faculty practice plan and vendor's defective products collided and resulted in a US Department of Justice investigation, a large fine, admission by the university that it lacked the appropriate IT management depth, and complete abandonment of a multimillion-dollar IT investment because of resultant defective billing practices.

Author's Analysis

Informatics specialists should be aware of the challenges of integrating cultures of healthcare systems and non-healthcare components of universities. Informatics experts should be aware that their expertise may be regarded as unneeded or perhaps frightening to officials in charge of EHR implementation, who often lack medical backgrounds and are being asked to do much more than they are really capable of doing. Informaticists should educate hospital and university officials that not knowing what you don't know about complex EHR issues, and placing too much trust in vendor promises, can lead to system failure—or worse.

Editor's Commentary

The merging of very different cultures under a single organizational umbrella is problematic, especially during the period immediately following the absorption of one organization into another. If positive action is not taken to unify the diverse entities into a productive whole, the entities may remain at odds indefinitely. This can result in employees duplicating effort, working at cross purposes, or not being utilized when appropriate, in turn resulting in excessive costs, reduced effectiveness, and decreased morale. This seems to have been the situation described in the case study. It is unfortunate that the medical informatics specialist, given her background, was not tapped for her expertise in EHRs, even though she offered assistance. In organizations with effective cultures, leaders recognize the gaps in their own and their teams' capabilities, and do what it takes to find and utilize the best expertise to solve problems. This did not happen in the organization described in the case study.

The challenges faced by the organization in this case illustrate the importance of clinical informatics as a distinct professional discipline that encompasses a unique set of skills and knowledge. The organization suffered a crisis of lost revenue due to inappropriate capture of data in the EHR. Had a trained and experienced clinical informaticist been involved in the project, she or he would likely have easily recognized the functional limitations of the software, understood their interrelationships with the provider documentation workflows, and grasped the revenue cycle implications.

This case also offers potential lessons for the informatics professional who wishes to avoid finding themselves in a similar situation. One is to recognize organizational dysfunction or a poor cultural fit before taking a new job. While this may be difficult to discern, the likelihood of an accurate impression can be optimized by speaking with as many potential colleagues as possible, at a variety of levels in the organizational hierarchy. Some individuals might still choose to take a position in a troubled organization, but making the determination in advance allows one to take a proactive approach about how to be effective. For example, as a condition for employment, an informaticist might require a contractual guarantee of membership on all committees that focus on the EHR within the institution. Also, one could identify and nurture relationships with colleagues of like mind who eventually could work together to move IT actions and policy in the desired direction.

Lessons Learned

- The professional discipline of clinical informatics presents a unique combination of knowledge and skills that can avert many serious HIT mishaps.
- The individuals with the most expertise in IT are not always the ones making the important IT decisions.
- Informaticists should carefully evaluate the culture of an organization when considering employment.
- Poorly led or poorly designed HIT initiatives can have broad and deep negative impacts across a health system.

Chapter 28

Culture Eats Implementation for Lunch: Chronic Care Model

Editor: Melissa Baysari
University of Sydney

Contents

Project Categories: population health and analytics

Lessons Learned Categories: implementation approaches, leadership/governance, training

The project in question was an attempt to engage primary care providers and care managers with electronic health record (EHR) supporting tools and a care management team approach to deliver coordinated care to a large population base in a Midwestern state. The Chronic Care Model (CCM), Wagner ACP, 1998, served as the framework for this project. Stakeholders included a large university-based health system, nine individual practices, and a large EHR vendor. A high-tech model with patient, provider, and care manager dashboards was proposed to give relevant actionable information at the point and time of care or care planning for each team member. The project was funded by a grant, and one feature of the grant included rapid implementation across all sectors of the community involved. Multiple advanced features were envisioned in the original grant proposal including patient electronic communications, online patient education, and patient health baseline and functional status surveys.

The success of this project was measured by surveys sent to providers and focus groups designed to identify barriers to and facilitators of implementation in each group. The Consolidated Framework for Implementation Research (CFIR) was used in the analysis of survey and focus group results.

We evaluated the adoption of a provider panel dashboard, designed to give patient-specific and panel-specific information to each provider. We also evaluated a clinical tool designed for use by nursing staff, which was added later for documentation and accountability purposes.

Physicians were offered training, but training attendance was not enforced, nor were physicians compensated for their time or performance. Conversely, the nursing teams were given specialized instruction in their dashboards, adequate training time, and asked for their opinions in the further development of their dashboards.

It became apparent early in the project that the physicians were not involved in the project, and efforts to involve them were stymied by funding issues between grant management, run by the medical school researchers, and the hospital management, which was responsible for day-to-day activities of the medical staff.

Results of the surveys showed that the implementation process involved little engagement of the physicians, and the dashboard data was described as inaccurate or incomplete. Furthermore, there was no clinical integration of the tool as there was no incentive for the physicians to use the dashboard. Efforts to intervene and get the physician participants on track were not successful.

Conversely, the tool was implemented and continually refined with the nurses' feedback to meet their clinical needs. The clinical communications tool also provided a means of documenting compliance with the patient care objectives for which the nurses were accountable and were given incentives to accomplish. The clinical tool was fully adopted by the nurses.

Author's Analysis

Justin Graham, in the first edition of this work, summarized a failed project with the following observations: "Health information technology projects are hard enough when everyone works together collaboratively. They are virtually impossible when people do not. Involve clinicians early and often in projects that will affect their workflow." This advice remains valid and should be the cornerstone of all project planning at the outset of a project. Experienced, expert project planning professionals should be deeply involved in all large information technology (IT) implementation projects, as their skills are not traditionally well developed in IT or medical staff teams.

The results and comparison of the two implementation processes highlight the importance of project-specific contextual factors that can undermine or enhance adoption. Nonengagement of physicians and physician management from the outset was a guarantee for failure. Physicians are incredibly busy, and asking them to do additional tasks without understanding their purpose, or the new care management paradigm central to the understanding of patient and population dashboards was doomed from the start. The forced, top-down approach to the physician community without the involvement of all levels of the community in implementation planning had the expected outcome of widespread nonparticipation. Conversely, full engagement of nursing management and line nurses allowed utilization and improvement of the nursing dashboard.

The different approaches to implementing the dashboard for nurses vs. the physicians predicted the failed and successful outcomes. These lessons are further explained by the CFIR (Damschroder, 2009), a comprehensive framework for analyzing an implementation process and systematizing the identification of barriers and facilitators and the established informatics sociotechnical evaluation framework (Sittig, 2010).

Editor's Commentary

This case study highlights a number of key lessons, most identified and described by the authors. Adopting the CFIR to identify barriers and facilitators proved to be a very useful approach.

But in thinking about the purpose of the dashboard for physicians (to give patient-specific and panel-specific information to each provider), one cannot help but wonder whether the dashboard was really needed. Following implementation, the dashboard was not utilized by physicians, and it was suggested that this was because they were not engaged in the implementation process, they did not participate in training, and there was no incentive for physicians to use the dashboard. If the dashboard was filling a gap or need, it is likely that uptake of the tool would have been greater.

With the almost unlimited potential of health information technology (HIT) to consolidate and analyze information, streamline processes, and display data, it is easy to get caught up in the hype and develop solutions to problems that may not really exist. There is a real risk that we design and develop technology because it is possible to do so. When thinking about HIT implementation, let's go to the users first, and ask them to identify where HIT is needed. HIT is not the panacea to all our problems in healthcare. If the problem is simple, let's ask ourselves whether HIT is really the answer. Why not use a needs-based approach to HIT implementation? Instead of inundating users with high-tech solutions, let's use HIT to address core problems.

Lessons Learned

- Employing frameworks to implement HIT can provide important guidance.
- Milestones throughout a project's duration should be established proactively to evaluate against an established implementation framework with time to address deficiencies.
- Engagement of the targeted end-users is critical for success.

Chapter 29

Shortsighted Vision: CPOE after Go-Live

Editor: Christopher Corbit
Team Health

Contents

Project Categories: inpatient electronic health record (EHR), computerized provider order entry (CPOE)

Lessons Learned Categories: communication, leadership/governance, staffing resources

Case Study

A small community hospital underwent implementation of computerizedprovider order entry (CPOE) in 2009, adding on to a major vendor electronic health record (EHR) system that had been in use for 5 years previously. From the start, the actual goals of the implementation were unclear. The vice president for medical affairs (VPMA) saw CPOE as a shortcut to improved safety and quality in a hospital that had problems with both. The chief information officer (CIO) saw his own worth measured in his success in implementing big projects, and saw this implementation as a means to burnish his reputation with his peers. The chief executive officer (CEO) liked to think of his institution as being cutting edge, and bringing advanced medicine to this semirural setting. CPOE and EHRs fit right in with that vision.

The hospital undertook the implementation with no external support beyond that provided by the vendor. There was no defined physician leader other than the chief medical officer (CMO). The CMO established a physician advisory governance group, but he essentially managed the entire process and personally authored the majority of order sets. Clinical goals and metrics for the project were established at the outset, but were not closely monitored.

The project was subject to several major delays and nearly failed entirely. However, thanks to long nights and heroic efforts put in by the information technology (IT) staff, the CMO, the lead nurse informaticist, and volunteer physicians, CPOE was fully rolled out to all inpatient settings, and ultimately achieved a 90% adoption rate. The build had many flaws and imperfections, but most of the medical staff, largely made up of contracted hospitalists, consented to using the CPOE system. Others developed workarounds (such as faxing in paper orders or moving entirely to verbal orders) or left the medical staff entirely.

The CPOE project had made no provisions for post-implementation maintenance or cleanup, and had no formal closure process for the identification of outstanding issues. As the project team began to disintegrate, there were over 250 order sets implemented, but many had flaws, some of which were major. Additionally, there were 20–30 specialty-specific order sets that were planned but never created.

Within a few months after go-live, attention began to drift. CPOE project meetings ended, with no regular replacement. The CEO turned his attention to other "advanced medicine" initiatives. The CIO and his staff moved on to other big projects, such as Meaningful Use, a patient portal, and an anesthesia module. The CMO's governance group began to lose interest, and the meetings became thinly attended. Aside from a few medication safety metrics, no other benefits were measured or accounted for.

The CMO hired an experienced chief medical informatics officer (CMIO) about 6 months after go-live to take stock of the situation and take over where he had faltered. The CMIO generated a list of over 200 necessary fixes, some urgent, and over 50 order sets desperately needing revision. He reconstituted the physician governance group and began to develop processes and procedures for EHR change requests and clinical content updates. However, the CIO would not make his staff available routinely to provide maintenance and enhancements. His focus remained on new big projects, and he neither knew nor cared about the day-to-day clinical operations of the medical center. The CEO also remained fixated on advanced medicine and never held his CIO or operational leaders accountable for the problems introduced by a CPOE system that could not be maintained.

Aside from a few pharmacy metrics, the CPOE system was not shown to improve quality and safety overall. Additionally, without sufficient maintenance staff available, all quality improvement initiatives became bottlenecked in the IT department. The queue of requests to improve, update, or enhance order sets grew longer and longer, and the quality of care drifted further and further from the ideal. Two years later, the original clinical goals and metrics had never been measured after implementation.

Nevertheless, the CIO (checking the box on a big project list) and the CEO ("advanced medicine!") remained contentedly ignorant of any problems as they moved onto their next big initiatives. In their eyes, it was "mission accomplished."

Author's Analysis

By many standards (including Stage 1 of Meaningful Use), this CPOE implementation succeeded wildly. The implementation was completed in a timely manner, and the hospital saw adoption rates approaching 90%. Many in the organization, including the CEO and CIO, would not disagree. But is the rate of adoption the only (or even the most important) metric of success?

The problem here is that CPOE was treated as a project, rather than a transformative event. Lacking vision and foresight, the organization could not see beyond the immediate implementation hurdles and failed to plan accordingly. A CPOE system requires regular maintenance and upkeep just to maintain a basic level of safety. And the radical transformation of healthcare delivery to enable the best, most efficient care requires a great deal more than physicians entering orders on a computer. Without sufficient resources devoted to improving the EHR, the organization cannot respond rapidly to clinical feedback or advance patient care through persistent application of quality improvement principles.

The hospital still suffers today from decisions made under the influence of poor leadership and inadequate governance.

Editor's Commentary

At the inception of this institutional transformative endeavor, an apparent lack of leadership and focus led to this project being a clinical failure. Every major administrator responsible for this transformation had different objectives and measures of success. This resulted in the lack of a true transformational team with only a very small core group of individuals responsible for major portions of the development. Even though by some measures the project can be considered successful, the actual users of the system endured extreme hardships in the entire process, possibly leading to poor quality of care.

In planning such a large-scale transformational event, several key steps must be taken to ensure the success of the project for all the stakeholders. One of the most important aspects, however, is a strong leadership to develop trust, earn credibility, and share their long-term strategy with absolute clarity. Without the support of the stakeholders and clear strategy from the leadership, any well-planned implementation is at risk of failure.

Transformational projects begin with the development of a long-term vision, a view of the best possible outcome that will inspire and give motivation to the stakeholders. These goals can be developed by one administrator, by the executive team, or may emerge from accumulative discussions among stakeholders. The most important factor is that the administrative team articulates a clear and unified vision of the goals and clinical measurements of success. This can serve as a roadmap for critical decisions on specific issues that come up. In this case, even though there was some attempt at defining clinical measures and goals, the author notes the lack of follow-through, which contributed to failing to meet them.

Keeping stakeholders dedicated to the vision requires significant energy and commitment. Initially, a few people will immediately accept the vision, but many others will take some time to accept the change. Therefore, the transformational team will need to take every opportunity to educate participants on the importance of the strategy and what their involvement can achieve.

Finally, it is important to remain involved and approachable not only during the implementation, but long after the system is in use. The actions and staunch commitment of administration to keep the stakeholders engaged, especially during the difficult times that most of these types of projects always seem to have, is crucial.

This lack of leadership and vision appears to have contributed to the extraordinary amount of work that was needed at the last minute to implement the CPOE system, in which the CMO had to do a majority of the work on order set creation and content. This extraordinary effort still required multiple workarounds developed by several members of the medical staff, with a number of these physicians leaving the medical staff altogether.

This leads to another issue, which is compounded by the fact that no clear goals or measures of success were predetermined. The CEO and CIO felt that the project was a success, despite all the internal evidence indicating that it was not. This is due to the fact that end-user experience and feedback is typically lost due to it being filtered through several layers on its way to administration. This "telephone chain" effect typically changes the original content of frustration and failure to acceptance and success once the original information is slightly changed in each step from user to supervisor to manager to committee to director to vice president and finally to the executive team.

This case highlights the issues and frustrations of users when transformational leadership fails to develop a clear strategy and appropriate methods to measure the achievement of goals. When this happens, the end-users, and ultimately patients, suffer. The executive team must develop a cohesive plan and vision for any large project of this size and make sure that they have the skills and ability to implement a large-scale institutional transformational event.

Lessons Learned

- Institutional transformation events require a clear vision and specific goals spelled out by the administration.
- Keeping all stakeholders committed to the vision is a fundamental, and ongoing, commitment.
- A well-defined vision provides a roadmap to guide decisions related to the project.
- The continued maintenance of CPOE systems is just as, if not more, important than the initial work required for implementation.

Chapter 30

Committing Leadership Resources: A CMIO and CPOE Governance

Editor: Gail Keenan
University of Florida

Contents

Project Categories: inpatient electronic health record (EHR), computerized provider order entry (CPOE)

Lessons Learned Categories: communication, leadership/governance, staffing resources

Case Study

Anticipating a computerized provider order entry (CPOE) go-live within 2 years, a medical center decided that it needed to move beyond just a committee of physicians. The medical center had a medical informatics committee (MIC) with a chairperson. However, no physicians were involved in the day-to-day leadership of the project. Governance structure consisted of a chief information officer (CIO), with direct reports of a chief nursing informatics officer (CNIO) and a director of medical informatics. No chief medical informatics officer (CMIO) was present due to the limited budget. It was determined that a physician needed to be centrally involved with the CPOE project, with a commitment of at least seven-tenths full-time equivalents (0.7 FTE). Recruitment of the individual was as follows:

- Internal candidates were interviewed, with no individual able to commit greater than 0.25 FTE to the implementation.
- The chair of the MIC was a 0.8 FTE physician administrator (chief of medicine) and 0.2 FTE in practice, and thus unable to fill this role.
- An executive search firm was engaged to find a "physician CPOE leader."
- Candidates were screened and an individual was identified and hired for the position (0.8 FTE CPOE role, 0.2 FTE clinical practice as ambulatory care physician).
- The physician CPOE leader was to report to the director of medical informatics (nonclinician).
- The physician CPOE leader had no formal reporting relationship within the clinical governance of the medical center.
- Responsibilities of the physician included providing physician input on CPOE design and build, assisting with the MIC, and establishing liaison relationships between clinical departments and information technology (IT).

As the build progressed, the physician's importance to the project grew, mainly due to this individual's ability to gather physician input and inform the CPOE build. Soon this individual was overwhelmed with managing physician requests for the build, managing MIC meetings, and being an ambassador to the physician community in addition to the 0.2 FTE clinical practice as an ambulatory physician.

Due to this individual's lack of bandwidth and the inability of the medical center to support a CMIO role, the physician leader of 16 months left to become a CMIO at another organization. The medical center was left with a large void, at both the project level and within the physician community. The CPOE project team sought to fill this void with two physicians who were able to contribute at 0.4 FTE each. The CNIO was able to step in and manage physicians, but only to a limited degree.

As a result of the fragmented leadership, there were project delays (including a several month delay of the CPOE go-live), a failed effort to standardize order sets, disparate physician communications, and chaotic MIC meetings. This organization has since retained physicians to assist with IT build optimization and hired a full-time CMIO.

Author's Analysis

The medical center's vision that a "project physician" could achieve success was shortsighted, in that physician input was required at two key levels: CPOE system design and build and physician "ambassador" duties. The project physician could not successfully focus on developing leadership relationships, communicating with physicians, and addressing cross-departmental issues without significant hospital support. Additionally, the physician struggled to provide sufficient input for the CPOE design and build. Both roles were full-time jobs and should not have been combined into one position. Having the project physician report to IT, rather than clinical leadership, further contributed to these problems because the project leadership (IT) lacked the management authority to address these challenges. The physician similarly underestimated the level of effort the role would take. The senior hospital management also did not effectively monitor the CPOE initiative and did not identify the evolving limits to the physician leadership for the project or address them. The MIC, as a leadership bridge for IT and clinical departments, should have served as another opportunity to identify the developing problems with the project, but that also would have required leadership accountable to the success of the CPOE project. Ultimately, the investment in the physician was lost when these bandwidth issues collided with the lack of medical center support for a CMIO.

Editor's Commentary

The author provides an example of the costly consequences of an organization's failure to take the long view on the infrastructure and leadership needed to support health information technology (HIT). As so many others have found, when there is no clear vision for HIT within an organization, poor decisions will occur due to the absence of a framework to guide effective decision making. The case suggests that the organization's leadership was not mindful of the factors associated with effective implementation of CPOE and also made no attempt to learn about the factors.

Though HIT failures can be instructive to those involved, the costs are sufficiently steep to warrant thoughtful planning and a search for feasible strategies that enhance decision making and minimize failure whenever possible. As was seen here, the management of an HIT project in isolation from an overall plan was a recipe for failure. It is in the interest of each healthcare organization to create an overall HIT vision and roadmap for achieving it that is updated at least annually. The vision and roadmap provide the basis for making sound decisions that link to the overall needs and HIT goals of the organization. As each new HIT-related problem arises, a solution can be devised that builds on the roadmap and knowledge gained through pursuing it.

In this case, the decision to hire the "physician CPOE leader" was a conclusion reached by a team anxious to see day-to-day physician leadership involvement on the CPOE project. The title of the position and job specifications suggested a short-term solution. Additionally, the combination of the narrow job scope, the physician leader being new to the organization, and the absence of formal ties to the clinical governance infrastructure made this position untenable. Ultimately, the new physician leader was beholden to multiple bosses and could not effectively carry out the role. Thus, it was no surprise to learn that the physician hired as the CPOE leader eventually moved to take on a CMIO role of greater bandwidth and administrative support outside the organization. There were clearly missed opportunities to avoid this fate during the recruitment and hiring phase. The organization used an executive search firm to help fill the position, but it is not clear that the expertise of the firm was used to the fullest. This type of consultant is typically paid a substantial fee to fill high-level job positions because of the consultant's specialized knowledge of the industry and talent in it. At the onset, the organization should have expected the consultant, as part of routine responsibilities, to evaluate the viability of the proposed position and present evidence-based recommendations for adjustments where needed. Had this been done, the position could have been revamped and better aligned with the organizational goals and resources before the hire. If, on the other hand, the consultant provided such feedback and it was not considered, then the organization needs to reexamine the efficacy of using costly consultant specialists whose advice is ignored.

In summary, the exorbitant costs of errors in the field of HIT suggest the need for thoughtful planning and the provision of solid evidence where possible to support decisions. This case provides a classic example of costs associated with the failure to build on existing knowledge; simply needing to recruit a new CMIO costs a significant amount of money. Even a simple review of the literature on CPOE implementation prior to designing the physician job specification could have dramatically altered the course of events in this case.

Lessons Learned

- Empower a physician leader to focus primarily on relationships, communication, and cross-departmental issues.
- Physician involvement at a project design and build level is important and time-consuming.
- Physician leaders require accountability to the clinical core of the organization.
- A MIC should continue in perpetuity and requires physician(s) to act as a bridge between clinical and IT departments.

Chapter 31

When to Throw in the Towel...ED Downtime

Editor: Richard Schreiber
Geisinger Health System

Contents

Project Categories: inpatient electronic health record (EHR), computerized provider order entry (CPOE), infrastructure and technology, laboratory information systems

Lessons Learned Categories: communication, leadership/governance, technology problems

The setting is a community hospital with close to 40,000 emergency department (ED) visits yearly, translating to just over 100 patients per day. It was a normal weekday morning in the ED. The ED was just starting to become busy when, out of the blue, the electronic health record (EHR) started to act erratically. At irregular intervals, it was not possible to place orders. The EHR popped up an unspecified error. Physicians and nurses were unable to save their notes, again with an unspecified error. Over that first hour, errors would arise at irregular intervals between events. In between those times, there were no issues with documentation or order placement, and laboratory and radiology results would cross at those times.

Calls to the local information technology (IT) department were left unanswered initially. A call to the regional IT help desk (which services several hospitals in the region) said that there were no issues with the EHR on their servers. Everything was working well on their end.

Over the next 3 h, the errors became more frequent and were lengthening in time and with decreased intervals between the episodes. Flow through the ED was grinding to a halt. Several calls to administration and IT, asking the question if downtime procedures were needed at that time, were not answered. The staff preferred to have worked out of the EHR, as the downtime procedures were difficult and required a different workflow (and worthy of another case study).

Finally, a call from IT stated that the internetconnection was unstable (externally to the hospital) causing intermittent disconnection to the EHR. There was not a timeline on resolution with the internet connection, and when asked about downtime, the response was to decide department by department to go on downtime procedures. Based on this non-recommendation, there was a half-hearted decision to use the downtime procedures as a recommended, but not definite, option.

The downtime procedures, in general, consisted of a dry-erase board to track patients in the ED, downtime forms for both physicians and nurses to document care, laboratory and radiology results via printouts from Lab/Picture Archive and Communication System (PACS) system either faxed or manually carried to the ED, handwritten prescriptions, and discharge instructions printed from an online resource.

Author's Analysis

Without a definite downtime decision, the ED workflow fell into disrepair. Since the EHR did work intermittently, and the ED workflow was based around the EHR, a few clinicians and nurses decided to work around the downtime and enter orders and document in the EHR when they could. One of the problems was that if the EHR lost connection just after orders were placed, there were sporadic instances where the orders would not finalize in the laboratory or radiology systems. Also, if the internet connection was down when attempting to save documentation, it would not save. Clinicians would have to keep their documentation active and save it when the internet connection was up.

The internet connection issue finally resolved after 8 h, but not without extreme difficulty in decompressing the ED. Long-term consequences included reviewing all laboratory and radiology tests to determine if any clinically significant results were missed. The biggest issue was missing documentation (both EHR and paper charts). The biggest single lesson for the facility was to have more concrete decisions around initiating full downtime procedures.

Editor's Commentary

Downtimes are either planned or unplanned, but in either instance require clear and definitive procedures. The most critical decision is whether to declare a downtime and to use downtime procedures. An institution must designate a single individual to make that decision. For a planned event, most institutions define an expected time frame which constitutes a need for downtime processes. Most often, IT can predict these time frames and recommend to senior administration whether downtime procedures will be needed.

By definition, unplanned downtimes are neither predictable nor can one predict their duration. In these circumstances, a senior administrator must make the crucial decision. In some circumstances, downtime procedures may be necessary for only one department (e.g., using paper laboratory requisitions during a laboratory information system upgrade). When it is unclear what the problem(s) may be, it is wisest to declare a full downtime and proceed to downtime processes.

This assumes that the institution has developed these processes and ensured they work. This requires that the institution practice downtimes. For some institutions with dual production environments, downtimes are rare. Personnel may be unfamiliar with downtime processes unless they have drills.

The other side of downtime is disaster recovery. Clear policy must exist to determine what information must be inserted into the EHR (e.g., it may be acceptable to save paper progress notes, or policy may include that these are scanned into the EHR). Once the electronic systems become available, there must be procedures for inserting key information back into the EHR (e.g., newly ordered medications). Policy must spell out clearly who is responsible for doing such "back-loading" and in what time frame. All interfaces must be checked to ensure proper function; often, interfaces, servers, and services require a reboot to resume. Spot-checking the EHR after a downtime will help to ensure completeness of the EHR.

In this case study, it appears that if there was a policy for downtime, it was not followed. The decision to perform downtime procedures department by department is unsound. It is also apparent that the IT departments were not aware of the issue(s), did not know what to expect, and did not know how and when the situation would be resolved. All those factors are triggers for higher administrative involvement and prompt decision making.

Finally, it seems likely that there was no defined process for disaster recovery. With every department on its own, it is probable that there was a mish-mosh of post-downtime documentation. This could prove even more disastrous for the institution with regard to billing and quality measures than the downtime itself.

Lessons Learned

- Downtime procedures must be definitive.
- Decisions regarding whether to declare a downtime must be clear, universal, and involve all team members.
- Communication is vital in addressing acute EHR issues during the day-to-day operations of a department.

Chapter 32

When Life Throws You Lemons, Make Lemonade: Voice Recognition

Editor: Christopher Corbit
TeamHealth

Contents

Project Categories: inpatient electronic health record (EHR), infrastructure and technology

Lessons Learned Categories: leadership/governance, training

Introduced in April 2014, adoption of templated provider documentation within our electronic health record (EHR) was slow. Hospitalists in our 150-bed community hospital began to use point-click-and-type templates to enter Progress Notes, but nearly all other providers continued to handwrite daily notes. Longer-form narrative reports, Admit and Consult Notes, Operative Notes, and Discharge Summaries were still dictated using back-end transcription. My colleagues had little warmth for using these tools.

> "The EHR templates break up my thought process too much to convey the patient's story coherently" was the top complaint.
> My eyes glaze over just looking at the complexity of these templates.
> There's too much junk I don't use in these templates.
> The finished notes look like [feces].

Voluntary use of front-end voice recognition (FEVR) to supplement the structured templates was added in March of 2016. A few users were passionate adopters, but overall progress stalled among the larger medical staff.

FEVR doesn't recognize my accent.
It's too complicated to understand how to use it.
I'm not a secretary, and I won't punctuate and format my dictation.

Using logic didn't change any minds. *Back-end dictation is expensive.* Our health information management (HIM) department estimated a cost of more than $500,000 per year. *Back-end dictation introduces unnecessary delays in note availability and subsequent care and transitions.* The turnaround time on a "STAT" dictation (often the rate-limiting step of a Rehab Center transfer) was at least an hour on a weekday, and often as long as several hours on the weekend. Routine H&P's and Consults were often delayed by 6–12 h. Important recommendations vanished into hyperspace for hours while reports were being transcribed.

Getting doctors to make changes that, at least initially, affected their efficiency in the name of lower hospital costs was not a motivating influence.

Although it was not clear at the time, conducting new provider EHR training and then separate FEVR application training hindered acceptance. Without appropriate demonstration within the EHR, users failed to appreciate the value of using FEVR to navigate the record, to enter search terms, and to free-dictate large portions of their notes.

Fourteen months later, FEVR logins and new EHR report rates had stagnated.

Over a July holiday weekend, my phone exploded with urgent emails and texts. Back-end dictation was down. Soon enough, the scope of the system failure was more clearly recognized.

Our hospital, part of a very large national corporation, used a shared back-end dictation service that had been corrupted by a malware exploit. After 48 h, the vendor declared that the service would be unavailable for 3 weeks if not longer while they reimaged their servers. To make matters worse, nearly 12h of saved but not transcribed dictations had been lost. Since hospitals cannot submit bills until patient charts are complete, a delay of even a day or two on completion of admission, discharge, and operative reports would have a disastrous effect on revenue.

As a remediation effort, the transcription vendor offered "unlimited" licensing to their FEVR product and a large supply of microphones. Within 2 days, our information technology (IT) staff had carpeted the hospital with application and microphone installations. With back-end transcription unavailable for several weeks, struggling physicians were faced with two choices: to handwrite extensive narrative notes or to try to use FEVR with the EHR documentation tools. This was a golden opportunity to rapidly enroll a large number of users and to drive adoption of FEVR.

As I crept into the operating room (OR) physician's lounge, the mood was low. One guy was typing a three-page operation note (op note) with two fingers. Another was laboriously handwriting a note.

"Anybody want to give FEVR a try?" I offered. A collective groan rose through the room. "Let me show you something." I proceeded to show how an op note from a prior dictation could be turned into a macro with fields for default normals and individualized variances. "VOILÁ! Instant op note!"

Eyes grew wide. Grins replaced frowns. Cognitive wheels turned. Failure had been turned into an "AHAH!" moment.

For the next 10 days, I showed my colleagues how to build personalized note templates that would allow them to tell patient's stories in their own words. These templates could be easily inserted in the EHR's awkward documentation tools.

Over the month of July 2017, there was a 30% jump in creation of notes via the EHR which remained sustained well after the transcription service came back on line in early August 2017.

There was an attenuated dip in revenue for that month which could have been disastrous had chart completion ground to a halt for 3 weeks.

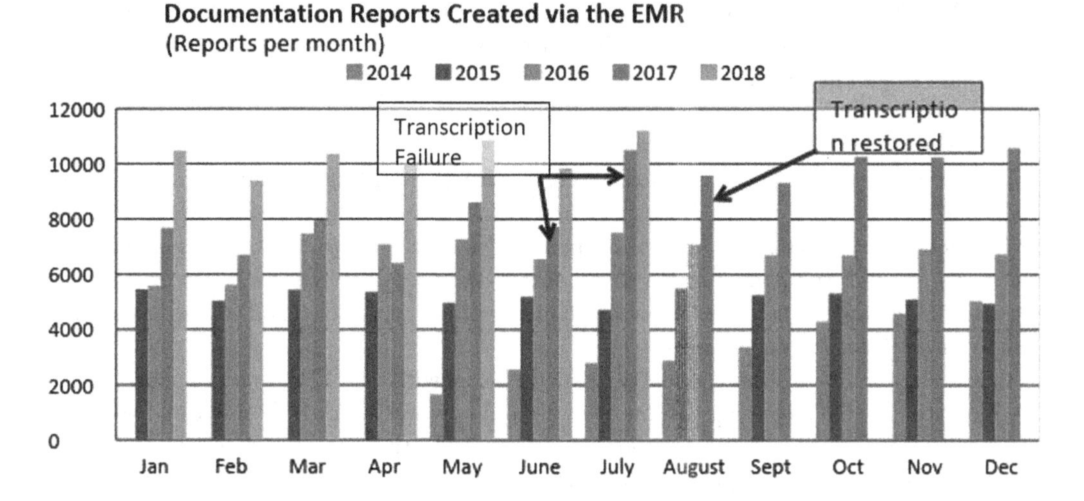

Kotter's eight-step process[1] begins with "establish a sense of urgency." Unplanned downtimes and other system or personnel failures can create the necessary environment to promote change. A flotation vest is bulky and uncomfortable—until one finds oneself in the water.

The additional steps followed naturally and with little effort.

- Form a coalition—establish a team of core users and analysts to drive adoption.
- Create a vision—understand how FEVR and macros can improve not just the efficiency, but also the experience of creating as well as reading notes.
- Communicate the vision—go to the places where the notes are written and offer at-elbow training and support to promote the transition.
- Empower others to act on the vision—encourage others to use the tools creatively to write better and more efficient personalized notes (while respecting documentation guidelines).
- Create short-term wins—getting home on time is a powerful motivator.
- Consolidate improvements—encourage sharing of macros; share feedback on transcription savings and timely discharges.
- Institutionalize new approaches—consolidating EHR training with FEVR training to demonstrate the benefits.

Once a core group of users began generating spare, readable notes, others joined in. Superusers evolved and shared macros with similar users within specialty areas. FEVR notes were immediately published in the EMR, shortening discharge times. Now, rather than optional and separate FEVR training, ALL new providers are issued FEVR licenses and trained to use FEVR as part of basic EMR competency.

Successful HIT projects are achieved with careful planning, messaging, execution, and support. Occasionally, unplanned system failures, with the right messaging and support, can help push stubbornly unfinished projects across the finish line.

---

[1] Kotter, John P., *Leading Change*, Harvard Business Review Press, November 2012.

Expert Commentary

FEVR allows the clinician to input information in a narrative form that enhances the usability for providers downstream. It can be integrated into the EHR and enhance the workflow. Unlike transcription, notes are immediately available with better documentation and more robust narrative sections. But all new technologies require training and new workflows—most notably, FEVR requires attention for translation errors (up to 10% error rates in some studies) and proofreading of dictated content.

Despite these drawbacks, steps can be taken to minimize these issues, such as training and a suitable microphone for the translation environment. Also, as noted in this case, one of the strongest features of FEVR systems is the use of macros. These can be set up to create an entire note framework, or small snippets of standardized text—best used in Physician Exam and Medical Decision Making (MDM) sections. However, clinicians must be engaged and willing to put in the effort to efficiently use these features.

The question in this case was not particularly the issues with the FEVR as noted above, but the implementation of the technology on many levels and why was it not fully supported and managed initially. While the crisis of dictation downtime drove them to implement the technology with an improved process, the main issue here was the overall lack of coordination and focus to fully support and implement around one process. The clinicians were given an option, and it is by no surprise that they chose the path of least resistance. The administration did not provide a clear decision on the workflow and processes around the FEVR implementation.

There was a lack of change management on an organizational level to incorporate all the processes aimed at successfully accepting and adopting new technologies and new workflows for clinicians. Effective change management enables the transformation of strategy, processes, technology, and people to enhance performance and ensure continuous improvement. A comprehensive and structured approach to organizational change management is critical to the success of any project that will bring about a significant change. Initially in this case, these necessities in change management did not occur. The process in this case was more reactionary than evolutionary. First, the point-and-click template was introduced without FEVR. Once FEVR was initially introduced, there were few processes to ensure its success. Only when the other processes failed was there effective change management to implement the FEVR technology successfully.

Effective organizational change management can positively impact achieving project outcomes. These outcomes must be anticipated and managed with the resources and education to implement new technology and workflows. This case clearly illustrates the importance of change management on an organizational level.

Lessons Learned

- Crises can be leveraged to drive new change, sometimes on a massive scale.
- People need an incentive to adopt new technologies—the greater the change, the greater the incentive needs to be.

AMBULATORY CARE FOCUS

What differentiates ambulatory care organizations today from inpatient health systems? Mostly, the lack of a 24 × 7 patient care schedule, a lower acuity of patient problems, and most importantly, usually fewer staff and financial resources to support and manage information technology infrastructure.

The Electronic Health Record Spotlight

Even if we had abandoned the entire implementation on the day of go-live, our institution would still be a far better place. By selecting, developing, and implementing an electronic health record (EHR), we examined almost every part of the organization. The EHR initiative shined a "spotlight" on every process, workflow, stakeholder, type of clinician, and piece of content in the entire institution and helped us understand our current state as well as develop a vision of the future.

Chapter 33

All Automation Isn't Good: CPOE and Order Sets

Editor: Pamela Charney
University of North Georgia

Contents

Project Categories: ambulatory electronic health record (EHR), computerized provider order entry (CPOE), laboratory information systems

Lessons Learned Categories: data model, staffing resources, system configuration, workflow

Case Study

An ambulatory care center was baffled by rising laboratory costs and erroneous laboratory test results. The center had hoped implementing an electronic interface between its electronic health record (EHR) and its off-site laboratory would decrease costs and errors. However, even after the implementation of the EHR, the center found that costs and errors were growing each day.

After implementing the laboratory interface, the ambulatory care center hired a physician informaticist to assist. The physician soon discovered many errors in the setup of the EHR orders screen and the laboratory interface mapping. Table 33.1 illustrates some of these errors.

These examples illustrate that laboratory test results the clinicians received were not what they expected when ordering the tests. Because of the errors in the laboratory interface setup, EHR

Table 33.1 Laboratories Ordered in EHR, Tests Mapped in Laboratory Interface, and Laboratory Results Received

Name of Order in EHR ***(What the Clinician Sees)***	*Name of Corresponding Test Mapped in Laboratory Interface* ***(What the Laboratory Runs)***	*Name of Laboratory Result Label Mapped in HL7 Messages* ***(What the EHR Saves for Clinician to See)***
CPK (creatine kinase)	Cockroach IgE	Creatinine
Chem Screen *Note: Providers thought this was "Basic Metabolic/Chem7."	Panel of tests including amylase, complete blood count (CBC), CD3, CD4, glucose, urea nitrogen, cholesterol, high- and low-density lipoproteins (HDL and LDL), triglycerides, alkaline phosphatase, gamma glutamyl transpeptidase (GGT), aspartate and alanine aminotransferases (AST and ALT), and lactate dehydrogenase (LDH)	Corresponding test results
GC Probe *Note: Specimen kit at this clinic is for RNA test.	Gonorrhea RNA	Gonorrhea DNA
HIV-1/2 antibody	HIV-1/2 antibody	HIV-2 *Note: The HIV-2 strain is very rare in the United States.
Hepatitis C antibody	Hepatitis C viral load	(Not mapped; results were faxed)

orders caused thousands of automated errors leading to significant frustration for clinicians and the diagnostic laboratory company due to:

- Unmet expectations
- Wasted time trying to look for the "correct" results
- Uninformed or misinformed clinical decision making
- Patient safety and risk management
- Unmet quality outcomes and pay-for-performance targets
- Unreliable data integrity of EHR results
- Costs of incorrect or unnecessary laboratory tests.

To make matters worse, the prior nonclinical EHR specialist set up disease-specific panels of tests with the intention of making it easier for clinicians to quickly order tests—but this resulted in the clinicians being able to quickly order the wrong tests.

For example, there was a prenatal laboratory panel that clinicians would order with one click at every prenatal visit (CBC + UrCult + RPR + Rub + ABO + Rh + HgBE + Lead + HBsAG/ABS + HCV). However, this panel was redundant to order at every pregnancy stage and was missing critical tests at specific gestational ages as recommended by obstetrical practice guidelines. Therefore, either the missing tests were not ordered, or the clinicians had to hunt through the EHR orders screen to find those specific tests.

Another example of systematizing poor-quality and high-cost care is a previous human immunodeficiency virus (HIV) laboratory panel that was frequently ordered for HIV patients: the "Chem Screen" described in Table 33.1 plus "HSVIgG + HepC + HBsAG + RPR + HIVAbw/WB." In this example, not only were some tests redundant and some tests missing, but also the hepatitis C screening test was erroneously mapped to the very expensive hepatitis C viral load test that would not be clinically indicated for patients without hepatitis C. In addition, the panel included an HIV antibody test, which was superfluous to perform on patients known to be HIV-positive.

The physician informaticist decided to tackle these laboratory order and result problems with a systematic approach instead of ad hoc troubleshooting for the following reasons:

- She recognized the profound impact these errors could have on patient safety, care quality, and operating costs.
- There were numerous errors discovered in every step of the laboratory order process:
  - Incorrect test and panel options listed in EHR
  - Incorrect mapping of orders to laboratory interface
  - Incorrect mapping of laboratory result HL7 messages into the EHR database.

The physician informaticist researched which laboratory tests ought to be orderable in the EHR based on the following:

- Analyzing reports of prior utilization of laboratory tests—how often was each EHR order selected by clinicians in the past year?
- Reviewing medical evidence-based guidelines (such as recommended tests for prenatal or HIV care); these were used to create new order sets instead of current panels that were not clinically useful.
- Reviewing quality measures including the managed care Healthcare Effectiveness Data and Information Set (HEDIS) and Meaningful Use metrics about hemoglobin A1c, creatinine, and drug monitoring.
- Conducting focus groups with the ambulatory care center clinicians to build consensus around which core laboratory tests must be included in the EHR orders.
- Weighing the cost of each test against the potential benefits to clinical decision making. For example, in the previous laboratory orders setup, more than half of the available EHR orders were obscure immunoglobulin E (IgE) tests for uncommon allergens. Not only were these very expensive and often not covered by the patients' health insurance, but they also were rarely ordered and would be more appropriate for complex allergy patients referred to outside allergy specialists.

The physician informaticist analyzed prior data about EHR laboratory orders and results, followed by remapping all the orders and results that the ambulatory care center was planning to include in the EHR:

- For every EHR order that a clinician can select, the physician informaticist had to check that the message the interface software sends to the laboratory company has the instructions for the clinically equivalent test (i.e., if a clinician orders "creatine phosphokinase/CPK" in the EHR, the interface map needs to tell the laboratory company to perform the test called "creatine kinase").

- For every incoming HL7 results message, a laboratory data map was created to tell the EHR where to save the result. For example, for an incoming "positive" result for HIV-1/2, the EHR needs to be set up to save that to the field with the label "HIV-1/2" instead of erroneously saving it to the "HIV-2" field or "HSV" field.

The physician informaticist also found several laboratory tests that were performed at the ambulatory care center. Instead of mapping those tests to identifiers for the outside commercial laboratory, she researched and mapped the corresponding Current Procedural Terminology (CPT) codes to the EHR orders to automate billing.

By removing the clinically problematic panels and remapping the EHR–laboratory interface, the physician informaticist empowered the clinicians to provide safer and more efficient care at substantially lower costs. The resulting order screen appears in Figure 33.1.

Provider feedback: *"This is awesome, so much easier than clicking around. It was well worth it!!!"*

Author's Analysis

The above story illustrates several notable lessons. While electronic automation of processes can increase efficiency, in this case it also quickly multiplied errors with serious clinical, operational, and financial consequences. The ambulatory care center created automated processes without a qualified subject matter expert, resulting in significant data integration errors ("garbage in, garbage out"). Fortunately, a physician informaticist was recruited who supplied critical expertise in the following domains:

- Current clinical knowledge about a broad range of laboratory tests used by multiple specialties (previous mapping was done by a nonclinician)

HIV Labs	☐ HIV Initial (plus above)
☐ HIV Quarterly	☐ HIV-1 GENOTYPE (NY)
☐ Comprehensive Metabolic Panel	☐ Hepatitis A Ab (total)
☐ CD4 / CD8 + CBC	☐ Hepatitis B Core Ab
☐ HIV-1 RNA,QN,RT-PCR	☐ Hepatitis B Surface Ab QL
☐ HIV Annual (plus above)	☐ Hepatitis B Surface Ag
☐ Lipid Panel (Chol + Trig)	☐ Hepatitis C Ab EIA
☐ RPR serology	☐ CMV Ab IgG
☐ Gonorrhea + Chlamydia URINE (Aptima)	☐ Toxoplasma IgG
☐ Urinalysis (UA + Microscopy)	☐ PPD/TUBERCULOSIS ID

Figure 33.1 Resulting order screen.

- Knowledge of evidence-based medicine guidelines and the ability to identify conflicting suboptimal practice patterns (previous panels were created by clinicians based on personal practices instead of evidence about which tests have high clinical utility)
- Expertise in EHR table structures, EHR database queries, large spreadsheets, and HL7 messaging (the prior clinical lead assisting the nonclinical EHR specialist did not understand the implications of interface mapping)
- Utilization and cost consciousness in making decisions about EHR options
- Coding, revenue cycle, and managed care incentives knowledge to bridge the gap between clinical operations and finance
- Policy and legal knowledge (such as whether federal initiatives prefer certain tests, or whether state regulations require special consent to order certain tests)
- Interpersonal and leadership skills to collaborate with the clinicians, technical staff, and laboratory company representatives
- Big picture vision that appreciated the enormous impact of system changes, while being detail oriented to troubleshoot and resolve specific problems.

In short, because nearly all health information technology (IT) projects automate processes at some level, it is imperative to involve physician informaticists with strong clinical, technical, financial, policy, and leadership skills.

Editor's Commentary

The ultimate goal of healthcare information technology is to support safe, high-quality, cost-effective patient care. Any EHR should make it easy for the clinician to do the right thing, for the right patient, at the right time. Clinicians at the ambulatory care center discovered quickly that creation of the interface between the clinic and the laboratory made doing the right thing more difficult.

The problems faced by the ambulatory care center illustrate that seamless integration of data between organizations is often easier said than done. Several mistakes were made along the way—had a clinical informaticist been involved from the beginning, these errors would likely have been prevented. However, all too often, individuals who have responsibility for making decisions regarding health information technology do not ensure that the right individuals are involved at each step of the process.

The ambulatory care center's new laboratory interface created a situation where errors in transmission of laboratory orders and results could have led to significant risk for patients. Table 33.1 illustrates just a few of the inconsistencies between tests ordered by providers, what was transmitted to the laboratory, and how results were sent back to providers. It is apparent that the laboratory interface system was not appropriately tested prior to use by providers.

It also appears that end-users were not included in the development of the orders interface. Most likely, the initial order sets were created based on the thought that providers order tests depending on the patient's diagnosis. The initial order sets appear to simply have been lists of any and all tests that might be ordered for a given diagnosis without thought to provider experience, evidence supporting use of the test, or cost of the tests. Including a consultant who had domain expertise in medical informatics and clinical practice improved the usability and safety of the system. The physician informaticist revised laboratory order sets to fit provider workflow while adhering to the tenets of evidence-based practice, ensuring cost-effective care. Thorough mapping of the laboratory test names and testing of the system vastly improved patient safety.

Inclusion of a clinical informatics expert during planning, building, and implementation of the new laboratory interface would most likely have prevented many of the problems that were experienced. In addition to understanding the complexity of healthcare information exchange, an expert in clinical informatics would have ensured that appropriate testing of the system would have been done prior to use in a clinical setting.

Lessons Learned

- Automation of processes can multiply errors with serious consequences.
- Qualified subject matter experts must be involved in complex process automation.
- Accurate mapping of data is critical for many healthcare processes and necessary to avoid potentially dangerous and costly errors.
- Clinical informaticists must draw upon expertise in workflow, evidence-based practices, regulatory oversight, leadership, consensus building, and other areas.

Chapter 34

Start Simple...Maybe: Multispecialty EHR Rollout

Editor: Eric Poon
Duke University Health System

Contents

Project Categories: ambulatory electronic health record (EHR)

Lessons Learned Categories: implementation approaches, system configuration

Case Study

The planning and oversight of a comprehensive electronic health record (EHR) implementation at a multispecialty academic medical group practice with 40 clinics, 1,000 physicians, and 2,000 other personnel was daunting. Which practice site should go live first? How long will each clinic's go-live take? Do we install a simple system first and add the "bells and whistles" later? How should rollout staff support both practices that have gone live and practices currently going live?

The authors of this case led a 2-year EHR rollout in the group practice arm of a large academic health center. This implementation represented the health center's first venture into EHRs; up until this point, both the group practice's and affiliate hospital's clinical information systems were largely paper-based. This case describes the post-EHR acquisition period in which leadership developed and executed a strategy for rolling out the EHR across its 40 clinic locations. The practice's size and the geographic spread of the clinics necessitated an EHR rollout that was staggered over time. The rollout plan initially called for bringing one clinic live each month. However, once implementation began, this timeline and the project plan were adjusted multiple times due to unexpected issues and lessons learned.

Practice leadership determined that the first clinic to implement the EHR would be a small family practice location that was geographically isolated from other primary care and specialty clinics in the group. The rationale was that the practice was not as complex as other sites. Patient volumes were relatively low, and clinic workflows were fewer and less variable. A small number of providers staffed the clinic, and the site did not participate in resident or fellow training. The expectation was that the implementation staff, including information technology (IT) builders, trainers, and managers, would obtain valuable yet manageable experience with a simple implementation and use that as a springboard for the more complex clinics that remained. Moreover, if the first clinic's experience was a bad one, its relative isolation from the rest of the group would minimize the spread of negative opinions about the project to staff at other clinics. Using this same rationale of relative simplicity, the next EHR go-lives were scheduled for a residency family practice clinic and then a pediatric primary care clinic, with more complex specialty clinics to follow.

A second major decision in the clinic-by-clinic rollout was the extent to which each clinic's EHR functionality should be modified from the vendor's "model" system. This was particularly a concern in the early stages of implementation when there was tension between providing the clinics with immediately useful systems that met their expectations and moving through each location's implementation in a timely manner. On the one hand, there were features of the model system that did not align well with the work processes of a given clinic or the group practice as a whole. Insufficient system customization resulted in poor acceptance of the EHR by physicians and staff. On the other hand, extensive customization at some clinics strained the capacity of the IT staff and reduced their ability to prepare the EHR for on-time rollout at upcoming clinics on the schedule. Moreover, excessive customization limited the opportunity to accomplish needed standardization of workflow and processes across clinic sites.

The implementation in the first clinic went well but a number of problems arose as the EHR rollout progressed. The implementation team struggled and user complaints increased as the EHR was installed in more complex practices, which, unlike the first practice, had resident physicians, rotating attending physicians who spent a minority of their time in clinic settings, incoming referrals, and more specialized care processes. Seemingly straightforward EHR system customizations were necessitated, such as the ability for a single provider to write prescriptions from multiple clinic locations. However, attempts to modify the model system's prescribing functionalities led to unintended malfunctions in other parts of the system that demanded significant time from IT staff and delayed the scheduled rollouts to other clinics. In such cases, where software-based solutions failed, the affected clinic's staff was forced to use unwieldy workarounds. By the time the final clinic's EHR was installed, the rollout schedule had been delayed multiple times, and the practice was planning for a new round of system customizations to address many problems that arose but went unsolved during the initial implementations.

Author's Analysis

Leading an EHR rollout in a group practice provided many lessons. Implementing a complex system that significantly changes care delivery processes may never be perfectly predictable, but there were two decisions in particular that we would have handled differently.

First, we would have chosen a more representative clinic for the first EHR go-live. Because the first clinic was the simplest, our implementation team developed a biased understanding of the implementation process. The team spent a significant amount of time preparing for the first go-live, and this created inertia that led them to force-fit solutions that did not work in more complex clinics. The decisions made for a basic primary care clinic did not translate to a complicated surgical practice. Because it was difficult to revise decisions and modify team member behavior on the fly, the more complicated needs of other practices were often accomplished using workarounds.

A better approach would have been to begin our rollout with a clinic that was maximally representative of our practice's processes, such as resident training and incoming referrals. One of our ear, nose, and throat (ENT) clinics, which is moderately complex, has significant procedural activity, and serves as both a physician referral and direct patient referral practice, may have provided a better starting point. This strategy would have exposed our team to an initial set of experiences that would better generalize to future implementations. Further, our training and build decisions would have been more representative of the practice as a whole, likely necessitating fewer workarounds.

Another potential improvement was our approach to customizing the vendor's model EHR system. A model system's functions are designed to work for the "average" patient, which ultimately means that it works for very few specific patients. However, our attempts to customize the EHR focused extensively on each clinic's idiosyncratic workflows. We failed to use our limited customization time and resources on solutions that would apply to the entire practice. Consequently, we failed to achieve key workflow standardizations that could have improved efficiency and quality of care. Tasks such as attending physicians' documentation in resident notes, effective communication with referring physicians, and the movement of patients and information between the practice and our hospital partner were not accomplished as expertly as possible. A better approach to the initial customization of our EHR would have been to identify and customize such practice-wide workflows. Instead, we focused first on each clinic's microsystem, which merely achieved clinic-level standardization on tasks that likely had lower overall value.

Editor's Commentary

This case calls to attention the different approaches EHR implementations could take. When the EHR technology is relatively immature and the outcome of its implementation uncertain, it is reasonable to start small and learn from early mistakes before scaling up the implementation to the rest of the healthcare organization. However, there is often a price to pay with this incremental strategy. First, the experience of early adopters of the EHR technology may exert disproportionate influence over its customization or ongoing development. If the needs of the early adopters differ from the rest of the larger organization, the resulting design could be less than optimal. The authors of the case stated that they wished they had started implementation at a more "representative" practice. That sentiment is understandable, but if workflow patterns have historically been developed organically in a parochial way in different practice settings, one has to ask whether a truly representative practice exists. Second, the incremental implementation strategy often serves to perpetuate the patchwork of idiosyncratic workflows, and deprives the healthcare organization the opportunity to design in a rational way a healthcare delivery system that truly serves the needs of its patient population.

One trend that is emerging with EHR implementations calls for design sessions up front that involve key stakeholders from the entire organization. This approach, which typically requires significant participation by both clinical leaders and front-line clinicians, encourages clinicians to think beyond the practice habits they have developed over the years at the local practice level and consider new approaches. During these sessions, critical issues such as interpractice communication, multidisciplinary care, transitions of care across different settings, patient and family engagement, and clinical performance improvement inform the group's thinking. If successfully executed, they offer the organization an opportunity to leverage the EHR implementation to optimize workflow and remove inefficiencies.

However, this comprehensive and inclusive approach to EHR customization and design brings its own risks. These design sessions can become unwieldy and unproductive if they are not well facilitated by those who understand the functionality of the EHR, its limitations, and different ways it could be used in different clinical settings. They also require the clinical participants to have a mature understanding of the goals of EHR implementation and what they can realistically expect out of an EHR. If the organization does not have the capacity to make design decisions quickly, or if the organization becomes overly ambitious by addressing too many clinical processes, these sessions can fail. In short, the comprehensive and inclusive design approach requires a fine balancing act.

Clearly, certain situations call for the incremental approach, and others call for a more comprehensive and inclusive one. As the EHR implementation experience broadens, one might expect a growing evidence base to inform future choices. Unfortunately, the EHR implementation experience (either positive or negative) is not well published and often remains proprietary knowledge for the EHR companies or implementation consultants. A national registry to track EHR implementation successes and failures would help advance the science of EHR implementation, but until that is developed, we will need to rely on anecdotal cases such as this one to inform implementation decisions.

Lessons Learned

- Implementing a complex system that significantly changes care delivery processes may never be perfectly predictable.
- Engage key stakeholders from the entire organization in design sessions.
- Evaluate an organization's needs for incremental versus comprehensive implementations to assess the risks and benefits of each approach.

Chapter 35

It's in the EHR...but Where?: Patient Records

Editor: David Leander
Dartmouth

Contents

Project Categories: ambulatory electronic health record (EHR)

Lessons Learned Categories: leadership/governance, system configuration, system design

A network of ambulatory care providers implemented an electronic health record (EHR) in time to receive the US federal government-sponsored Meaningful Use incentive payments. The organization provided primary care, behavioral health care, dental care, and even some specialty care to over 40,000 patients across multiple sites. The organization was recognized as an early adopter of technology, achieved Meaningful Use status, and even received hundreds of thousands of dollars of grant funding to support further development of its EHR program. Over time, the health care organization leadership requested that the EHR team add more and more features to track more and more patient information in the EHR—data fields were created to document a patient's diabetes care plan, birth control preference, tobacco-use history, whether or not a controlled substance agreement or advanced directive had been completed, and many others. A governance committee was formed to oversee all new requests, as well as new features and functionality to be developed in the EHR. The committee included leadership from all clinical departments, medical records, operations, information technology (IT), quality improvement, and the EHR support team. New features were proposed, discussed, and voted upon. Over time, the functionality for clinical staff documentation, storing outside records and results, tracking test orders, and referrals grew in both number and complexity. The complexity led to several years of consistent complaints from providers about the difficulty reviewing a patient's record and finding information in the EHR, and feeling insecure about being unaware of patient information stored in the EHR.

Outside Consult Reports, received on paper, were scanned and saved to a "Consult Report" folder in a patient's chart in the EHR to be available whenever and wherever needed. However, the Consult Reports were organized by date, and each report had to be individually opened and viewed to reveal the source of the report (i.e., cardiology, sleep laboratory) or find other identifying information. Imaging tests, from magnetic resonance imaging (MRI)to echocardiography, were treated similarly. This process became complex and laborious, particularly for patients with multiple medical problems or patients with multiple consults from varying specialties over time. For patients with multiple medical problems and cared for by multiple consultants from multiple specialties over time, this became very complex and laborious. Providers had different practices on updating the chart to reflect recent consults. Some noted the most recent date in the problem list, while others did not. Sometimes these notes were outdated. The varied practices created new challenges to assessing a patient's current clinical status and care plan.

Extensive screening examinations for behavioral health were developed that included the PSQ9, GAD7, alcohol and substance abuse screens, and others, in support of the mission of the organization to serve patients' medical and behavioral health needs. The goal was to screen all patients and either treat newly diagnosed problems or refer to behavioral health as needed. To see that a patient had completed these screening tests and to review the results (either positive or negative), a provider had to remember to click through several icons when reviewing a patient's record. Providers began to raise concerns about missing patients who had been identified through unreviewed screening tests, even potentially those with life-threatening behaviors.

To address the complexity of the EHR referral workflow, quick and easy consult order processes were requested for popular internal programs such as Breast Health and visiting nursing. The EHR team designed a workflow for these that used a single-line message in the EHR's internal messaging system. Providers became confused about when to use the standard referral workflow and screens or the messaging system and sometimes tried to use both. The Referrals Department did not know what to do with the standard referral requests for programs that were supposed to be contacted by the messaging system. If a patient was referred with the messaging system, a provider had to document the action in a free text note in the EHR in order to assure that the issue was reassessed at the next visit. If there was no next visit or the note was later missed, and the message-based request did not occur, no one knew and the patient did not receive the referred service.

When these concerns were raised to the EHR team and the EHR governance committee, the answer remained, "it's all in the EHR."

Ultimately, a staff survey showed that providers and other members of the care team were statistically *more* likely to be dissatisfied with their EHR than similar people at similar organizations.

Author's Analysis

The failure to appreciate the organization's own limits to expertise in EHR design and configuration was the foundation for later mistakes.

- "Just document it" is not a good mantra for EHR workflow development or clinician workflow design. Poorly designed user interfaces (UI) and required data entry fields have caused many providers and other care team staff to spend more time picking and checking boxes in an EHR than assessing important clinical issues with patients and often create misleading documentation.

- If information about a patient is important, so is the presentation of the information to the care team. If the information is stored, but not effectively presented, it will be missed. Not only does this enable bad care, but also it can create liability for the organization in case of adverse events that could have been avoided with the knowledge of such information.
- Records, results, and other patient information need to be stored and curated similarly to periodicals in a library, or even an airplane cockpit dashboard—they need to be simply organized, easily found, reviewed, and understood; otherwise, they provide little value in caring for a patient.
- Training multiple people on how to use complex systems, like which process applies to which type of referral, is unlikely to succeed in a complex health care environment. Processes for common tasks should be easy to figure out and perform, not require memory-based training.

Editor's Commentary

Innovation in the EHR can lead to an unmanageable amount of information to process as this case highlights. This case also raises the issue of creating multiple places in the EHR to find information, leading to individual clinicians coming up with their own way to process information in the chart and leading to disparate methods of using and entering information. Thus, more work is needed in this area to streamline workflows and understand how users are actually using the software.

Another element of this case is the divide that often presents between EHR teams and clinicians. Often, workflows are envisioned a particular way by EHR teams and then reimagined by the clinicians. Similarly, when certain needs are identified by clinicians, these requests are reinterpreted by EHR teams, often leading to common phrases like "works as designed" or in this case "it's in the EHR." This case highlights the need for improved understanding and expectations across EHR team and clinical staff, as highlighted by the survey results showing dissatisfaction.

Ongoing training is a key to ensuring that all users are aware of the most current practices and can avoid some of the variation in how certain tools are used. Having regular, department-wide touch-base sessions could bring these variations to light, and as a group, a unified method could be established. For example, the issue of the problem list documentation could have been raised and discussed as a group, and a common methodology to use it could have been implemented. From a quality perspective, this also could ensure that documentation in the EHR is of high quality.

Lessons Learned

- Complex UI can make it difficult to document a patient's clinical care and to review prior information.
- EHRs require constant skillful curating for effective structure and organization.
- Training will unlikely solve end-user problems with an overly complex EHR, especially in a large organization.

Chapter 36

All Systems Down...What Now?: Ambulatory EHR

Editor: Christopher Corbit
TeamHealth

Contents

Project Categories: ambulatory electronic health record (EHR)

Lessons Learned Categories: communication, leadership/governance, technology problems, training

Case Study

A large, multisite ambulatory care health system with over 50 physicians and mid-level providers implemented a market leading electronic health record (EHR). Within 2 years, the health system is using the EHR for all clinically focused processes: patient visits are scheduled in the EHR; patients are checked in and triaged in the EHR; and clinicians document all aspects of patient care in the EHR, including communications with nurses and other colleagues about patient management. All orders are entered and managed within the EHR, such as prescriptions, diagnostic tests, and internal and external consult requests. The EHR is digitally linked to pharmacies through a statewide e-prescribing system. Additionally, the health system has leveraged problem lists and procedure codes for clinical decision support alerts that guide an individual patient's care. Outside records are either received by the EHR via direct data interfaces (i.e., laboratory results) or entered as scanned documents. Staff use both mobile and fixed devices supported by a wireless network, depending on their workflow needs. Beyond regular office hours, providers use remote access to the EHR to help manage patients when on call. Occasionally, there are problems with the system's slowness and performance, but mostly the EHR functions well and has become a critical resource to the health system. The health system has started the process to attest for Centers for Medicaid and Medicare Services (CMS) Stage 1 Meaningful Use dollars.

One morning, around 9:30 a.m., clinicians and administrative staff at a large site in the health system begin to experience EHR freezes; "hourglasses" spin on the display screen for seconds and sometimes minutes, orders "hang" before completing, and other data entry steps or data review tasks become very slow. Providers and administrative staff at the site ask each other if the problems are site-wide or just affecting a few people. After another hour, they learn that everyone at the site is experiencing the same problems. A call is placed to the information technology (IT) help desk. The EHR functions slowly, but is usable during patient care. As the morning progresses, the system delays worsen and providers report that the entire EHR is freezing and shutting down. One physician says he rebooted his laptop three times without any improvement. Another physician reports feeling embarrassed when a patient in an examination room asked about a recent magnetic resonance imaging (MRI) result, and it took 3 min to open the MRI report. A nurse complains that it took 5 min to pick up an order for a flu vaccine and document it was given to a patient, instead of the typical 1–2 min. Two physicians discuss whether or not the site should revert to paper, but they are reluctant to do so, given that all patient information is only available in the EHR and that any data manually collected would need to be entered into the system eventually.

One local site administrator announces that due to the problems with the EHR, the site will not schedule any more patients that day because they are already two-thirds booked (which is typical for a busy morning). By 11:30 a.m., the site learns that the entire health system is being affected by the EHR performance problems. Each task a clinician enters takes up to 5 min and occasionally the entire EHR freezes, at which point the computer must be rebooted. Before 12:00 p.m., the director of IT sends an e-mail to all staff that the health system is experiencing major problems with EHR performance and that the IT team is working with the EHR vendor to address the problems. The director of IT sympathetically notes that he "feels your pain." Another local site's providers agree that they will document all visits on paper. Prescription pads are found and distributed to providers. A nurse practitioner suggests deferring coding of visits until the system resumes normal function.

A physician notices that the next three patients to arrive have multiple, complex medical problems, take many medications, and have frequent diagnostic tests to review. He asks the patients to reschedule for another day, explaining that the EHR is down. The registration desk at the local site is instructed to inform patients as they arrive that due to problems with the computer system, only brief visits and medication refills will be provided. A nurse fields a call from a pharmacy—a physician had renewed a patient's narcotic pain medications for a much higher dose than the patient usually receives. The physician writes a new prescription and recognizes that he misunderstood the patient's reported dose, which could not be verified without the EHR. For the next few hours, physicians and nurses struggle to treat patients with diabetes, heart disease, and mental illness without access to past records, medication lists, test results, or care plans. The staff spends much of the day apologizing to patients, some of whom are angry. Most patients must reschedule to return another day.

Author's Analysis

After an extensive review of the problem by both the health system's IT team and the vendor, a plan was set to upgrade servers and modify database configurations that were identified as the cause of the poor performance of the EHR. The health system made several key errors that caused the downtime to be a bigger organizational problem than it had to be. The health system did not realize that with a fully implemented EHR, care could not continue "as usual" when the EHR went down. Without the EHR, providers made mistakes, potentially harming patients. Health system productivity suffered, which not only affected the organization as a whole but also could have affected the staff since all employees receive productivity-based incentive compensation. Staff also felt insecure and unsupported by the organization, having felt forced to provide less than optimum care.

The health system did not have any triggers for clinician and administration leadership to make decisions about what to do at different stages of system outages, including when to revert to paper documentation, when to reschedule patients, and even when to stop providing care. Inadequate communication meant staff was not informed about problems with IT as they evolved and did not know how to respond to the problems. Lastly, the patients' response to the outage should not be overlooked—if events like this continue with any regularity at a health system, patients will likely start going elsewhere for care.

The health system should have prepared and practiced for downtime, just like fire drills are practiced in case of a fire. Without practice drills, neither clinicians nor administrators can know what to do during downtime. Downtime drills should include all aspects of downtime management, including communication protocols and paper-based documentation processes.

Editor's Commentary

As EHRs become "mission-critical" elements of patient care, downtime is an extremely disruptive process and significant issue for most patient care settings. As we move away from paper charts, there is an increasing reliance on EHR for clinical information and workflow. If not adequately planned for, downtime may be considered such a disruption in services as to threaten the safety and welfare of patients. Therefore, policies and procedural support that exemplify best practices during downtime are absolutely necessary.

Downtime may happen at anytime—even a few hours after go-live! Thus, you need to plan and test your downtime procedures at the same time you are implementing your EHR, which is not an easy task and normally overlooked by project management. In development, focus on best practices and guidelines to provide uninterrupted service in an efficient manner before, during, and after downtime.

Although a detailed plan on developing a downtime plan is beyond the scope of this discussion, presented here is a generalized framework either to begin your downtime policy and procedure creation, or to review what you already have in place and help augment it. The creating of downtime procedures can be broken down into four main categories:

1. **Provider and staff communication:** Once downtime has been identified, consistent communication is vital throughout the downtime and its recovery among all stakeholders affected by the downtime.
2. **Availability of historical clinical data:** Access to patient information by the clinical and office staff is vital to maintaining patient safety and optimal care throughout the downtime.
3. **Continuing operational activities:** Ongoing clinical care and support for business activities must be maintained within the framework of a downtime, episode as exemplified in this particular case presentation.

4. **Recovery and reconciliation of data:** After the downtime is over, the reconciliation of data back into the EHR is fundamental for continued patient safety and quality of care.

With the focus on these general areas, divide the work into discrete phases and address specific workflows (such as order entry or documentation). Systematically tackle questions about how each group of stakeholders (physicians, nurses, office staff) responds in each downtime phase across each process, with a focus on workflow. Each group will need to specifically identify the areas where they are dependent upon the other groups for information or logistical planning.

One of the first priorities in assisting the delivery of clinical care during system downtime is providing clinicians access to historic clinical information. The downtime solution should be able to provide as much historical information as is feasible. This needs to be as up to date as possible and easy to access, or a frustrating situation can be made worse and patient safety can be further compromised. Even if you have designed and implemented your EHR backup with a near-real-time incremental update system, pieces of information may be lost. It may be possible to have a regularly scheduled extract of data including demographics, medications, problem lists, and immunizations saved to a secure computer at a defined time frame that can be printed in the event of downtime.

There may be other sources of historical data that can be accessed outside of the EHR. For example, ancillary systems may have a direct log-on or portals that nonlaboratory personnel can access. Also, picture archiving and communication systems (PACS) frequently store diagnostic imaging reports as well as the images internally. Transcribed reports are frequently stored in scanning or document management systems outside the integrated clinical system.

Maintaining operational activity during downtime may be one of the most difficult tasks to achieve, but if planned for accordingly and practiced (just like fire or disaster drills), the challenges can be minimized. There are several critical areas that need to be addressed in your plans, which include the clinical and office staff. Downtime forms need to be accessed quickly; these are entered later or scanned depending on the EHR or policy. Laboratory and radiology results will need to be reported on paper, as well as any standing orders held for later entry into the EHR. Also, it is imperative to have prescription pads always accessible, along with medication and allergy lists. Finally, have the most commonly used patient instructions preprinted and available to give to patients at discharge.

Another priority during downtime is providing clinicians the tools to document and implement treatment plans. Once clinicians begin using an EHR, they have a tendency to forget even deeply embedded knowledge. This can be one of the greatest hazards of EHRs. Most EHRs have clinical decision support tools built into the system. An example of this is to have specific reminders within the documentation, such as asking about influenza or pneumococcal immunization. Without being prompted by the documentation, either the physician or the nurse may not be reminded to ask this question since they are accustomed to being prompted to do so. The office staff is already working without their customary tools, so anything that can be done to simplify and make the processes more efficient is very beneficial.

When switching to paper for documentation, preprinted templates and flow sheets should maintain the same design style and embedded clinical decision support as in the EHR. With the same style as the EHR, it will be easier for the clinicians to maintain their workflow. It is important to remember that once you have your paper downtime forms finalized and ready to go in the event of downtime, all preprinted clinical documentation forms must follow regulatory guidelines. Therefore, they need to be incorporated into any guideline and regulatory updates applied to the EHR.

Addressing order workflow is another priority during downtime. Physicians have become somewhat dependent on order sets to improve quality and efficiency in the ordering process. These order sets should be printed for ordering during downtime, or at the very least, as information resources. These should be maintained as close as possible to the electronic order set, as studies have shown that even the order of a pick list of items or the location of an order within an order set influences which ones are chosen.

As hectic and agonizing as the downtime episode may be, the recovery can be even worse. In addition to providing continual care for patients, the staff is burdened with the task of data reentry. In addition to improving workflow for clinicians during downtime, documentation tools that closely resemble the EHR will also facilitate data reentry and recovery. Items that can be reentered into the EHR can include, but are not limited to, paper clinical documentation, flow sheets (vitals, nursing assessments), orders, and problem lists. Thus, it is worthwhile to define a minimum data set that can be initially reentered into the system quickly so that other areas may begin data reentry. A second pass can then be taken to update remaining information. So, the practice needs to have a clear resource strategy that addresses what information will be entered into the EHR.

Depending on the time frame of the downtime episode, a substantial amount of information can be documented. Subject to the features of the EHR, it may be possible to input data normally entered discretely in a nondiscrete format. Some EHRs allow for storage and retrieval of scanned images. As such, it may be possible for your group to scan large quantities of information and reference this information in the patient's EHR chart, and thus not add the burden of manually entering the information into the EHR. However, some critical information should be discretely entered back into the EHR. Examples include allergies or adverse drug reactions identified during the system downtime, problem list changes, and medication changes. Information that could affect coding and billing might also be important to reenter to aid in chart processing.

In an ideal world, development of an EHR is designed with downtime issues in mind. The tools developed within the EHR to improve and enhance quality and efficiency need to be addressed when designing downtime workflows and documents. Without an adequate downtime procedure in place and practice with these procedures, a downtime episode will adversely affect patient care.

Lessons Learned

- Once a health system has a fully implemented EHR, care cannot continue "as usual" if the EHR goes down.
- Different stages of system outages should create clinical and operational triggers.
- Communication is essential in managing downtime.
- Health systems must prepare and practice for downtime.
- Downtime directly affects and is noticed by patients.

Chapter 37

Weekends Are Not Just for Relaxing: Reconciliation after EHR Downtime

Editors: Justin Graham
Hearst Health

Eric Rose
Intelligent Medical Objects

Contents

Project Categories: ambulatory electronic health record (EHR)

Lessons Learned Categories: communication, staffing resources, training

Case Study

Interconnected health care is a large integrated delivery network that owns two larger (greater than 400-bed) hospitals, multiple smaller rural and community hospitals, and over 60 clinics. A "big-bang" implementation was its strategy for an electronic health record (EHR) implementation, with all functionality rolled out to all clinical staff at each location on the same day. The go-live schedule was designed to implement a group of clinics first, and then the hospital to which those clinics primarily referred.

The system had only been implemented in two 60-bed rural hospitals, including their clinics, plus several clinics associated with a larger community hospital when the first unscheduled downtime occurred. It lasted for several hours on a Sunday afternoon, when none of the ambulatory sites were open. If an end-user had been working in the system when it went down, they had no idea there was anything wrong, but the moment they secured their workstation or ended their session they could not get back in. The call went out immediately to the hospitals to log out and implement downtime procedures. Once the system came back online, it rebooted with the backup from the moment it had gone down. Leadership breathed a sigh of relief when the system was back up and focused their recovery efforts on the two hospitals that had been affected. That is until Monday morning.

Providers in every live clinic came into work on Monday morning and found many of their completed charts still open. Multiple providers called the help desk with complaints that they had finished the charts over the weekend and their work had been lost. The information about the downtime eventually reached the clinics' leadership, who then had to pass on the information that any data entered during the downtime had been lost. Since the clinics were closed at the time the downtime occurred, no one had reached out to any of the ambulatory staff. The estimate of charts with lost data numbered in the hundreds, and the providers were extremely unhappy about not just the lost data, but also the amount of effort that had to be duplicated to reenter the information. Some clinics offered to have other staff perform the data entry, but most providers declined because they either had to enter subjective information or felt like it took so long to fill out the downtime forms that it would be easier and less risky to enter the information themselves the first time.

The negative word of mouth generated by the affected providers was perpetuated throughout the physician community at meetings for months. Leadership calculated this error in communication led to hundreds of hours of lost physician productivity and an inestimable loss of credibility and faith in the project and the system.

Author's Analysis

Ensure that your communication plan for issues and emergencies includes all locations. This problem would likely have been prevented if the clinics' leadership had been notified and instructed to contact their providers about the downtime. A new business continuity plan was put into place with a set of downtime procedures that included clinic managers and physician leads as well as processes for downstream communication to all end-users via message alerts and pop-ups.

Do not underestimate the amount of time spent outside office hours performing work. The leadership assumed that because the number of open charts was small, their success with meeting the goal of charts being closed within 72 h meant the providers were proficient with the system. This event highlighted the error in that assumption. The organization's Physician Engagement Team developed an Optimization Program after this event, with one goal being that of increasing provider efficiency and reducing the amount of time providers spent on their charting outside of office hours. This attempted to ameliorate some of the negative aftereffects of the event by reassuring physicians that organizational leadership cared about their work–life balance and wanted them to be able to finish their work in the same amount of time they did prior to the implementation of the new system.

Editors' Commentary

Many advantages exist for using electronic medical records, but one disadvantage that was not foreseen by this hospital administration was the increased amount of time needed to document a case by physicians in the outpatient setting. In this situation, the physicians were not able to complete their charts in the normal time frame of the workweek, and thus were pushed to off-hour times, including the weekends, where this downtime event occurred. A lack of specific downtime procedures, specifically in the area of communication, resulted in an event that, while it had a negligible effect on outpatient care, caused a significant issue with the outpatient providers.

Downtime can happen at any time and every system experiences some sort of downtime, crash, and other issues from time to time. It is how the downtime is planned for and handled that is important. Communication is vital to keep system users up to date about system downtime. A focus on best practices and guidelines to provide uninterrupted service in an efficient manner before, during, and after downtime is essential.

Communication channels are key, but they tend to be one-way and unsatisfactory for users. There are several fundamental aspects to consider when communicating during downtime:

- All stakeholders need to be involved in the development of downtime guidelines and procedures; they must be notified of any downtime, whether or not they are considered directly involved in the downtime.
- State clearly what the underlying cause of the downtime is (hardware, software, network, and such).
- Highlight likely consequences or lack thereof for the downtime (data loss, database corruption, prolonged downtime).
- Keep the tone very neutral. Do not place blame. Ideally, this conveys acknowledgment of the problem with professionalism in addressing the issues leading to the downtime.
- If you send the announcement out by e-mail, your notification will be forwarded to several people. Make sure that the IT team and help desk understand the issues and consequences of the downtime. An executive summary to the C-suite helps them deal with any questions that can come their way. Technical details should be focused on those that understand them.
- Provide contact details (preferably someone who has the time in the midst of the downtime) for further questions, and ask for patience in the same sentence (this often works).
- Promise updates when the situation changes.

When the cause of the downtime has been addressed, send a summary including a list of all the possible consequences so that the users can review their data. This should also include the actions taken and changes implemented in the short term and those planned for the future ("lessons learned"), based on technical root-cause analysis.

Training for downtime is vital. The first downtime training should occur when the system is being implemented. All system users should receive refresher training on a regular basis. Often overlooked, new employees hired after system implementation need to be trained on these procedures as part of their system training as well. In addition to all system users receiving regular training on downtime procedures, the channels of communication need to be tested on a regular basis to ensure they are viable options. E-mail addresses, phone extensions, personnel responsibilities, and physical office space can and frequently do change.

Once a downtime situation has been identified, consistent communication is vital throughout the downtime and its recovery among all stakeholders affected by the downtime. Regular testing and updating the communication channels is an absolute necessity to ensure that the system users adhere to all planned downtime procedures. Without key channels of communication, a well-planned downtime procedure will most likely fail.

Lastly, this case offers some lessons regarding system selection. It is concerning that a system failure could occur without it being obvious to end-users who were using the system during the failure. Software applications should, when such failures occur, provide unambiguous indications to end-users that the data they are in the midst of entering cannot be saved. In addition, many current-generation software applications save data with every user action (keystroke, mouse-click, etc.), minimizing the amount of data lost with any system failure, and such capabilities should be sought in EHR systems as well.

Lessons Learned

- Ensure that communication plans for issues and emergencies include all locations.
- Remember that work is often performed outside of office hours.
- Train for downtime.
- Seek out clinical information systems designed to minimize data loss in the event of system downtime.

Chapter 38

104 Synergistic Problems: An Enterprise EHR

Editor: Eric Rose
Intelligent Medical Objects

Contents

Project Categories: ambulatory electronic health record (EHR), inpatient EHR

Lessons Learned Categories: contracts, leadership/governance, project management, technology problems, workflow

Case Study

This health information technology (HIT) story describes an implementation of an integrated electronic health record (EHR) system in a large university teaching hospital. The project started in 2001, and the implementation progressed slowly from one hospital unit to the next. The main parts of the system were Orfeus, for controlling and administrating healthcare processes, and Medeia, for recording the care planning, realization, follow-up, and evaluation. The software provider had missed delivery dates and the parts delivered had not always met the original specifications. These challenges, combined with technical and integration problems, caused resistance among the hospital staff.

The resistance peaked in the surgical outpatient clinic and surgical inpatient unit where our story took place. The implementation was carried out in two of the surgical units during November 2005, but the situation was soon called a crisis by the staff members and the implementation came to a halt. In order to restart the project successfully, an assessment was performed to identify problems and recommend potential solutions. When studying the situation's problems, we interviewed surgeons, nurses, administration, and other EHR project stakeholders and identified 104 different issues of concern. These issues were classified into first-, second-, and third-order groups after the issue order model presented by Star and Ruhleder (1996).

First-Order Issues

First-order issues are often easily visible, and solutions to them are practical. These issues were grouped according to the themes of redistribution of work resources and working time, arranging user training, and technical problems during the implementation.

After the implementation of the EHR, a main issue in information access was caused by workflows that were impeded. The process to use the EHR was slower than using the paper records at hand. One of the system features that slowed workflow was the structured character of the EHR. For example, there were more than 50 headings for recording a nursing action. One of the nurses described the situation as follows:

> Now I have to open Medeia, to open the nursing records. Now I'll create the record, that takes many clicks—like surgeons' names, date, and cause this and cause that. Then I'll have to choose the right headings, and then I can go and record the day visit by the patient … and then I'll have to choose the next suitable heading… I have many workflow steps here, steps that I have never done before … Before I just wrote, for example, 'covering letter' and 'breast cancer' on the paper and that was it.

The slowness of use affected workflows in various ways. For example, in the surgical outpatient department with continuous patient visits, half of the working time consisted of documenting patient records. In contrast, this took only about one-eighth of the working time in the surgical inpatient unit.

Second-Order Issues

Second-order issues can be caused by unpredictable contextual effects, that is, a collision or combination of two or more first-order issues. The unexpected effects may be caused by technical choices made or by the differences between the various cultures of practice that are working together in the implementation.

Combined effects of technical features that caused user resistance were, for example, the way the EHR logged off users, how the technical devices were arranged in the inpatient areas, or other problems that might have been caused by a constant need to repeatedly log in to the system. Constant technical problems caused the staff to think that the EHR did not ease their documenting load but rather interfered with their workflow and caused unwanted periods of waiting for the system to open or to find the next patient's data. Technical problems were further illustrated by the varied practices during downtime of the EHR system. During downtime, the patient records could be written as separate text files that could then be added into the EHR when the system was up again. Problems emerged when the separate text files were attached only as printouts to the paper version of the patient records and not entered into the EHR. The result was that the EHR was not necessarily up to date, and the staff could not trust the information in the EHR as complete or accurate.

Third-Order Issues

Third-order issues are often political or social by nature. Their nature dictates that these problems are also hard to solve. Such problems can be caused by the historical reasons behind the choices made in the implementation project or distinct features in the organizational culture.

The staff in the surgical clinic thought that they had no influence on system design and development. While working bedside, both a surgeon and a nurse might record information quite fluently and not consider whose user account was used to access the system. Problems of responsibility emerged when mistakes were made in the records. The one whose username was logged into the system was held responsible. On the other hand, surgeons feared that the slowness of use could cause malpractice in situations when patient information could not be accessed as easily as needed. A surgeon might have to make a decision on patient care with insufficient information.

Author's Analysis

This conflicting situation was caused by a combination of multiple and intertwined sociotechnical issues. Emergence of such issues demanded attention on several levels in the organization, in this case, for example, by the information management department and hospital administration. The preliminary results suggest that social structures affecting the interaction in a hospital unit affect how the emergence of intertwined problems, handling the issues, and resolving the crisis takes place.

With previous manual patient records, the staff members were used to interpreting the paper records. Now with the EHR, feelings of insecurity emerged as well as the fear of ignorance as the previously usable interpretive schemes were insufficient in the changing context of interpretation. With the EHR, the patient information was "hidden" behind different headings of new nursing classifications and behind the views in the new system environment. Furthermore, the EHR was designed as independent system components. These components can work quite well by themselves, but the integration had caused some unexpected effects. Uncertainty combined with technical problems caused user resistance to reach its peak, and thus, the implementation and use of the EHR came to a halt.

The case study shows that a new, unfamiliar information system can be accused of shortcomings or problems that may not actually be caused by the technology. In a crisis situation, it is a human reaction to find a "scapegoat" that can be accused. Instead of simply labeling the new information system as a "scapegoat," we want to ask whether the implementation of an information system is a catalyst that makes it possible for other sociotechnical issues to emerge in the organizational context. The case study indicates that technical problems, such as slowness of use, can cause user resistance or at least increase users' doubt about the new information system. On the other hand, issues concerning professional values, such as fear of malpractice because of missing or inaccessible patient information, can lead to the decision not to use the system at all.

Editor's Commentary

This fascinating case history of a HIT project that went seriously awry offers a smorgasbord of cautionary points. As the title suggests, it seems that every possible mishap that can occur in such a project took place.

It would be interesting to know what the decision-making process was for selecting the system used and its configuration. It seems likely, given the outcome, that involvement of the end-users—at least from the surgery department—was minimal. If there had been such end-user involvement, the usability issues described herein would likely have been recognized even before the purchasing decision was made, and the system would probably have been tailored to more closely match the true needs of the clinical staff.

The references to "slipped schedules" and the vendor-supplied software "not always meeting specifications" point to the importance of careful negotiation of vendor contracts. Such happenstances are not uncommon, and often are unavoidable (to be fair to the vendors), and this serves to underscore that organizations relying on vendor-supplied software should ensure that purchasing contracts clearly stipulate what remedies will be offered in such circumstances, and also include contingencies in their implementation plan for them.

The "issue order model" used to group the problems encountered in this project helps to differentiate problems that are straightforward and practical (though not necessarily easily solved) from those that involve interactions among several factors, such as the issue with adding the text files, which were created during periods of downtime, back to the EHR. This latter issue requires a consistent workflow outside the use of the EHR, which is often hard to achieve. The "third-order" issues in this case history describe a collision between the EHR system's characteristics and the professional realities of medical practice and serve to remind us of the high stakes where the safety of real patients and the professional standing of real healthcare practitioners are involved.

Lessons Learned

- Stakeholder involvement in project planning and technology selection is critical.
- Technology-driven workflows must fit the needs of clinicians.
- Costs of project delays to both health systems and vendors should be reviewed prior to a technology implementation.
- HIT initiatives exist within the complex sociopolitical culture of the healthcare delivery system and are influenced positively and negatively by the organizations involved.

Chapter 39

What Defines "Failure": Small Practice EHR

Editors: Larry Ozeran
Clinical Informatics Inc.

Jonathan Leviss
Greater New Bedford Community Health Center

Contents

Project Categories: ambulatory electronic health record (EHR)

Lessons Learned Categories: system design, technology problems, training

Case Study

A young primary care physician, after practicing for several years at the same urban community health center where he had undergone residency training, decided it was time for a change. Despite having no experience either in solo private practice or in the use of electronic health record (EHR) systems, he decided to establish his own solo practice and to use an EHR system from the first day, with no paper records. The decision to purchase and install an EHR system required a substantial capital investment and was a highly unusual step for a solo, private-practice physician in that city (itself a rare breed there).

The physician cited two main factors in the decision to adopt an EHR: efficiency and effective charge capture. "I wanted to be able to get my [visit] notes done quickly and bill electronically, and also not have the overhead for storage of paper charts." He also cited quality and patient-safety benefits such as drug–drug interaction warnings offered when using the EHR to generate prescriptions, and reminders regarding preventive interventions for which the patient is due. The initial installation and configuration of the EHR was uneventful, and the physician and staff received training from the EHR vendor at the time of initial installation.

Over several years, the practice grew to three physicians and two mid-level practitioners. A physician with some informatics training joined the practice. The new physician made some noteworthy observations:

- Although newer versions of the EHR system were available, the practice continued to use the version that was current when the practice was founded years before.
- Some processes (such as generating outside referrals) were being handled with paper, despite the capability of the EHR to handle them electronically.
- Certain configurable content, such as the rules on which automated reminders regarding preventive care are based, had not been changed since being automatically set during the initial software installation, despite changes in the evidence-based standards of care on which they were based.
- Certain basic security practices—such as assigning each user a separate user account and not sharing passwords—were not being followed.
- Many of the features of the software, some among them frequently cited as conferring the most important benefits of an EHR, were being used rarely or not at all: e-prescribing and computerized provider order entry (CPOE), assignment of discrete codes to patient diagnoses and problems, population-based reporting tools, creation of custom data fields to record discrete data of interest, and customization of documentation templates.
- Aside from an inbound laboratory results interface, no other interoperability features of the EHR system were used.

When these observations were pointed out to the practice's founding physician, he thought that although true, these observations were not of serious concern. "The program is effective for what I need it to do. I realize it can do a lot more, but I'm pretty happy with what I get out of it now, and I don't really have the time to get into all the details" of utilizing features such as those just mentioned. However, he acknowledged the potential value of such functionality, particularly in promoting patient safety and improving quality:

> I realize that a lot of the quality experts want us to use EHRs to do patient recalls, population-based care, and quality measurement … and I want to do all that too. I think sometimes what the experts don't realize is that physicians, particularly those in private practice, where we're responsible for everything, need help just getting through the day taking care of our patients, and we focus on the aspects of an EHR that let us do that. I hope we can get to the rest of it someday soon.

More recently, the practice started taking steps to get more out of their EHR. They have upgraded to the latest version, started using the EHR's electronic prescribing capability (i.e., electronic transmission of prescriptions directly to pharmacies, rather than printing or faxing prescriptions from the EHR), and began participating in a quality improvement initiative that will provide reports on key quality measures extracted from data in their EHR. The growth of the practice to its current five providers has increased the level of product knowledge among the providers, as each gradually (often accidentally) discovers new aspects of how the EHR can be used and shares it with the others.

Author's Analysis

The case history raises the question of what "failure" means in the adoption and use of health information technology (HIT). Specifically, this case illustrates that there are gradations of failure short of complete abandonment or deinstallation of a system, and that failure is, in some cases, a matter of context or expectations. The practice's founding physician absolutely does not see the practice's use of an EHR as a "failure." Quite to the contrary, the specific goals in mind when the decision to use an EHR was made, to allow documenting care more quickly than on paper without the expense of a transcriptionist, to avoid the space and associated expenses entailed by paper records, and to minimize accounts receivable through electronic claims submission, by any analysis were met.

On the other hand, many "experts" in clinical informatics and clinical quality improvement, blanching at the thought of the most valuable (from their perspective) features of an EHR going underused or unused, would look on this case history as a failure to obtain the maximum benefit from an EHR (Zhou et al., 2009). There are few published data on the frequency with which specific features of ambulatory EHRs are actually utilized (Simon et al., 2009). However, abundant anecdotal experience suggests that the case study is not unusual, and this might explain recently published data suggesting that the use of an EHR alone is not associated with quality of care.

Practicing physicians and the experts do agree on one thing: the quality benefits obtained through capture and storage of discrete data in the EHR, being able to share that data across organizational boundaries, and leveraging of that data for just-in-time decision support and population-level care management are significant and worth striving toward. The question of "failure" in this case, then, becomes a simple matter of perspective on the pace of this evolution of the healthcare process. However, challenging questions remain: How can EHRs be engineered so that these more "advanced" features are easier to use? How can the organization of healthcare services and their financing be restructured to increase the feasibility of more effective utilization of EHR technology? How can physicians, particularly busy ones trying to run a practice on their own and who may need training and assistance, be identified, and how can that training and assistance be provided to them?

Editors' Commentary

The author's final questions resonate with the concerns of HIT advocates and policymakers that care providers make use of the sophisticated capabilities of HIT that have the potential to transform healthcare and improve outcomes, rather than simply using the most rudimentary capabilities of those systems. This idea is enshrined in the phrase "meaningful use," which is commonly used to identify a specific U.S. governmental program that provided financial incentives to providers who adopted EHR technology, but only if they demonstrated the use of certain key capabilities of those systems. While this program has since been superceded by other programs, the idea of "meaningful use" remains a highly relevant concept in HIT adoption.

Regarding the assessment of this case study, it might be instructive to know how much the physician paid for the system and support services as a percentage of revenues. Similarly, it might be useful to know how many patients the physician was seeing and how many hours were spent in the clinic each day compared to after being in solo practice for 1 year. This would provide more concrete evidence that the system was, in fact, a success for the goals the physician initially set.

The bigger issue, as the author has accurately noted, is how this scenario plays out across the country, which has implications for our entire nation's healthcare system. As physicians and informaticists, we usually have two primary goals for EHRs: better care and lower costs. If we can provide the best care at the right time, we can likely achieve our goals. If decision support relies on old data or is not considered, both the nation's healthcare system and the patient lose. Unfortunately, all EHRs require training, and training requires time and resources. Most physicians currently feel overwhelmed by the amount of clinical and administrative work they must complete and often feel underpaid for their efforts. This is not a situation that encourages individuals to dedicate time without compensation to benefit the nation's health system, even if a quality-of-care "moral imperative" advocates such efforts.

Lessons Learned

- A successful EHR meets the needs of the practice.
- EHR functionality may go unused or underutilized if the cost to implement appears to be greater than the benefit.
- Training requires a time commitment that must be seen as worthwhile to the trainee.
- EHR features that may benefit the healthcare system in aggregate may not be a priority for busy physicians who do not see the benefit as worth the cost.
- Increasing use of underused EHR features may require an easier user interface, repair of our healthcare system, or direct compensation to physicians for use.

Chapter 40

Digital Surveys Don't Always Mean Easier...Patient Surveys

Editor: Richard Schreiber
Geisinger Health System

Contents

Project Categories: ambulatory electronic health record (EHR), population health and analytics

Lessons Learned Categories: contracts, implementation approaches, project management, system design, workflow

A multisite ambulatory healthcare organization (HCO) needed to collect information on Social Determinants of Health (SDOH) for the patient population it served. Drivers of the need included the following:

- The HCO, and the accountable care organization (ACO) it recently joined, needed to more accurately predict clinical needs of patients and future costs of care.
- The HCO wanted to better understand the SDOH needs of its patients for future services.
- The HCO wanted to implement a new standardized SDOH survey it had helped to develop through a national collaborative.

The HCO had an electronic health record (EHR) for several years and had received Meaningful Use incentive payments. However, patients were still completing paper-based medical history questionnaires and a multipage behavioral health screening survey at preventive care visits. Medical assistants (MAs) then entered the survey data into the EHR for providers to review. The medical and EHR leadership wanted to build on the EHR success and use a digital approach to gather the SDOH information instead of adding another paper survey for patients to complete.

The HCO believed that if the survey was presented to patients digitally, data collection would be more standardized, efficient, and complete, and analyses would be more effective. Once live, the digital survey platform would be expanded to include the existing patient surveys, eliminating a time-consuming MA task of logging the results of the paper surveys into the EHR plus providing a flexible platform for future surveys.

The main EHR vendor recommended a partner technology company to develop the survey on a tablet device in a manner compatible with the data structure of the EHR. The partner company had built many tablet solutions with the same EHR for patient registration and billing. The company proposed using a custom tablet for the survey, with embedded software that would gather and store the data in the EHR for providers and other members of the care team to review and for population analytics.

A new EHR support manager was assigned to manage the project, including providing the SDOH survey to the technology vendor, developing an implementation plan, training HCO staff, and managing the overall effort. The HCO and vendor signed a contract with a 3½-month trial period followed by a 3-year maintenance commitment. The original project plan appears below:

Week	*Milestone*
1	Sign contract with vendor
5	Technical kickoff—create access process for vendor, discuss roles/responsibilities, review scope of project
7	Technical modifications to the SDOH template are complete. User acceptance testing (by EHR team is complete)
11	First test complete using tablets in TEST environment
15	Signoff of test phase. Import tablet solution into PRODUCTION environment
17	Successful test in PRODUCTION (using test patient)
20	Successful test in PRODUCTION (using real patient)
21	User training complete for pilot team(s)
25	Go live—using tool across all adult primary care physical visits

Following the Week 17 "test in PRODUCTION," a physician informaticist joined the HCO and was asked to lead the project due to its importance to medical leadership. During the next week, a workflow to use the technology was developed and MAs and other members of the care team were trained. During the first week of pilot use, problems were identified quickly:

- The MAs frequently did not have time to have a patient complete the tablet-based survey in addition to the paper surveys already in use.
- Several survey questions included terms or addressed issues patients did not understand, preventing patients from completing the survey without staff assistance.
- Providers felt unprepared to address issues identified in the survey, like homelessness.
- Rubber padding clipped to the tablets for protection prevented easy cleaning between patients.

- Patients accidentally shut down the application frequently—the "Quit" button was adjacent to the answer button for the survey; once clicked, the application would shut down immediately, requiring the MA to reboot the tablet.

The project was temporarily put on hold and reassessed, and the physician informaticist developed a plan to address these problems. Over the next 2 months,

- The survey was reassessed based on the national standard and key differences were identified and corrected; unclear language was simplified.
- The clinical value of the survey was discussed with providers, who endorsed the concept.
- The vendor determined that the "Quit" button could not be moved to a different part of the tablet screen, despite the obvious design flaw.
- The vendor proposed a newer tablet, with a built-in padded cover, that was easier to clean and more durable, but also much more expensive.
- The HCO Nursing Director raised concerns about the additional work the survey added to already-overtaxed MAs.

After much discussion, the HCO decided to end the project and asked the vendor to terminate the contract and allow for the return of the tablets. The vendor reminded the HCO that it had signed off on the test phase months before and committed to a 3-year maintenance contract. Negotiations ensued, involving both HCO and vendor executive management.

Author's Analysis

The well-intended EHR team and healthcare organizational leadership unfortunately had taken on a development and innovation project that was beyond their expertise, including the importance of managing a new initiative within the scope of a vendor–customer contract. Most of the problems that were encountered could have been averted, even if that meant not taking on the effort at all. However, like many other organizations, the group needed more discipline and expertise to understand what was within their skill set and what was not when it came to solving problems with IT. The failure to do so not only caused this project to fall short, but also diverted financial and staff resources from other efforts that might have been better suited to the organization's capacities, efforts that could have succeeded.

Editor's Commentary

This case highlights the importance of involving experienced physician and nursing informatics specialists early when selecting or changing information tools. Their insights augment the success of any informatics project. It's likely this could have averted some or all of the issues this organization endured.

There were a number of red flags that could have alerted the organization that trouble lay ahead. The partner company had developed registration and billing functions, but apparently not patient-facing technologies that require different usability features. Had this company ever built such functionality? If so, had the organization spoken with some other sites that had used the product? Perhaps the experience of other sites that had used similar devices would have helped this organization. The pros and cons of the location of various buttons, ease of cleaning, and the ease or difficulty of navigating the survey would have surfaced earlier.

The EHR team completed testing, but it is crucial that real users test a program and the devices themselves. Perhaps many of the usability issues would have arisen earlier if real users had tested the solution.

Never sign off a project until it has been live in the production environment for a reasonable period of time. Test environments rarely reproduce real live scenarios; at best, they screen for technical and overt user and usability errors. Until one uses a program in the wild, one cannot know its full capabilities and deficiencies. How long is it sufficient to use a program in the wild? That depends on the program, the number of users, the time it takes to flesh out all aspects of the program and how complex it is. Vendors prefer early sign-off; users want to delay as long as possible. There is a negotiated middle ground. For a survey and use of a device for that survey, a reasonable period of time might be 1–3 months.

Beware the bait and switch. It seems evident that the devices would see heavy usage and require maintenance and replacement. Such a contract should include clear pricing for device upgrades. In this case history, the initial device was unsatisfactory. It should have been clear in the contract that if this was shown to be the case during testing, then a price increase should not have been allowed.

A good contract requires explicit terms for early withdrawal. If the organization knew that the vendor would require a full 3-year commitment and payment even before the survey was in full production, perhaps the risk would have been more obvious to them before signing.

Lessons Learned

- Proper assessment of preexisting and future state workflows is critical to successful HIT implementations.
- Hardware design must meet the requirements of the healthcare environment in which it will be deployed.
- Critically review all contracts, regardless of project size and cost.[1]

[1] Note—for more insights on HIT contract review, refer to Chapter 48 "Exploring HIT Contract *Cadavers* to Avoid HIT Managerial Malpractice."

COMMUNITY FOCUS

As healthcare expands from the healthcare organization into the community and across regions, so does health information technology (HIT). This means that projects involve multiple organizations, large and small, with new levels of complexity and challenge.

"It's the Workflow, Stupid"

If you do not study your workflow ahead of time, you will not be prepared for the disruptive changes Computerized provider order entry (CPOE) causes. By hospital policy, when a patient went to the operating room, all preoperative orders were to be canceled. Before CPOE, the ward clerk moved all active order sheets and the medication administration record to the back of the chart, safely out of the way and effectively discontinued. After the CPOE go-live, many postoperative patients had duplicate orders. Providers entered new postoperative orders, but no one had discontinued the existing preoperative orders. Without detection, order management workflow had shifted from the ward clerk to the provider, causing critical patient safety risks.
Leviss (2008)

Chapter 41

Push vs. Pull: Sharing Information across a Physician Referral Network

Editor: Jonathan Leviss

Greater New Bedford Community Health Center

Contents

Project Categories: inpatient electronic health record (EHR), community-facing technologies

Lessons Learned Categories: implementation approaches, system design, workflow

Case Study

Over 5 years, a large multihospital-integrated delivery healthcare system, with tertiary care centers of excellence, implemented an inpatient electronic health record (EHR) and a large medical archive repository. The organization had a large, experienced information technology (IT) department, including development teams. Both the clinical teams and the IT department were very capable users and demonstrated the ability to create and support a variety of complex applications. Because of this, the quantity of electronic data and documents about each patient treated at the health system was considerable.

The health system relied on patient referrals for both inpatient volume and to maintain the organization's ability to support the tertiary care referral center. There were approximately 4,000 referring physicians, and most of them did not have medical staff privileges at the health system hospitals. The health system provided easy referral access to care, but referring physicians were vocal and consistent about what became known as the "black hole," or their feeling that they were frequently uninformed about the care given to their patients at the referral center. In addition, communication about the handoff back to the community physician and expectations for follow-up care were largely missing. It was not that the organization did not have the will or understand the benefit associated with improved communication. Rather, the organization determined that finding solutions to improve communication was very difficult. Even with focused initiatives, such as capturing the primary care provider (PCP) at the time of admission, operations fell short, as evidenced by data indicating that staff recorded the PCP of the patient only about 60% of the time.

The organization spent some time deciding how to address this issue of information flow back to the referring physician population. There were discussions involving the use of the current EHR vendor's physician portal and another methodology that required more effort and a heavier reliance on data quality. The second option was a clinical messaging strategy, but it required a significant amount of continued development effort. The two solutions had fundamentally different methods to accomplish the task of provider communications. The physician portal was primarily a "come and get it" philosophy, making documents and results available to those who wanted to look for them (the pull method). The clinical messaging strategy focused on delivery of certain documentation to the physician (the push method). In the end, due to the difference in the time required to deploy each solution, the ease of deployment, and the cost, the final decision was to brand the available physician portal and roll that out as a strategy to combat the "black hole" phenomena.

The goals of the physician portal were to (1) improve communication of patient care-related information to referring physicians, (2) facilitate patient care and follow-up with the PCP after discharge, and (3) increase the accuracy of the recorded patient–physician relationship (i.e., identify the PCP). To use the physician portal, providers were required to either be a member of the medical staff or remain referring providers and enter into an agreement that involved privacy, security, and use criteria. Once these requirements were met, the referring physician would be given a username and password for access. There was no classroom training available, but there were written training materials and an outreach liaison that could respond to questions, but did not have the capability to provide significant support. The password would reset every 90 days, due to system policy. Additionally, the physician portal permitted access to all patients and required a valid moral compass on the part of the provider to comply with the requirement that only patients that they were actively caring for would be viewed.

Although referring providers vocalized a need for improved follow-up information, further evaluation of their baseline experience (without the portal) was actually better than what was provided to them through the physician portal. Referring providers received copies of dictated discharge summaries, letters, and operative reports that were placed in an envelope and mailed to them. Within their offices, there was already a workflow process in which office staff would receive and triage the inbound information, marry it with the paper chart, and place the information in the same place every time. When it was convenient for the physician, they could locate new information, review historical information from their records (if necessary), write a quick note in the chart, and use sticky notes to notify staff of any actions that needed to be taken with the new information. This workflow process repeated itself several times a day and seamlessly integrated inbound documents from multiple locations (radiology, outpatient laboratory, telephone calls) into a single workflow for the physician. This was efficient, reproducible from day to day, and actually fulfilled the criteria for unified messaging, in which multiple communication pathways came to the individual as a single pathway, although with the shortcomings of paper-based records.

Geographically, the location of these offices varied from rural to urban, and the size varied from single practitioners to multispecialty groups. Due to the nature of the healthcare industry in this region, these physicians had options to admit their patients to multiple hospitals in their community, and when tertiary care referral was necessary, they had a choice of referral centers, as well. At this time, most of the offices had electronic practice management systems, but less than 10% had any EHR functionality.

The demographics, local and regional choices, and practice patterns resulted in a highly competitive environment where relationships with providers were extremely important. The physician portal was meant to enhance this relationship by providing the referring physicians with faster, greater, and more flexible access to follow-up information on their patients. Although anticipated to be a big success for this health system, actual results were quite different from the expectation.

Far fewer physicians even registered for access than expected because they just did not want to have to deal with another username and password. Of the physicians who did sign up, many of them did not attempt to access the portal and most of the remaining only tried once or twice. Since they were not using the portal every day, just remembering the world wide web address (URL) to access the site became a frustrating chore for most, and the health system lost users when their passwords expired. Not knowing one's password meant calling a help desk at a number that was not easy to find. This was just too much hassle to locate a document on a patient that previously was found in the office chart. In addition, referring physicians felt they were doing extra work for information that the health system should be supplying to them (and in fact, used to deliver to them) rather than just providing a portal to look it up.

Even when the username and password issues were improved and some physicians frequently viewed documents, the feedback revealed another critical flaw in the deployment. A large part of the rationale for the physician portal was that it would make it easier for the health system's medical records department and might reduce some expenses. The health system could eliminate personnel stuffing envelopes, save on postage, and have more records available than before, but the physician practices had to absorb a newly fragmented workflow.

Reports still came to physician offices from many sources by fax, mail, and courier, requiring the continuation of the prior paper workflow. Now, the health system was also asking for a separate workflow for its portal-based documents. In order to integrate reports from the health system's portal into a patient's chart, the referring physician needed to search the portal for a new document, print out the document, and hand it to office staff to marry it with the paper chart. Next, the office staff would bring the full chart containing the printed document from the portal back to the physician for review. Alarmingly, this change alienated the physicians, made them less efficient, and actually impacted referrals. A frequently heard referring physician complaint was, "Why do I have to work so hard to find something that you should be delivering to me?"

Fortunately, in parallel to the early work with the physician portal, the health system continued to pursue the clinical messaging strategy. More evaluation of office workflow was done to understand how to deliver documentation electronically and seamlessly into the existing office workflow to minimize or extinguish disruption. This was accomplished with the clinical messaging system and enhanced by adding an additional layer of personal preferences that allowed the health system to leverage the customer relationship management (CRM) successes of other industries. For example, some physicians did not want to automatically receive operative notes, but discharge summaries were okay. Other physicians only wanted notification that their patients were in the emergency department (ED), but did not want to receive the ED note. What resulted was a very successful customer-focused deployment of messaging services that delivered documentation to physicians, only about their patients, the way they wanted to receive it. As more and more offices started to implement EHRs, work was planned on how to utilize the messaging infrastructure to insert documents directly into their EHRs. But there were customer service issues that needed to be solved before this could become widespread.

Author's Analysis

The health system in this case failed to understand how users were thinking and did not initially monitor if what was deployed fit their needs. This case demonstrates the importance of a user-centric approach into adoption of technical solutions in healthcare. If you understand the needs and work environment of your users, you may find that you design, configure, and deploy your solutions differently than if you attempted to deploy a one-size-fits-all solution.

The workflow implications for the physician user population should have been understood before a particular solution was selected to solve the business problem. In this example, the business problem was fixing the "black hole." Portal access to documents could be a solution but there was not enough understanding of how it would be accessed and the environment it would be accessed from. It ended up having an opposite impact than what it was designed for. The health system should have focused more on the potential impact of the portal on referring providers and less on the personnel benefits from the deployment.

Insufficient effort and attention to data quality were committed to effectively personalize a service to a large group of care providers. Organizations must have a commitment to these operational components in order to make a more personalized deployment successful. But in at least this example of provider messaging, the organization's ultimate commitment to these operational details resulted in better physician relationships and increased referrals from those relationships.

If the health system had not assumed to know how the referral physicians were thinking or how they would respond to a certain situation or offering, but had asked, the project failure might have been averted.

Editor's Commentary

While this case occurred in a setting that is now rare in the United States (a major medical center whose referring physician base has not yet widely adopted EHRs), the lessons it offers are still highly relevant. The author emphasizes the importance of tailoring a solution to the customer or end-user and asking the customer for input in solution design. Experiences in health IT repeatedly demonstrate that the complexity of our workflows and the high expectations of clinician users make buy-in and adoption of less-than-ideal solutions extremely challenging. Optimal outcomes require engaging clinicians in the process of implementing health information technology (HIT), which is more than simply asking for input. Health systems usually recognize that ED physicians must be involved in the planning, design, and go-live of ED rollouts; similarly, nurses must be part of project governance and implementation for medication systems. Community-based physicians, therefore, should be part of the project governance for initiatives intended to address their needs. If members of the referral physician community had been involved in the project oversight, several key challenges might have been identified early in the project:

- Referring physicians likely would have known that they would still be managing paper documents even if the health system went "paperless."

- Referring physicians would have anticipated the concerns the hospital faced by requiring complex data access agreements for portal use.
- Referring physicians would have balked at the idea of requiring another password, especially one that changed frequently and was difficult to reset.
- The health system could have identified and addressed project barriers before wasting extensive resources and antagonizing the physician referral base.

Committees that identify barriers to a project early create the opportunity to address these barriers, compromise on solving them, not solve them, or even agree not to move forward on a project.

Without end-user adoption, projects with new technologies will never move forward. Sometimes the end-users are correct in rejecting the new technologies, but rarely is a health system correct in rejecting the input from the end-users.

Lessons Learned

- Engage the customer before, during, and after deploying a new solution.
- Understand how customers are thinking and then closely monitor if deployed solutions fit their needs.
- Fully assess the workflow implications of a proposed solution prior to rollout.
- Ongoing effort and strict attention to detail are required to personalize service to a large group of care providers.

Chapter 42

Disconnecting Primary Care Providers: HIE Alerts

Editor: Richard Schreiber
Geisinger Health System

Contents

Project Categories: community-facing technologies, population health and analytics

Lessons Learned: communication, data model, implementation approaches, system configuration, training, workflow

A state-wide health information exchange (HIE) received grant funding to participate in a national pilot for better coordination of care between hospitals and primarycare providers (PCP). The goal was to provide an automated communication that would enable the PCP to better coordinate care as part of a broader program to prevent avoidable hospital admissions, decrease hospital readmissions, and reduce overall health care expenditures. Specifically, the HIE would work with its main technology vendor to develop a system to alert a PCP when an affiliated patient was admitted to and discharged from any hospital participating in the HIE. The HIE already received a data feed of all hospital and emergency department admissions and discharges from participating hospitals, which would provide the basis for communications to PCPs.

The HIE and its technology vendor developed the functional requirements for the communications and designed the following approach:

A patient is admitted, discharged, or transferred at *hospital* participating in the HIE

⇓

A registration event occurs in the hospital's ADT (admission, discharge, or transfer) information system

⇓

The ADT event is communicated to the HIE by HL7 interface

⇓

HIE sends communication to PCP by Direct Message

⇓

PCP receives Direct Message and acts accordingly to coordinate care with hospital care team and/or patient

- Direct Messages included details about the ADT event as well as clinical summaries generated by data available in the HIE.
- In the case of admission or transfer—PCP communicates with care team to provide background information on patient, guiding care as appropriate (including avoiding unnecessary admissions or long acute care stays).
- In case of discharge—PCP communicates with patient to coordinate prompt follow-up care and reduce hospital readmissions.

The HIE began to introduce the "Provider Notification" solution to PCPs across the state using the state's Regional Extension Center staff who were already assisting the same PCPs with EHR adoption. Several PCPs, including a 100+ physician Medicare Pioneer Accountable Care Organization (ACO), agreed to participate and pilot the solution. Within months, however, PCPs reported the program lacked value and almost all wanted to disenroll from the program:

- Most PCPs thought they already received similar notifications from their preferred affiliate hospital and did not want to spend effort getting redundant information.
- PCPs complained it was too burdensome to log into a secure Direct Message website that required a unique user name and password to check for Provider Notifications.
- Provider Notifications were voluminous—messages did report ED and hospital admissions, discharges and transfers, but most messages were for registrations for laboratory tests, X-rays, and diagnostic services done at hospital outpatient sites.
- Even PCPs who valued the admission and discharge notifications were frustrated by the effort spent pouring through less important events.
- Provider Notifications included a PDF summary of all information available on the patient in the HIE, which could include years of laboratory results, diagnoses, and medications, most of which was criticized as out of date and not relevant to recent event.

The grant funder raised concerns about the failing program at the HIE. The HIE hired a medical informatics consultant to assess the program.

The consultant met with the HIE staff and reviewed the overall project plan, sample Provider Notifications, and the design and configuration of the HIE solution. Additionally, the consultant met with PCP offices that were pleased and displeased with the solution and observed workflows at their offices.

Author's Analysis

The consultant identified several key problems:

- Most Provider Notifications were for hospital registration events for outpatient laboratory and radiology tests, not the intended admissions or discharges. The configuration to generate the messages identified all new ADT patient registration events at participating hospitals, including registration for outpatient diagnostic testing at nonhospital locations.
- PCPs were the target recipients of the information about patient admissions and discharges, but in most PCP practices, a nurse, care manager, or other member of the care team could more effectively and efficiently act on the information to coordinate patient care, exchange patient information, or schedule follow-up appointments. When necessary, this person could escalate an issue to the PCP.
- The PDF HIE summaries were several pages long with years of data, most of which was not relevant to the admission or discharge event; however, most PCPs felt obligated to review the data.
- PCP offices, large and small, did not know how to design or implement a new workflow based on information involving the Web-based Direct Message portal that was not part of their core EHR, email, or other office technologies. The ADT alert rollout plan lacked a formal implementation process, or provide training to PCPs and their staff on how to use the solution.

The consultant advised the HIE to either address and resolve these core concerns or shut down the HIE's Provider Notification program.

Editor's Commentary

The medical informatics consultant identified all of the key problems that the vendor, in conjunction with the HIE, did not. The initial project plan, and in particular, the functional requirements for communications, did specify several components in enough detail. For example, the configuration plan for messages identified all new ADT patient registration events at participating hospitals, including registration for outpatient diagnostic testing at nonhospital locations. The plan should have specified that messages should be sent only for hospital admissions and discharges. Rather than targeting the PCPs themselves, the plan should have been to direct messages to the practices' staff, for example, a nurse, care manager, or other member of the care team. Staff members can more effectively and efficiently act on the information to coordinate patient care, exchange patient information, schedule follow-up appointments, and escalate to the primary care providers (PCPs) if necessary. Finally, an implementation plan should have been included to accomplish the following: show the practices how to incorporate the Web-based Direct Message portal into their workflows, explain to PCPs how to effectively skim the PDFs for only the relevant admission or discharge event rather than reviewing the entire document, and provide training to go over these critical aspects with PCPs and their staff. The vendor might have benefited from consulting with a medical informatics expert, and PCP Subject Matter Experts during the development of the configuration plan. In addition, the vendor, in conjunction with the consultants, could have pilot-tested the process, even if briefly, with a small number of PCPs, and evaluated it prior to rolling out the HIE across the state.

Lessons Learned

- Designing HIT requires interdisciplinary teams, including clinical informatics experts and clinicians.
- Too much information does not help busy providers to care for patients.
- Small provider groups have limited resources and capacity for HIT implementation, so need external support and assistance.

Additional Reading

Feldman SS, Schooley BL, Bhavsar GP. Health information exchange implementation: lessons learned and critical success factors from a case study. *JMIR Med Inform.* August 15, 2014;2(2):e19. doi:10.2196/medinform.3455.

Byrne CM, Mercincavage LM, Bouhaddou O, Bennett JR, Pan EC, Botts NE, Olinger LM, Hunolt E, Banty KH, Cromwell T. The Department of Veterans Affairs' (VA) implementation of the Virtual Lifetime Electronic Record (VLER): Findings and lessons learned from Health Information Exchange at 12 sites. *Int J Med Inform.* August 2014;83(8):537–47. doi:10.1016/j.ijmedinf.2014.04.005. Epub April 28, 2014.

Maloney N, Heider AR, Rockwood A, Singh R. Creating a connected community: Lessons learned from the Western New York beacon community. *EGEMS (Wash DC).* October 27, 2014;2(3):1091. eCollection 2014.

Chapter 43

Loss Aversion: Adolescent Confidentiality and Pediatric PHR Access

Editor: Eric Poon
Duke University Health System

Contents

Project Categories: community-facing technologies

Lessons Learned Categories: communication, implementation approaches, system design

Case Study

A large, nonprofit, multispecialist physician practice provides care for over 500,000 individuals in rural and urban communities spread over several states. Healthcare is provided at 1 acute care hospital and 25 primary care practices that encompass family medicine, pediatrics, and most medical and surgical subspecialties. Primary care is provided by nurse practitioners and family physicians at all 25 clinics, while pediatric and subspecialty cares are provided at 7 clinics distributed over the service area.

The practice prides itself on being an early adopter of a clinical information system that includes an integrated personal health record (PHR). Extensive advertising is done that highlights the practice's use of health information technology (HIT) and how use of PHRs strengthens the patient–provider relationship. Patients have access to the following via a web-based portal:

- Secure messaging with healthcare providers
- Online appointment scheduling
- Laboratory and test results
- Immunization status
- Health maintenance reminders
- Problem lists, including drug allergies
- Post-visit summaries.

In order to demonstrate its commitment to using PHRs, the practice provides financial incentives for providers who use secure messaging with patients. The practice also promotes the benefits of PHR use via posters in clinic waiting areas, recorded voice mail messages, and inserts included in mail sent to covered and prospective patients. Patient use of PHRs has gradually increased, and in general, patients and providers report satisfaction with PHRs.

More recently, the practice moved all patients into a patient-centered medical home model. This care model continues to focus on use of the PHR as a means for patients to act in partnership with care providers in coordinating care. The practice's PHR system is seen as central to optimizing care.

One group of patients is kept from full participation in their care management. Citing concerns regarding privacy and confidentiality, the practice removes access to PHRs for adolescents as well as their parents and caregivers. Practice managers made this decision based on legal requirements restricting access to an adolescent's medical information. Current system functions make it difficult to control access to information in PHRs and meet Health Insurance Portability and Accountability Act (HIPAA) requirements fully. This means that families who were utilizing the PHR to schedule appointments, communicate with providers, access laboratory and test results, check immunization status, and monitor routine screening requirements lost those capabilities when their child turned 13. At the time, this decision was made it was felt that parents would have no problem moving back to "traditional" methods of communicating with pediatric providers. Thus, no plans to mitigate unintended consequences were made.

Parents of adolescents living with chronic health conditions reported significant roadblocks to obtaining care following the loss of parental access. Immunization reminders cannot be sent without PHR access. Unless there is an appointment scheduled or a specific request made via telephone, there is no way for parents to quickly determine immunization status for school or sports activities. Customer service staff and pediatric clinic administrators reported receiving complaints from parents who had been using online appointment scheduling. Other services have been impacted as well. As one parent stated, "The only way I knew we were moved from a case management model to the patient-centered medical home was because the complex case management nurse stopped calling me."

At this point, the practice has determined that there is a need to provide parents/caregivers access to some components of their child's PHR. However, due to other "pressing" HIT projects, work on this is not expected to begin until the next fiscal cycle.

Author's Analysis

Review of the situation revealed the need for parents or caregivers to have access to certain functions of their child's PHR while ensuring that other areas of the PHR remain secure. Key lessons learned include the following:

- Development of a PHR for use in pediatrics involves confidentiality concerns not typically faced when developing PHRs in care settings that do not include pediatrics.
- Parent or caregiver needs for communication and information sharing must be considered when building pediatric PHRs.
- There is a need to provide access to the PHR for parents or caregivers to utilize online scheduling, check immunization status, communicate with providers, and view reminders and alerts as needed.
- Pediatric PHRs are much more complex to build and maintain than PHRs used for adult populations. The need for multiple layers of access control is one reason for this complexity.
- Thorough testing is vital to ensure that protected health information is not inadvertently viewed by individuals who do not have authorization to do so.

Editor's Commentary

This case demonstrates an episode of "growing pains" in an otherwise successful implementation of PHRs to support patient-centered care. As the PHR (or any form of HIT) is used more broadly, issues and risks are bound to emerge. In this particular case, privacy concerns were raised on behalf of adolescent patients who might not want their parents (or legal guardians) to access their records through the PHR. Because the PHR lacked the necessary functionality and processes to allow adolescents and their parents (or legal guardians) to negotiate and control who could access their records online, all PHR functionality was taken away for the adolescent population.

It is all too easy for us to second-guess the decision made by the "practice managers" to remove PHR access for adolescent patients. Although the HIPAA legislation was passed more than a decade ago, the hodgepodge of federal and state laws and regulations continues to evolve. Legislators, regulators, privacy advocates, legal experts, healthcare administrators, health information management professionals, and health information system professionals are all challenged to shape, interpret, and implement privacy laws and regulations. It is quite understandable that a practice manager whose domain expertise is in neither privacy nor HIT might err on the side of caution to minimize risk exposure to the practice.

With the benefit of hindsight, however, it might be instructive to examine more closely the decision-making process. It is not clear from the case whether the appropriate stakeholders were consulted before the decision was made. For example, did the medical director help the practice manager anticipate the impact of withdrawing PHR access on the care model the practice was transitioning towards? Were informatics professionals on hand to help define alternative approaches to the problem? Was the larger HIT community consulted on how other healthcare systems have addressed this concern? Did legal counsel help quantify the degree of risk if adolescents and their parents continued to use the PHR? It is very possible that the same decision might have been made even if additional resources were brought to the decision-making table. However, one could have expected practice leaders to appreciate the consequences of this decision and to spend the appropriate amount of time on making this decision.

If we assume that no technical solution was immediately available within the PHR to address the privacy concerns, other process-driven approaches might have allowed the practice to preserve PHR access for adolescents and their parents (or legal guardians). For example, the practice staff could ask adolescent patients (while alone from their parents or legal guardians) whether they wanted continued access to their PHR. If the practice could develop simple decision aids (e.g., a short list of benefits and risks for the adolescents, or talking points for staff), the resource draw on the practice might be minimal. Alternatively, PHR access could be taken away for all adolescent patients and be granted back only if both the adolescent and adult review the benefits and risks of PHR access. While these and other alternatives might not have mitigated all the risks, they may be sufficient as interim measures as technical solutions are developed.

We might infer that the practice was surprised by the negative reactions from patients and their parents (or legal guardians) when their PHR access was taken away. In retrospect, insights from the field of behavioral economics might have anticipated this as people have a tendency to strongly prefer avoiding losses to acquiring gains, a phenomenon known as "loss aversion." If PHR access had never been offered to the adolescent population, the patients and their parents (or legal guardians) might never have complained. However, when functionality is taken away, one could expect dissatisfaction from at least a vocal minority. Had the practice anticipated this, they could have pursued more aggressively mitigation strategies, such as communicating the loss of PHRs proactively to patients and their parents or guardians and reminding parents or legal guardians how they could otherwise obtain immunization records. Alternatively, a summary of the patient's record (such as medications and immunizations) could be proactively given to the patient at every visit.

Lessons Learned

- PHR use in pediatrics involves unique privacy and confidentiality concerns.
- Parent or caregiver needs for communication and information sharing must be considered when building PHRs.
- Stakeholder input is critical for successful HIT initiatives.

Chapter 44

Improved Population Management Requires Management: Care Coordination

Editor: Catherine Craven

Mt. Sinai Health System

Contents

Project Categories: population health and analytics

Lessons Learned Categories: communication, implementation approaches, leadership/governance, workflow

This project, which took place within a medium-sized regional hospital system that included several primary care practice sites, was designed to combine advanced population health analytics with improved care coordination as a patient is discharged to or from the hospital and to or from another facility, including home or a nursing home. The project goals were (1) improvement of the management of chronic disease for severely chronically ill patients with more than four medical conditions, with one condition requiring improved management; (2) fewer emergency room visits; (3) and fewer inpatient hospitalizations.

Project implementation consisted of three main components: (1) accelerated hiring of two data analysts, (2) hiring of 12 nurses with advanced practice experience (APNs) for 10 clinics, and (3) development of an electronic health record (EHR)-based care management application that would aggregate patient data. The application would provide the clinician and clinical care team with a view of the entire patient panel, their health status, and the presence or absence of completed preventive care measures. The APNs received additional training to enhance care coordination, such as communications, team building, and workflow for the specified primary care sites. The APNs were added to the existing teams at each of the primary care clinics, and served as the care coordinator for that team. Their main function was to facilitate navigation of care transitions and assist with monitoring of care measures that could help to improve patient health outcomes, thereby reducing emergency room visits and inpatient hospitalizations. The new application was expected to provide up-to-date and even real-time patient data for clinicians and care teams, as well as a data set that included all patients in a clinician's patient panel. The new EHR-based application would provide clinicians and care teams real-time information on health status, needed preventive measures for individual patients, all within the providers' EHR interface display. Patients could be grouped by age, health status, and preventive care measures needed or up to date.

The project team planned a project evaluation for 6 months after initial deployment. Elements evaluated included the number by which of emergency department (ED) visits were reduced, reduction of inpatient admissions, and cost savings. Following the evaluation, the plan was that new care processes, procedures, and EHR-based application would be disseminated throughout this growing healthcare system.

Although the intention of the leadership was rapid deployment, multiple delays occurred early in the project. First, although the trained data analysts hired had appropriate technical education, they did not have the appropriate healthcare system knowledge or experience to be effective. This caused significant delays with the integration of disparate data sets to create patient panels and combine the health status and preventive care data early in the project, which set back all other deliverables. It was more difficult than anticipated and took longer than expected to develop consensus among stakeholders surrounding clinical practice guidelines, which caused delays that drove up project costs. Subsequently, unneeded, even inappropriate tests or procedures were noted as not compliant with the guidelines, reflecting poorly on the clinicians.

Staff training and engagement was a major challenge. The collaborating EHR vendor that developed the application provided a training center and focused training for physicians. Physicians, however, were not effectively trained for many reasons, including a lack of a set scheduled time for training and a lack of communication about the availability of training. Half of the involved physicians did not even know there was training available. The number of APNs needed was difficult to find and hire in this geographical area, and there was greater than anticipated turnover among those hired. Only half of the needed personnel were on-boarded within the goal of 6 months of project launch. The APNs were absent from clinic two half days a week to complete care-coordination communications training and other related training and group discussions about lessons learned throughout the project. Although patient education and care transitions were the primary responsibility of each new APN team member, there was no mechanism to record their training time or care-coordination work efforts, or ensure accountability. Clinical workflows were inconsistently reworked to integrate APNs into the clinical team. All of this led to confusion in clinical administration and operations, patient scheduling, direct patient care, and follow-up care; it was not even clear when the APNs should become involved in managing the patients' transitions to other community-based care organizations.

Ad hoc measures were put in place to record training time and work effort for care-coordination data, but the measures were not integrated with the patient care data and workflows in the EHR, making it difficult to effectively analyze the financial impact of the program. When the initial grant funding for the program ended, the health system ended the program.

Author's Analysis

Key errors made this project unlikely to succeed.

Several pre-implementation tasks were neglected: there lacked detailed implementation, data testing, and data validation plans. The plans used had not been agreed upon by the parties involved, specifically members of leadership, clinical administration, EHR system developers, APNs, data analysts, and clinicians. Missing were regular interdisciplinary meetings for project participants or regular occurring task-focused meetings, so as the early problems occurred, they were not solved and were instead compounded. The members of the existing primary care teams did not receive adequate training in care-coordination-related communications, and change management, or even team building, to foster adoption of the needed workflow and care-transitions support. Finally, the evaluation plan could not be used to analyze the implementation plan, personnel, or data tasks to identify problems earlier in the program as it was developed at the project's end.

Ultimately, leadership's engagement with and support for the project was insufficient, so when the key challenges surfaced, from staffing to training to workflows, the clinicians lost trust and confidence in their own organization; this became a significant barrier to future system improvement efforts.

Editor's Commentary

This case demonstrates a plethora of basic change-management mistakes, ranging from a lack of leadership engagement from the outset, to poor understanding of skills needed for one type of position, a delayed hiring process for another, inadequate education among some stakeholders, vastly uneven levels across the stakeholder groups, and an after-the-fact evaluation "plan" to name just a few. The EHR vendor that was collaborating on this project and provided a training center may not have done enough to actively ensure that the physicians came to training sessions. This stands out as a factor because EHR vendors are well versed in such tactics, including the development of multimodal communication plans, to encourage/drive physicians to critical education and training sessions as a key part of system implementations. The need for this is not unfamiliar to them at all. It's unclear whether the vendor just did not do much, or if they offered more advice, but project leadership ignored it. In addition, the lack of an integrated mechanism to track APN time and effort spent on coordination activities is notable given that capturing time spent on all types of patient-care activities has always been a central function of all EHRs. It begs the question: Was this prototype system rushed into deployment because of the project's deadlines, or was the vendor simply focused on another aspect of the care-coordination system development for their own benefit? Many lessons were learned in this relatively early care-coordination project, but to be fair, many of these issues and missteps still occur surrounding implementation of care-coordination applications that are now far more sophisticated than this one.

Lessons Learned

- Full engagement of front-line personnel or their representatives, as well as members of the leadership team, is essential during all phases of planning and deployment.

- Implementation planning should begin "with the end in mind," including a consensus-based, detailed evaluation.
- Data integration for population health management purposes is nearly always more difficult than expected.

Additional Reading

Damschroder LJ, Aron DC, Keith RE, Kirsh SR, Alexander JA, Lowery JC. Fostering implementation of health services research findings into practice: A consolidated framework for advancing implementation, science. *Implementation Science* 2009; 4: 50.

Feldstein CA, Glasgow RV. Practical, robust implementation and sustainability model (PRISM) for integrating research findings into practice. *The Joint Commission Journal on Quality and Patient Safety* 2008; 34(4): 228–243.

Middleton B, Bloomrosen M, Dente MA, Hashmat B, Koppel R, Overhage JM, Payne TH, Rosenbloom, T, Weaver C, Zhang J, American Medical Informatics Association. Enhancing patient safety and quality of care by improving the usability of electronic health record systems: recommendations from AMIA. *Journal of American Medical Informatics Association* 2013; 20(el): e2–e8.

Samal L, Dykes PC, Greenberg JO, Hasan O, Venkatesh AK, Volk LA, Bates DW. Care coordination gaps due to lack of interoperability in the United States: A qualitative study and literature review. *BMC Health Services Research* April 22, 2016; 16: 143.

Sittig DF, Singh H. Defining health information technology-related errors: New developments since to err is human. *Archives of Internal Medicine* 2011; 171: 1281–1284.

POINTS OF VIEW

Chapter 45

Theoretical Perspective: A Review of HIT Failure

Authors: Bonnie Kaplan
Yale University

Scot Silverstein
hcrenewal.blogspot.com

Jonathan Leviss
Greater New Bedford Community Health Center

Larry Ozeran
Clinical Informatics Inc.

Health information technology (HIT) projects are highly complex social and technical endeavors. Knowledge about people, organizations, and implementation, as well as technological and maintenance issues, has grown over the years, both within medical informatics itself and through contributions from other disciplines (Ash et al., 2008; Kaplan and Shaw, 2004). There is an emerging consensus that problems are caused by social, cultural, and financial issues, and hence, are more managerial than technical (Kaplan and Harris-Salamone, 2009). For that reason, they should be analyzed by attention to both social and technical factors, as well as how they interact in the particular setting in which the project occurs.

A theoretical framework that does just this sort of analysis is useful for understanding the stories of HIT success and failure. From the many useful theories and frameworks (Kaplan and Shaw, 2004), two are popular among informaticists analyzing the kinds of issues that our case studies illustrate. Both are practical and well grounded in research (Kaplan, 2001a). One is Rogers's Diffusion of Innovation (DOI) (Rogers, 1995) and its extensions to address gaps relevant to HIT implementations (Lorenzi et al., 2009). It is one of "the most important and widely used models which explore technology adoption, acceptance and diffusion" (Ward, 2013; Zhang et al., 2015). Another is sociotechnical systems STS) theory (Harrison et al., 2007). The Institute of

Medicine recognizes that HIT is part of a complex of STS (Committee on Patient Safety and Health Information Technology Board on Health Care Services, 2011).

These theories have proven their value as the foundation for studies of different kinds of technologies in different kinds of institutions in a range of countries, including Canada, Saudi Arabia, the Netherlands, Australia, and the United Kingdom. For example, a quick web search identified studies of electronic health record (EHR) implementation in long-term facilities (Cherry et al., 2008), shared EHRs, summary of care records (Greenhalgh et al., 2008), and consumer eHealth (Zhang et al., 2015) that draw on DOI; and STS-based studies of CPOE (Aarts, 2012), the NHS National Information Infrastructure (Aarts, 2012), business intelligence system implementation in a healthcare organization (Foshay and Kuziemsky, 2014), the NHS's HealthSpace personal health records (Greenhalgh et al., 2010), hospital EHR implementations (Boonstra et al., 2014; Chan et al., 2016; Black et al., 2011), and a variety of computer-supported cooperative work in healthcare (Fitzpatrick and Ellingsen, 2012). Additionally, recent studies (e.g., Abouzahra, 2011; Lapointe et al., 2011) and literature reviews (e.g., on Black et al., 2011; Ward, 2013) identified reasons for outcomes as due to a combination of social, contextual, managerial, and technical issues.

This mix is consistent with the social interactions nature of both DOI and STS (Kaplan, 2001b). Social interactionist theories in informatics were developed and extended by the late Rob Kling, the father of social informatics (SI), during his tenure at the University of California, Irvine, and then at Indiana University.

Kling thought that many information and communications technology (ICT) professionals have an inadequate understanding of ICT, the actions and interactions of people who use them, and the organizational and social contexts in which they are used. SI refers to the interdisciplinary study of the design, uses, and consequences of ICTs that takes into account their interaction with institutional and cultural realities. Kling also recommended that communicating SI research to others is important because the value of SI theory, insights, and findings has relevance across a range of disciplines. He defined a major challenge in drawing SI work together and beginning to make it known to other academic communities (Kling et al., 2005, 107–108).

The principles of SI can be summarized as follows:

- The context of ICT use directly affects its meaning and roles.
- ICTs are not "value neutral"—they create winners and losers.
- ICT use leads to multiple and often paradoxical effects that are multifarious and unpredictable.
- ICT use has ethical aspects.
- ICTs are configurable.
- ICTs follow trajectories, often favoring the status quo.
- ICTs coevolve before and after implementation; all are social activities.

Most important of all is critical thinking about ICT projects; that is, developing the ability to examine ICTs from perspectives that do not automatically and implicitly adopt the goals and beliefs of the groups that commission, design, or implement specific ICTs. Critical thinking also entails developing an ability to reflect on issues at a number of levels and from more than one perspective (Kling et al., 2000, 123). For these reasons, according to Marc Berg, one of STS theory's main expositors, the idea of "success factors" becomes problematic, as they entail the idea that a fixed list of activities and characteristics will ensure "success." "Success" depends both on the point of view of users who may differ in whether and to what degree they consider a system "successful," and on the specific situation and the complex processes of addressing the kinds of insights Kling identified (Berg, 2001).

These principles explain why Kaplan's review of individual, organizational, and social issues identified the fit of ICTs with other contextual issues surrounding their development, implementation, and use as crucial to their success. Research on these principles includes the importance of fit in the following areas:

- Workflow and routines
- Clinicians' level of expertise
- Values and professional norms
- Institutional setting, history, and structure
- Communication patterns, organizational culture, status relationships, control relationships, division of labor, work roles, and professional responsibility
- Cognitive processes
- Congruence with existing organizational business models and strategic partners
- Compatibility with clinical patient encounter and consultation patterns
- The extent to which models embodied in a system are shared by its users.

Authors have also addressed (in various ways) fit between information technology and how individuals define their work, user characteristics, and preferences (such as information needs), the clinical operating model under which a system is used, and the organization into which it is introduced. Others have focused on interrelationships among key components of an organization (i.e., organizational structure, strategy, management, people's skills, and technology) and compatibility of goals, professional values, needs, and cultures of different groups within an organization, including developers, clinicians, administrators, and patients. In addition, studies have been done on ways in which informatics applications embody values, norms, representations of work and work routines, assumptions about usability, information content and style of presentation, and links between medical knowledge and clinical practice, and how these assumptions influence system design (Kaplan and Shaw, 2004; Kaplan, 2001b).

Kaplan's research also identified the same four barriers—insufficient funding, technology, and knowledge; poor project management; the organization of medicine and healthcare; and physician resistance—blamed for lack of diffusion of ICT in healthcare since the 1950s. These barriers are characterized by looking to external causes for the problems in our field (Kaplan, 1987). They are evidence of beliefs Kling and Iaconno characterized as computerization movements that too often characterize the driving forces behind HIT (Kling and Iaconno, 1988). Among these beliefs is the technologically deterministic view that ICT in and of itself, not SI principles, will cause organizational and individual change in healthcare delivery and the practice of medicine. A close relative of technological determinism is the "magic bullet" theory, where people believe they are change agents if they initiate or develop IT because they think IT itself has the power to create organizational change. These people describe IT as a "magic bullet" and believe that they have built the gun (Markus and Benjamin, 1997). Unfamiliarity with the findings of SI research and beliefs in technologic determinism directly contribute to healthcare IT failure.

Some authors in the healthcare informatics sphere have begun to challenge the dominant paradigm (Koppel et al., 2005; Han et al., 2005), but not without raising significant controversy and receiving considerable criticism (despite significant problems in local and national EHR initiatives in the United States and abroad) (Freudenheim, 2004; Peel and Rose, 2009). Yet there is new interest in information on HIT difficulties, as illustrated by the success of the first edition of

HIT or Miss, many presentations on HIT failure at small and large professional society meetings, inquiries by members of the US Congress into HIT failures (Conn, 2010), and opinion articles in leading national newspapers and academic journals.

Assessments of failures must continue and the lessons learned must be shared broadly if we are to meet the call to leverage HIT to dramatically improve health systems across the United States and the world.

Chapter 46

EHR Transitions: *deja vous*

Author: Richard Schreiber
Geisinger Health System

As of the end of 2016, over 95% of US hospitals have at least a basic electronic health record (EHR) and have achieved meaningful use/promoting interoperability, as have about 90% of physician office practices but only about 60% have demonstrated meaningful use.[1] Many hospitals and practices have or are considering changing their EHR vendor. In a survey of 1,181 office practices in mid-2015, 61% were using their first EHR, 29% were using their second, and 11% their third. Another survey of office-based clinicians at the same time found that 18% of providers intended to replace their EHR by 2016. There is no available data for hospitals but our experience is that migration from one EHR to another is common, especially as mergers and acquisitions continue to dominate the landscape.

There are numerous reasons for choosing to migrate from one EHR to another. The most common include vendors going out of business, products that no longer meet regulatory muster, a facility that has outgrown the EHR, or a merger in which one facility joins up with the EHR of the purchasing company.[2] Other reasons for EHR migration include the costs of maintaining multiple systems, a desire to change the EHR structure (e.g., to cloud computing), sheer dissatisfaction with the current EHR's usability, billing structure, availability of advanced modules, or a desire for newer technology.[3]

There is a paucity of empirical evidence to guide implementers when transitioning from one EHR to another. There are anecdotal reports, conference presentations, blog posts, opinion pieces, web articles, and a few surveys regarding transition experiences. What is clear is that such transitions are fraught with challenges:

- The cost is high. Expenditures from the initial EHR become sunk costs; purchase of the new EHR is expensive, and costs are not limited solely to the purchase of the product itself. Estimates of the true cost of purchase, configuration, testing, optimizing, and ongoing

[1] Health IT Dashboard. Adoption. Office of the National Coordinator for Health Information Technology. Found at: https://dashboard.healthit.gov/quickstats/quickstats.php Accessed 21 June 2018.
[2] Penrod LE. Electronic health record transition considerations. *PM R* 9. 2017;S13–S18.
[3] Penrod.

maintenance of a new system are at least twice the cost of the EHR software, and possibly as high as fivefold. Often, there are network and hardware upgrade costs to support the new software, which may be necessary anyway, but which add to the immediate financial investment.

- There is often a scarcity of resources,[4] especially personnel to do the installation and configuration, both on the vendor and on the hospital or practice side.
- Training and support when the EHR comes on-line are often inadequate or too brief to ensure success.[5]
- The hegemony that hospitals and practices undergo during mergers also involves major cultural shifts.[6] This disruption is an added strain complicating implementation of a new EHR.
- Although costs may be lower if a facility migrates to an already-built EHR, opportunities for customization are fewer, and workflows will change. This may have advantages (workflow changes may enhance care; workflow may become more streamlined), but this means that an EHR transition will also involve disruption of care delivery.

One contentious aspect of such migrations is whether to convert data from one system to another. Some have decided to maintain the old system in a read-only mode; others have migrated data—electronically, manually, or by both methods—from one to the other. For the latter, the question arises regarding which data types, how much, and how far back one should import.

Time and cost requirements to migrate data must be weighed against the benefits of physician productivity and continuity of patient care. There is often an assumption that migration increases productivity and care, but this does not always occur.[7] There is no question that data needs to be retained for both medical and legal reasons. Data retention requirements range from 3 to 25 years, depending on the state and patient age.

If implementers decide to migrate medication, allergy, and problem lists, what research exists suggests that the process can be "daunting."[8] Clinicians must still curate these data in the new system to ensure accuracy, efficiency, consistency, and patient safety. Clinicians are not always convinced that these goals are attained.[9] This can affect not only patient care, but also physician satisfaction as well.[10]

Then, there is the question of how much data to migrate. As with a new implementation from paper to an electronic system, physicians often want "all the data" moved from one EHR to the next. This is both arduous and potentially dangerous—no one wants old data that someone may have superseded. Much old data are never accessed, and not worth the cost to migrate.[11]

---

[4] Priestman W, Sridhara S, Vigne H, Collins R, Seamer L, Sebire NJ. What to expect from electronic patient record system implementation: Lessons learned from published evidence. *J Innov Health Inform.* 2018;25(2):92–104.

[5] Priestman.

[6] Healthcare Finance. With healthcare mergers, joining workplace cultures can be a difficult transition. Found at: www.healthcarefinancenews.com/news/healthcare-mergers-joining-workplace-cultures-can-be-difficult-transition Accessed 21 June 2018.

[7] West S. Need versus cost: understanding EHR data migration options. *J Med Pract Manage.* November–December 2013;29(3):181–183.

[8] Bornstein S, 2012.

[9] Zandieh, 2012.

[10] Pfoh, 2012.

[11] Bresnick J. EHR data migration: 5 steps for a successful conversion. Found at: https://ehrintelligence.com/news/ehr-data-migration-five-steps-for-a-successful-conversion Accessed 21 June 2018.

Likely to be the greatest dissatisfier among caregivers is that institution of a new EHR may not preserve individualized workflows.[12] Sometimes this is good, especially where old workflows were poor, inefficient, or risked poor patient outcomes. Where efficiencies existed, but workflow is disrupted, discontent erupts. This may lead to physician burnout,[13] or early retirement.[14]

Newer methods of data preservation may supplant conversions. Big data storage and computing platforms such as Hadoop, Spark, and MapReduce may supplant costly, difficult, and technically complex interface connections. Beyond anecdotes, there are few or no prospective data to guide us.

EHR migration issues are a subset of the interoperability problem. If somehow all EHRs used the same database structures, configurations were mutually compatible, and all products could protect discrete data fields, switching from one EHR to another would be a financial and administrative exercise. If we define[15] interoperability as the capability to exchange data within and between disparate computer systems, with semantic preservation and the ability to use and interpret data, then we immediately see the inherent difficulty—it is not now possible to preserve semantic meaning between systems reliably.

A research survey in 2017[16] revealed that respondents felt that they could obtain complete information from another facility using the same EHR only 51% of the time. When the facilities used disparate EHRs, that rate was only 23%. These data involve exchange of information from and to an outside facility, but consider the implications when one facility tries to move data from one EHR to another. Deep interoperability and semantic meaning are easily lost.

The MITRE corporation in their JASON report "A Robust Health Data Infrastructure" recommended public application program interfaces (APIs), such that "interoperability issues can be resolved only by establishing a comprehensive, transparent, and overarching software architecture for health information."[17]

In theory, an open and fully interoperable EHR would be able to extract patient records yet maintain data granularity, transmit such data to a different EHR while maintaining semantic meaning, exchange data bidirectionally in a standard format, move records to a new EHR, and embed functionality using APIs to access, manipulate, and store new data.[18] Such open architecture software might also resolve the data conversion issues of EHR transitions, but no empiric data exist to support this hypothesis.

What is the role of the executive, especially the chief medical informatics officer (CMIO), in EHR transitions? For some, there is no choice: if the legacy system is out-of-date for whatever reason and cannot be updated, or if the vendor is no longer viable, certified, or able to support the legacy system, change is inevitable. The same is true when affiliations or mergers impose a change.

---

[12] Bornstein S.

[13] Verghese A. How tech can turn doctors in to clerical workers: The threat that electronic health records and machine learning pose to physicians' clinical judgment—and their well-being. New York Times. May 16, 2018 Sunday magazine.

[14] Crowson MG, Vail C, Eapen RJ. Influence of electronic medical record implementation on provider retirement at a major academic medical centre. *J Eval Clin Pract.* April 2016;22(2):222–226.

[15] What is interoperability? HiMSS. 2013. Found at www.himss.org/library/interoperability-standards/what-is-interoperability Accessed 25 October 2017.

[16] Interoperability 2017. Found at: https://klasresearch.com/report/interoperability-2017/1215. Accessed 27 October 2017. NB: only available to subscribers.

[17] A Robust Health Data Infrastructure. JASON. The MITRE Corporation. http://healthit.gov/sites/default/files/ptp13-700hhs_white.pdf.

[18] Sittig DF, Wright A. What makes an EHR "open" or interoperable? *J Am Med Inform Assoc.* 2015;22:1099–1101.

Even when there is a perceived need for change from clinicians or management, the CMIO has numerous informatics shoes to fill:

- Identify gaps: the new EHR may not have desirable configurations that were useful workflows in the legacy system. Likewise, the new EHR may have added benefits not previously possible.
- In either case, the CMIO must focus on and reanalyze workflows, and vigorously support workflow redesign. This should be completed long before the new EHR undergoes final configuration so that the workflows can be trained and support arranged for after deployment.
- The CMIO should lead to a deep investigation regarding data conversion—is it worth it? It may be desirable, but must make everyone aware that such conversion may be fraught with difficulties.
- Carefully set expectations. There is variability in perceptions of efficacy of a new EHR by providers, and positive perceptions often wane over time.[19] "Under promise but over deliver" is a good mantra to follow, but research also shows[20] that those with low expectations will probably have those expectations fulfilled. Although those with high expectations may find those unrealized, these clinicians nevertheless often have greater satisfaction with the new system.
- Training and support are paramount for a successful transition.
- Careful and studious attention to unintended consequences after implementation[21] is critical.

[19] Krousel-Wood M, et al. Implementing electronic health records (EHRs): Health care provider perceptions before and after transition from a local basic EHR to a commercial comprehensive EHR. *J Am Med Inform Assoc.* June 1, 2018;25(6):618–626.

[20] Zandieh.

[21] Whalen K, et al. Transition to a new electronic health record and pediatric medication safety: lessons learned in pediatrics within a large academic health system. *J Am Med Inform Assoc.* April 23, 2018; doi:10.1093/jamia/ocy034. [Epub ahead of print.]

Chapter 47

User Interface: Poor Designs Hinder Adoption

Author: Kai Zheng

University of California-Irvine

Contents

> Usability represents an important yet often overlooked factor impacting the adoption and meaningful use of electronic health record (EHR) systems. Without usable systems, doctors, medical technicians, nurses, administrative staff, consumers, and other users cannot gain the potential benefits of features and functions of EHR systems.
>
> *National Institute of Standards and Technology*

Introduction

User interfaces (UIs) are "the means by which the user and a computer system interact, in particular the use of input devices and software."[1] In healthcare, cognitively efficient and visually appealing software UI is essential to time efficiency, user satisfaction, and quality of care and patient safety. Unfortunately, it has been widely acknowledged that healthcare UI, particularly of those complex applications such as electronic health record (EHR) and computerized provider order entry (CPOE), is often poorly designed and not well aligned with clinicians' mental model of documenting, information assembling, and decision making.[2,3] For example, a 2016 survey of nearly 1,400 clinicians found that over half of the respondents were unsatisfied with their EHR system. Among those who indicated dissatisfaction, 90% reported that their EHR was difficult or very difficult to use.[4]

The lack of usability of current-generation health IT systems not only hinders their adoption and use, but is also a principal cause of unintended adverse consequences. Since 2004, a large body of literature has reported the detrimental effects of health IT as a direct result of human–machine interface design flaws.[5,6] For example, a study conducted by Koppel et al. found that cluttered CPOE screens made it easy for clinicians to write medication prescriptions under a wrong patient[7]; another study conducted by Campbell et al. found that complex UI led busy clinicians to enter data in wrong places.[8] Prompted by mounting concerns, in 2012, the Office of the National Coordinator for Health Information Technology (ONC) commissioned the Institute of Medicine (IOM) to convene a committee to explore how to make health information technology (IT)-assisted care safer. In the report subsequently issued, "Health IT and Patient Safety: Building Safer Systems for Better Care," the committee concluded that poor UI design, poor workflow, and complex data interfaces are three key threats to patient safety.[9]

While usability is known to be a crucial factor for successful adoption and meaningful use of health IT, it has not historically received as much attention compared to functional requirements.[10] Recognizing this issue, several organizations, including the National Institute of Standards and Technology (NIST),[11] the ONC,[12] the Healthcare Information and Management Systems Society (HIMSS),[13] and the American Medical Association (AMA),[14] have all attempted to create guidelines to improve health IT usability. Further, the ONC included safety-enhanced design requirements as part of the Stage 2 and 3 Meaningful Use criteria to require EHR vendors to report their use of formal user-centered design (UCD) processes in designing, developing, and testing their products.[15] However, the lack of adherence to usability guidelines and the variability among vendors' adoption and application of UCD remain an under-addressed problem.[16–18] In a recent study conducted by Ratwani et al. at three pediatric hospitals, the authors found that usability issues continued to be a major cause of patient safety events, constituting nearly two-thirds of safety reports related to EHR and medication received between 2012 and 2017.[19]

Methods for Studying and Improving Healthcare UI

In the health informatics research literature, there is no shortage of methods for studying and improving healthcare UI. Many of these methods were originally developed in domains such as ergonomics, human factors, cognitive science, and human–computer interaction. For example, Kushniruk and Patel proposed to use cognitive engineering to improve the usability of clinical information systems[20]; Johnson, Johnson, and Zhang described a user-centered framework for guiding the redesign of healthcare UI[21]; and Sittig and Singh developed a socio-technical model for studying health IT in complex adaptive healthcare systems.[22]

In "Applying Human Factors and Usability Engineering to Medical Devices: the Guidance for Industry and Food and Drug Administration (FDA) Staff," the FDA specified a set of human factors and usability engineering methods for enhancing the usability of medical devices.[23] Many of the methods curated by the FDA, such as task analysis, heuristic analysis, contextual inquiry, interview, cognitive walk-through, and simulated-use testing, can be readily applied to improving the software UI of health IT applications. A comprehensive review of research methodologies that have been used in studying the usability of health IT can be found in Yen and Bakken (2012).[24]

On the concept level, HIMSS provides a set of "EHR Usability Principles"[13] to inform the development and evaluation of EHR systems, namely:

- Simplicity
- Naturalness
- Consistency
- Forgiveness and feedback
- Effective use of language
- Efficient interactions
- Effective information presentation
- Preservation of context
- Minimize cognitive load.

Similarly, AMA has laid out nine "Priorities to Improve Electronic Health Record Usability"[14] to optimize EHR design to support efficient and effective clinical work:

- Enhance physicians' ability to provide high-quality patient care
- Support team-based care
- Promote care coordination
- Offer product modularity and configurability
- Reduce cognitive workload
- Promote data liquidity
- Facilitate digital and mobile patient engagement
- Expedite user input into product design and post-implementation feedback.

Lastly, "Test Procedure §170.314(g)(3) Safety-Enhanced Design" of the Stage 2 and 3 Meaningful Use criteria requires EHR vendors to report their practice of incorporating UCD in their product design and testing processes.[15] The §170.314(g)(3) requirements specifically focus on the following eight areas, which are believed to be particularly susceptible to human–machine interface design flows:

- CPOE
- Drug–drug, drug–allergy interaction checks
- Medication list
- Medication allergy list
- Clinical decision support
- Inpatient setting only—electronic medication administration record
- Electronic prescribing
- Clinical information reconciliation.

Challenges and Future Work

Unlike functional requirements that can be readily assessed using scripted test scenarios, usability of health IT can be difficult to measure and generalize. First, usability is, to some extent, a subjective and personal matter; the perception of what is usable vs. what is not could vary largely depending on a person's role, training background, clinical experience, and computer proficiency.

Further, clinicians across different medical specialties may have different preferences; even for those within the same specialty, the opinions on what constitutes a good UI can also differ.[25,26]

Second, usability is difficult to quantify. While researchers have used quantitative measures such as task completion time, completion accuracy, and the number of mouse clicks and keystrokes needed to complete a task as proxies to evaluate usability, these measures do not fully reflect the potential misalignment of healthcare UI design with clinicians' cognitive models and workflow requirements. In addition, UI is only one source of usability pitfalls. Some usability problems may originate from other factors, such as intersystem dependencies and the lack of consideration of the socio-technical contexts in which users and software systems are situated. All of these issues may manifest as unusable human–machine interfaces. However, they cannot be fully eliminated through UI redesign if their root causes are not properly treated.

Third, UCD-based usability testing is often conducted in controlled laboratory settings. As a result, the number of test users involved is often very small, test scenarios are limited, and usability deficiencies due to the complex interplay between users, the system, and the use environment may not surface. Further, conventional UCD methods heavily rely on soliciting the input from prospective end users, the results of which are, however, susceptible to subjectivity, cognitive biases, and recall errors.[27,28] Furthermore, even the most experienced clinicians may not be able to foresee all design flaws that may lead to catastrophic results under unanticipated circumstances.[29,30]

In conclusion, the UI of current-generation health IT systems is often poorly designed and not well aligned with clinicians' mental model of clinical work. Applying UCD-based principles and practices can help to mitigate the issue by uncovering certain design flaws early in the process. However, UCD is not the panacea for all usability deficiencies, due to the complex nature of clinical practice and different cognitive and workflow requirements across specialties and settings. Therefore, in addition to enforcing UCD, we also need more field studies to examine how clinicians interact with deployed health IT systems *in situ*. We also need a "postmarketing surveillance" mechanism to systematically collect and analyze usability pitfalls of health IT, especially those associated with adverse patient safety events. The only way for us to succeed in combating health IT usability problems is to learn from the failures.

References

1. New Oxford American Dictionary.
2. National Research Council. *Computational Technology for Effective Health Care: Immediate Steps and Strategic Directions*. Washington, DC: The National Academies Press. 2009.
3. Middleton B, Bloomrosen M, Dente MA, Hashmat B, Koppel R, Overhage JM, Payne TH, Rosenbloom ST, Weaver C, Zhang J; American Medical Informatics Association. Enhancing patient safety and quality of care by improving the usability of electronic health record systems: recommendations from AMIA. *J Am Med Inform Assoc*. 2013;20(e1):e2–e8.
4. AmericanEHR. Survey on physician use of EHR systems—Ease of use baseline data. www.americanehr.com/research/reports/use-of-ehr-systems-ease-of-use-baseline-data.aspx; accessed November 17, 2018.
5. Bloomrosen M, Starren J, Lorenzi NM, Ash JS, Patel VL, Shortliffe EH. Anticipating and addressing the unintended consequences of health IT and policy: a report from the AMIA 2009 Health Policy Meeting. *J Am Med Inform Assoc*. 2011;18(1):82–90.
6. Zheng K, Abraham J, Novak LL, Reynolds TL, Gettinger A. A survey of the literature on unintended consequences associated with health information technology: 2014–2015. *Yearb Med Inform*. 2016;(1):13–29.

7. Koppel R, Metlay JP, Cohen A, Abaluck B, Localio AR, Kimmel SE, Strom BL. Role of computerized physician order entry systems in facilitating medication errors. *JAMA*. 2005;293(10):1197–1203.
8. Campbell EM, Sittig DF, Ash JS, Guappone KP, Dykstra RH. Types of unintended consequences related to computerized provider order entry. *J Am Med Inform Assoc*. 2006;13(5):547–556.
9. Institute of Medicine. *Health IT and Patient Safety Building Safer Systems for Better Care*. Washington, DC: National Academy Press. 2012.
10. Armijo D, McDonnell C, Werner K. Electronic health record usability: Interface design considerations. AHRQ Publication No. 09(10)-0091-2-EF. Rockville, MD: Agency for Healthcare Research and Quality. 2009.
11. Lowry SZ, Quinn MT, Ramaiah M, Schumacher RM, Patterson ES, North R, Zhang J, Gibbons MC, Abbott P. Technical evaluation, testing, and validation of the usability of electronic health records. NISTIR 7804. Washington, DC: National Institute of Standards and Technology. 2012.
12. Office of the National Coordinator for Health Information Technology. ONC change package for improving EHR usability. www.healthit.gov/sites/default/files/playbook/pdf/usability-change-plan.pdf; accessed November 18, 2018.
13. Healthcare information and management systems society EHR usability task force. defining and testing EMR usability: Principles and proposed methods of EMR usability evaluation and rating. 2009.
14. American Medical Association. Improving care: Priorities to improve electronic health record usability. www.ama-assn.org/sites/default/files/media-browser/member/about-ama/ehr-priorities.pdf; accessed November 17, 2018.
15. Office of the National Coordinator for Health Information Technology. Test procedure for §170.314(g)(3) safety-enhanced design. www.healthit.gov/sites/default/files/170.314g3safetyenhanceddesign_2014_tp_approved_v1.3_0.pdf; accessed November 18, 2018.
16. McDonnell C, Werner K, Wendel L. Electronic health record usability: Vendor practices and perspectives. AHRQ Publication No. 09(10)-0091-3-EF. Rockville, MD: Agency for Healthcare Research and Quality. 2010.
17. Ratwani RM, Benda NC, Hettinger AZ, Fairbanks RJ. Electronic health record vendor adherence to usability certification requirements and testing standards. *JAMA*. 2015;314(10):1070–1071.
18. Ratwani RM, Fairbanks RJ, Hettinger AZ, Benda NC. Electronic health record usability: analysis of the user-centered design processes of eleven electronic health record vendors. *J Am Med Inform Assoc*. 2015;22(6):1179–1182.
19. Ratwani RM, Savage E, Will A, Fong A, Karavite D, Muthu N, Rivera AJ, Gibson C, Asmonga D, Moscovitch B, Grundmeier R, Rising J. Identifying electronic health record usability and safety challenges in pediatric settings. *Health Aff (Millwood)*. 2018;37(11):1752–1759.
20. Kushniruk AW, Patel VL. Cognitive and usability engineering methods for the evaluation of clinical information systems. *J Biomed Inform*. 2004;37(1):56–76.
21. Johnson CM, Johnson TR, Zhang J. A user-centered framework for redesigning health care interfaces. *J Biomed Inform*. 2005;38(1):75–87.
22. Sittig DF, Singh H. A new sociotechnical model for studying health information technology in complex adaptive healthcare systems. *Qual Saf Health Care*. 2010;19(Suppl 3):i68–i74.
23. Food and Drug Administration. Applying human factors and usability engineering to medical devices: guidance for industry and Food and Drug Administration staff. www.fda.gov/downloads/medicaldevices/.../ucm259760.pdf; accessed November 18, 2018.
24. Yen PY, Bakken S. Review of health information technology usability study methodologies. *J Am Med Inform Assoc*. 2012;19(3):413–422.
25. Hultman G, Marquard J, Arsoniadis E, Mink P, Rizvi R, Ramer T, Khairat S, Fickau K, Melton GB. Usability testing of two ambulatory EHR navigators. *Appl Clin Inform*. 2016;7(2):502–515.
26. O'Connell RT, Cho C, Shah N, Brown K, Shiffman RN. Take note(s): Differential EHR satisfaction with two implementations under one roof. *J Am Med Inform Assoc*. 2004;11(1):43–49.
27. Mayo E. *The Human Problems of an Industrial Civilization*. New York: MacMillan. 1933.
28. Schwarz N, Oyserman D. Asking questions about behavior: Cognition, communication, and questionnaire construction. *Am J Eval*. 2001;22:127–160.

29. Han YY, Carcillo JA, Venkataraman ST, Clark RS, Watson RS, Nguyen TC, Bayir H, Orr RA. Unexpected increased mortality after implementation of a commercially sold computerized physician order entry system. *Pediatrics*. 2005;116(6):1506–1512.
30. Zheng K, Hanauer DA, Padman R, Johnson MP, Hussain AA, Ye W, Zhou X, Diamond HS. Handling anticipated exceptions in clinical care: Investigating clinician use of 'exit strategies' in an electronic health records system. *J Am Med Inform Assoc*. 2011;18(6):883–889.

Chapter 48

Exploring HIT Contract *Cadavers* to Avoid HIT Managerial Malpractice

Author: Henry W. Jones III
Law Office of Henry W. Jones, III

Contents

What's the Problem?

First-year medical school students study gross anatomy to seriously immerse themselves in the guts and sinews of dead bodies. To enable competence in the diagnosis and treatment of *humans'* infrastructures, and to meet their ethical and legal commitment to quality, these prospective professionals study not only the piece-parts of the body-ecosystems, but also pathophysiology—*what went wrong.*

Can we learn from traditional medical training, to deliver better health information technology ("HIT")health and lifespan? Do you have *HIT* projects *postmortems* in your, your team's, and your advisers' skill sets, yet?

Probably not, per both arguably *inadequate* health industry traditions and the consensus belated, federal-financing-triggered move of most U.S. health providers into "modern, normal" IT automation.

But, going forward, why not?

Are HIT and organizational leaders, managers, and boards actually, demonstrably serious in their proclaimed aspirations to plan, fund, build, launch, and then operate *safely* their new HIT-dependent infrastructures? Do confident self-described HIT professionals desire to *optimally* manage the software, databases, and other digitized, nonbiological components of modern-day health care operations? If so, then why not require, fund, implement, and habitualize the close, useful study of actual *"ill" and "dead" HIT projects*?

Chief Information Officers (CIO), information technology (IT) departments, health provider boards, HIT consultants, and their advisers hop to claim competence and fluency in HIT On what basis? (There exists no formal education path or certification system for "Guru in IT Procurement.") Can they really assert professionalism if they haven't hunted, found, and mined available, robust, independent documentation of the many electronic health record (EHR), clinical application, health information exchange (HIE)health plan, and other HIT projects that have *foundered*?

Where's the Diagnostic Data?

The *good news* is that human deaths aren't necessary to provide "HIT cadavers" for useful HIT study. Granular, clear documentation—which doesn't require training or fluency in the "foreign languages" of anatomy, biochemistry, or genetics—is available to HIT students, managers, servant-leaders, and others, today.

Where exactly are such extenders to the "nutrition," health, and likely lifespan of *your* HIT? How can such intellectual and commercial "vitamins," or even "business vaccines," be located and digested?

Three different, large, *historically underutilized* data sources offer opportunities to upgrade HIT planning, training, procurement, project execution, cost controls, and outcomes.

First, American commercial litigation often grinds "exceedingly fine" (albeit often slowly and at large cost). Many, varied, unpublicized lawsuits reveal *HIT-specific* useful documents, available to be "mined" from courthouses and studied. This diagnostic data trove includes HIT contracts, project budgets, project initial plans, project revisions, post-problem expert reports, "smoking gun" emails, financial impact calculations, and other relevant data. These *real-world, it-happened-in-our-industry* disclosures can be mustered for more realistic, IT-aware project planning, team design, recruiting, team training, budgeting, vendor negotiations, contract drafting, and risk mitigation.

Second, the fact that so many U.S. hospitals are government-owned, operated, and/or financed means that prudent researchers, executives, and leaders have access to helpful IT guidance materials. "Open records," "public records," "citizen access," and "government transparency" laws enable diligent individuals and teams (if they plan ahead and act in a timely fashion) to determine the real challenges and outcomes—the actual "commercial morbidity and mortality"—of HIT. In particular, HIT can "mine" documents from government-owned local, state, and/or federal health providers to collect evidence-based data and estimates for their challenges and projects. By extracting documentation from peer organizations, they can better assess options, norms, and useful variations in contract terms, long-term inclusive "total cost of ownership" ("TCO"), predictable project stressors, and the frequency and causes of post-kick-off contract amendments.[1]

[1] These "IT biopsies and radiology reports" are *not* so available to professionals in other industries with limited government ownership. This opportunity for optimization is relatively unique to the health industries. While most non-health industries have more years (decades) of IT efforts and failures, researchers generally cannot leverage "sunshine" laws to "biopsy" customer-spending, customer-outcomes, and customer-negotiation-outcomes disclosures from those sectors.

Third, American capitalism yields useful "medical records" from some larger businesses. Specifically, publicly traded HIT-specific and other IT vendors must disclose to potential and current investors many of their key corporate challenges, plans, problems, and prognostications.[2] Easily researched are IT vendors' specific, segmented disclosures on their respective risks self-analysis, financial health, competitive challenges, personnel, and significant legal proceedings. Health provider leaders can do free "cross-training" and "business epidemiology," merely by reading the federally required "commercial confessions" of EHR, health plan, pharma, and other impactful publicly traded vendors in HIT ecosystem.

Responsible HIT managers and operators needn't merely *assume* and *hope* about the "business mortality and morbidity" trends and troubles of their prospective vendors. Rather, doing necessary preliminary homework on the commercial health of potential suppliers requires only Internet access and web browser software.[3] For many years, IT customers in other, non-health industries have done such easy "due diligence" before procurements.

The public availability of these documents and details enables HIT leaders to avoid the unnecessary limited-data (shame and secrecy?) history of past HIT problems. Using these tools, HIT professionals can begin to practice evidence-based "preventive medicine" in their HIT operations.

This chapter "dissects" and delivers only a *small subset* of the publicly available, actionable, verifiable documents and disclosures that smart, serious HIT leaders can and *should* deploy to better understand and enable the better health (i.e., plans and operations) of health providers' "organs" (i.e., software and IT systems) and "blood" (i.e., patient and financial data).[4]

1. "My Later, Inclusive Hospital-Stay Bill Will Be What?!": Coat-Tailing On Others' Prior Projects' Costs

   What will be our full project-long cost, for this HIT initiative?—is a common question.

   Experienced IT participants in every industry already know that IT project costs always exceed the mere initial, out-of-pocket vendor up-front costs. Foreseeable, necessary extra project costs include semi-customization, integration with previously installed applications, later software upgrades and versions, new testing, new documentation, internal training

---

[2] These published data are a *quid pro quo* for the power to raise capital by selling shares, per the U.S. Securities Act of 1934. Vendor-specific searching is available free at www.sec.gov/edgar/searchedgar/companysearch.html. Key-word searching (albeit less robust than some databases, but still sometimes effective for researching contract vocabulary, IT industry jargon, and vendor names) is available at https://searchwww.sec.gov/EDGARFSClient/jsp/EDGAR_MainAccess.jsp. However, actual contracts only must be filed for customer or supplier relationships that are deemed "material" to the publicly traded company's economic prospects (which some commentators summarize as "constituting at least 10% of income or spending"). One admitted constraint of such research is that United States Securities and Exchange Commissiont (SEC) registrants may, and usually do, redact from these public disclosures particularly sensitive contract content, such as pricing, price discounts, or technical secrets.

[3] Such easy data mining will only be a subset of smart tasks in any significant procurement or deployment involving a publicly traded vendor. Beyond the scope of this article is the many other customary (at least in more IT-mature industries), helpful "due diligence" action items regarding a prospective vendor's dependence on "upstream" commercial component licensors, dependence on open source software, intellectual property (including its exposure to patent attacks from third parties), prior customers' satisfaction, and other issues.

[4] Per length limitations, this chapter omits many available other "commercial autopsies" arising from alleged medical malpractice, medical software patent, medical software trademark, state physicians billing system, medical marijuana dispensary management software, former employer hospital versus ex-employee physician-researcher software intellectual property ownership, and many other, diverse H.I.T.-project litigations.

(for both IT professionals and actual health care providers), data reformatting, renegotiation of impacted prior supplier relationships, and more tasks and spending.

But by how much will "TCO"[5] exceed the supposed project "ticket"?

Good news! Project budgeting and costs forecasting materials can be "mined" from available materials from others' prior efforts.

For example, when the New York City public hospital system shopped for and selected its EHR provider, a disappointed (not chosen) potential supplier sued. The losing bidder alleged that only bureaucratic bungling prevented its selection. The good news for you? Free downloadable court papers show, with granular detail, the up-front quantification, estimation, and evaluation efforts of the New York Health and Hospital System, before it chose its EHR vendor.[6] If your colleagues want to compare your initial cost hunches with the actual experiences of "those who've gone on before," then mining the pleadings of the Manhattan courthouse can yield "full-time equivalent" (FTE) staffing, Gantt chart, and other expectations of another EHR effort.

And follow-on open records requests can "biopsy out" what was later actually spent. Ongoing supplemental statements of work, change orders, and contract amendments are frequently found in medium- and large-scale projects for software installation (either the supposed "commercial off the shelf" or more custom or semi-custom applications). To set realistic, even honest, expectations of all-in, multiple-years foreseeable spending, diligent planners can "tag" nearby and distant government hospitals, state health agencies, and other tax-dollars-at-work health providers, requesting and ultimately receiving their respective initial internal budget estimates, spending forecasts as received from prospective vendors in their bids and "request for proposal" (RFP) responses, initial actual contracts (particularly those important, granular pricing and invoicing exhibits), and post-transaction cost-supplementing authorized amendments.

2. Read An "HIT Autopsy Report" Recently?: The Benefits Of Pre-Procurement Rubber-Necking Others' Prior HIT "*Trainwrecks*"

Vaccines, seat belts, and stair railings are standard components of American and global risk mitigation. What risk reduction tools, wisdom, and processes are included in your HIT projects, contracts, training, and budgets? (Or in your competition's?)

The walk-around "rounding" of resident physicians may be mostly impractical for HIT leaders, given the geographic dispersion and long duration of many comparable HIT projects. But documents assessing concluded HIT efforts are available—for those HIT professionals who care to inquire and improve.

For example, a 16-page report from a grand jury's analysis explains the human errors, inadequate planning, and troubled history (and perhaps organizational myopia and/or hubris?) of a large government EHR effort that grossly exceeded its initial duration and cost forecasts. Perhaps reading the Ventura County (California) "Final Report—Health Records Processes and Procedures" is "mandatory homework" for present and future HIT leaders.[7]

---

[5] However, avoid thinking licensed-in software is ever "owned." Its use is rented.

[6] The hospital system's reply, contesting the disappointed bidder, is available free at http://iapps.courts.state.ny.us/iscroll/SQLData.jsp?IndexNo=654362-2012 (i.e., the February 15, 2013 Answer and its Exhibits).

[7] The grand jury report, regarding an EHR project in which the duration and spending significantly exceeded initial beliefs, is available free at https://vcportal.ventura.org/GDJ/docs/reports/2013–14/Healthcare_Records-05.29.14.pdf.

IT professionals from non-health domains for decades have known and studied large-dollar enterprise requirements planning (ERP) application failures, the precursors to the EHR 1.0 births and young lives in HIT. But HIT leaders need not look outside health care to find a nine-figure example of project failure. Industry press and vendor financial disclosures confirm that a hospital's automation aspirations can actually result in project failure and a $106,000,000 refund.[8]

Pacemaker replacement in your family member's chest: cause for concern, or just another day at the office? After initial adoption of a first-time EHR (usually eased by partial federal "Meaningful Use" financing), many health providers now must consider and "go under the knife" of undertaking "EHR 2.0" overhauls. Such institutional changes can be triggered by mergers among providers, "end-of-life" "aging-out" transitions by vendors of older products to newer offerings, or efforts to achieve greater interoperability among patient records, billing/collections, and clinic-specific applications.

Is diagnostic documentation available to assist in assessing and executing such rarely-in-a-lifetime, industrial-scale, "legacy application" transitions? Yes. HIT executives and their teams can find and mine litigation pleadings where hospitals have claimed pain and suffering, beyond the foreseeable efforts and discomfort, in EHR transitions.

For example, regarding a new, replacement computerized physician order entry module, the Denver government hospital system sued its many-years vendor Siemens, following original procurement in 1996 and many contract amendments and cumulative spending over $100,000,000. The customer-plaintiff alleged (Soarian) product failure for months and significant financial and operational damage.[9]

Perhaps your timely (early) delivery of such daunting documentation to senior executives, before an RFP is published or a vendor contract is signed, can help drive more realistic project duration and funding allowances from senior management.

3. Surgical Supplies Secured, Before Beginning?: What *The Checklist Manifesto* Suggests For Accurately Assessing Actually Involved HIT Project Participants

   "What lies beneath?" sounds like horror movie marketing.

   But do you *really* know the piece-parts of your vendor's offerings?

   To what extent are anticipated deliverables to your health provider entity actually *aggregations* of many *indirect* vendors? How healthy and stable are the supply lines that create and connect the subsystems of your vendor's product's "anatomy"?

   To what extent do your current contracts and controls accurately manage and monitor the inclusion of "free and open source" software in your vendors' offerings?

   To what extent have your would-be vendors actually analyzed and confirmed the components of their proposed deliverables, given that most IT projects include diverse, significant piece-parts from upstream suppliers?

   Many HIT "old hands" have heard that Epic's EHR historically is founded on one particular upstream supplier (i.e., the Cache programming language developed and licensed by

[8] Cerner's settlement of an arbitration over a troubled transaction with Trinity Medical Center, a small North Dakota hospital, is described in industry publications (e.g., www.beckershospitalreview.com/healthcare-information-technology/cerner-trinity-settlement-totals-106m.html and https://ehrintelligence.com/news/cerner-settles-financial-software-dispute-for-106-2-million) and the vendor's S.E.C. filings (e.g., www.sec.gov/Archives/edgar/data/804753/000080475315000009/a201410-k.htm). The customer hospital had asserted damages of $240,000,000.

[9] *Denver Health and Hospital Authority v. Siemens Medical Solutions, Inc.*, U.S. District Court for Colorado, case 1:13-cv-02923—RBJ (filed October 25, 2013, settled May 16, 2014).

InterSystems). Cerner EHR customers encountered lengthy contract supplements specifying varying commercial terms for third-party applications redistributed by Cerner. IT veterans recall that the IBM personal computer launched in the early 1980s with 50% non-IBM components.

Smart IT customers increasingly contractually require *granular* disclosures and *supplemental* protective provisions from IT suppliers—unlike suppliers of *non*-IT resources where the components of deliverables more often are fungible and modular, where supplier underperformance or failure consequently is a smaller risk. (There likely are multiple, easily substituted sources for scrubs, sutures, and stents, but not so for the source code components of your licensor's software.)

Operational safety suggests special contract exhibits explaining your immediate (direct) supplier's degree of dependence on its upstream suppliers. Unlike physical non-IT product provisioning, professionalism in HIT procurement merits special contract terms requiring adequate durations of the links in upstream supply chains, prompt notice of upstream supply-link terminations, and often other terms (e.g., reprioritization of limited inventory, special insurance coverages, staff hire-away rights).

4. Is Your Supplier Sterile (Safe And Acceptable For Your Surgery)?: The Duty To Do Detailed Upstream "Due Diligence"

Will you inadvertently choose for your child the surgeon with the most malpractice lawsuits? Or, as a smart professional, will you first check the national registry for patient complaints, before placing yourself or a loved one under a particular physician's scalpel or care?

Smart software and other IT customers require both more preselection data and post-selection protections than the narrowly drafted, sometimes ambiguous warranties, indemnification, and insurance coverage terms that will be found in vendors' form contracts. Savvy shoppers seek more meaty risk-diagnosis information, before believing (or assuming) that their prospective supplier and any particular product are safe for its own patients.

In your next procurement, consider committing to better risk mitigation by beefing up each of (i) your organization's published RFP (or perhaps even its request for quotation (RFQ) or request for information (RFI)), draft contract, and negotiation plan, to seek many of these supplemental terms:

- Warranty and disclosure of any litigations (including arbitrations) in prior 10 years (even though vendors will push back, seeking limitation to fewer years and/or only then-unsettled lawsuits)
- Warranty and disclosure of any product termination in prior 10 years (vendors later may claim that past product "roadmaps" won't accurately reveal their plans for future innovations and customer satisfaction, but prospective customers will consider the scenario of recalls of implanted pacemakers or orthopedic prostheses)
- Warranty and disclosure of particular product components created out-of-house and licensed-in (a newer best-practice, even in transactions among IT vendors themselves)
- Duration and key terms of "upstream" sub-supplier contracts (in order to assess the safe "runway" duration of the current product configuration or version)
- Audited financials for past 5 years
- For identified key upstream sub-suppliers, audited financials for last 5 years
- Other terms that depend on the particular transaction and deliverables.

5. HIPAA Compliance Flowdown: Vetting Vendors For Your Better Cybersecurity Compliance

The well-known federal "Wall of Shame" for inadequate safekeeping of patient data isn't where any health provider wants to be.[10] Already, competent health provider boards, compliance departments, in-house lawyers, and trade groups have exhorted and explained "how" to seek United States Health Insurance Portability and Accountability Act (HIPAA) compliance.

Can HIT planning, procurement, and administration contribute to privacy and cybersecurity requirements?

Can penetrations, leaks, and other failures suffered by HIT *suppliers* inform and enable your *better* HIPAA compliance?

Yes. The *Epic v. Tata* litigation saga suggests that prudent HIT leaders should supplement their supplier agreements, if they aspire to support evolving, difficult privacy and cybersecurity requirements. The well-known EHR vendor learned only belatedly, and luckily, from a bold whistleblower inside a competing, offshore-based HIT company, that its software was being illegitimately mined, remotely, inside the infrastructure of both-vendors common customer, well-respected Kaiser Permanente.[11] In assessing the adequacy of your HIT "health," why not ask: if large, sophisticated HIT market leaders like Kaiser and Epic can be penetrated and misused, can't you too, a mere intermittent and perhaps smaller HIT customer, without the internal staff, sophistication and focus on software?

So, upgrade your contracts, to require prompt, granular notifications of any discovered (or even suspected) vendor deficiency in its product or network security that might compromise the security of your operations. In any HIT outsourcing project, negotiate additional details and documents to govern and track ongoing adjustments and collaborations in cybersecurity standards, tools, processes, reporting, and planning.

And, contractually mandate that your supplier funds any resulting investigation, remediation, testing, new documentation, and retraining costs.

6. Calling The Surgical Patient Dead: Pulling The Plug On A Dying EHR Project

   "Extraordinary measures" to attempt to extend the end-of-life of a dying patient is an expensive and arguably futile fact of the American heath industries, argued Atul Gawande, M.D., in his most recent book (*Being Mortal*). When an HIT project is dying—that is, when the frequent-encountered "over budget, missed phased deadlines, and lost confidence in the vendor and/or the product—can the customer (health provider) 'call it' and walk away without painful financial and legal consequences"

   When a struggling, extended EHR implementation effort is apparently doomed, can the software licensee-to-be hospital cancel the contract? And receive some reimbursement of money already paid to the vendor? (How much reimbursement, after likely interim approvals of prior deliverables, joint responsibility for many decisions and tasks, and possible project stressors unrelated to vendor performance such as changes in regulations or local health market economics?) Can the CIO quantify the project "heartbeat," "brain activity," or other "vitals" to confidently conclude the prospect of fully functioning survival?

   Probably not, if the project is founded on an inadequate contract.

---

[10] www.hhs.gov/hipaa/for-professionals/compliance-enforcement/agreements/index.html.

[11] Best explained in the July 27, 2016 66-page court ruling—the 944th pleading filed in this large litigation!—in *Epic Systems v. Tata*, in the U.S. District Court for the Western District of Wisconsin, after many months of intense discovery (required disclosure of records, depositions of employees, and other "business record biopsies," many contested, including allegations and proof of defendant vendor impermissible destruction of required evidence [i.e., "spoliation"]). www.wiwd.uscourts.gov/opinions/pdfs/2014/Epic%20v.%20TCS_No.%2014-cv-748_Amended%20MSJs.pdf.

That's how a hospital CIO got sued, individually.

And that's how an academic medicine center spent $2,869,000 in unexpected litigation defense costs, on top of initial software procurement, plus internal labor and related costs.

The University of Virginia at Charlottesville launched implementation of the IDX EHR software. At that time, the vendor was publicly traded and independent. But roughly 80% into the planned project duration, and with roughly 80% of the budget spent, only about 20% of the expected features had been built. Executive leadership decided to "pull the plug" and "change horses" to another vendor. Which got not only "The University" (as it's called throughout the state), but also the CIO sued by the rejected vendor.[12]

The moral from this arguably "commercial morgue?" Modify contracts to include "commercial euthanasia" terms. Negotiate and specify up-front what's a "dying" or "dead" project enabling withdrawing your "life support" of funding, staffing, time, and opportunity cost. Expect the possible need to build in timing, process rules, and funding for an independent third-party review and report. Make sure vendor form contracts, don't include any subtle or other "both sides bear their own costs," and modify any term providing "In event of dispute, loser pays all related enforcement costs" to include such fault-allocation external and even internal (e.g., staffing) costs.

7. Pained Yet By Budget-Shocking, Operations-Threatening "Involuntary Business Imaging"?: Do Vendors' On-Premises Software License "Compliance Audits" And Resulting Pay-Offs And Litigations Prove Inadequate IT "Self-Care"?

   Is your organization "living on borrowed time"?

   Regardless, it's dependent on "borrowed" technology. Business software products are rented, not bought.

   Not only hospitals and other health providers, but also many hundreds of non-health corporations, government units, and non-governmental organizations (NGO) have been audited by their software suppliers. What's the assessment question?: compliance with licenses. Such application vendors press, with vigor, discipline, and mature processes, to assess whether there's an accurate match between *purported* (i.e., reported and paid-for) and *actual* types, numbers, and timing of their customers' deployment of licensed application software.[13]

   Extensive audit-generated evidence very frequently establishes a significant, expensive gap between appropriate and actual stewardship of third-party provider (i.e., software vendor) intellectual property and customer custody and assumptions. Budgets, careers, and ongoing organizational operations are regularly threatened by software suppliers whose auditing technologies and vendor-leaning contract interpretations trigger often multimillion-dollar "true-up" payment demands. (And if IT leadership doesn't know its *actual* utilization of contractually provided applications, can there be realistic confidence regarding meeting cybersecurity challenges?)

---

[12] Open records research by the author (specifically, email to the author's in-state researcher from the University of Virginia System).

[13] Slides from an October 23, 2018 presentation at the 1,700-attendees annual conference of the Society for Corporate Compliance Ethics on this topic by the author are available without charge at www.corporate-compliance.org/Portals/1/PDF/Resources/past_handouts/CEI/2018/406_jones_2.pdf. The extensive article "Software Licenses Non-Compliance and Audits: Growing Hazards and New Action Items" is available without charge upon email request to the author, at memphishank@gmail.com. It was published in the December 2017 issue of the monthly magazine of the global Association of Corporate Counsel (i.e., *The Docket*), and co-written by this author and H. Ward Classen, Esq.

Will it hurt?

A $6,300,000 unfair vendor demand was alleged by Hospital Corporation of America, claiming inaccurate auditing and contract interpretation by its software supplier Informatica.[14]

Over $9,900,000 was paid to settle an audit by famous (and, to some, infamous) software supplier Oracle by the Texas Health And Human Services Commission.[15]

For example, a single, long-established software vendor has litigated with *over a dozen* U.S. hospitals and health providers.[16] One academic medical center was shocked that its decades-long supposed "business partner" (i.e., licensor) demanded $2,100,000 for its "entitlements gap," in 30 days from delivery of the vendor's postaudit analysis, for a now mostly obsolete product.[17] That provider was further frustrated that the vendor's pressures required a $621,195 payment to resolve the "declaratory judgment" lawsuit brought by the hospital system, even after negotiations plus 6 months and 22 pleadings of initial court actions, and even despite litigating in the hospital's hometown. And a large urban government medical authority paid *seven figures cash* to escape and end a federal court lawsuit that this hard-auditing licensor had filed in the vendor's hometown, far away at the other side of the country.[18]

---

[14] Amended Complaint, 9/22/11 (noting original 1999 transaction [license, not purchase], 2010 audit demand by the vendor, following a 2007 alleged vendor inspection and approval of the customer's implementation of "repository services" features) (case 3:10-cv-01155, USDC TNMD, 12/9/10–6/1/12, 151 pleadings filed).

[15] Results of open records research by the author. The payment was not ever reported in the general or IT industry press to the author's knowledge.

[16] *Weirton Medical Center v. Micro Focus, Attachmate, Cerner & Siemens Medical Solutions* (4/13/18-TBD per ongoing at this writing, USDC PAWD) (health provider alleging that IT outsourcing services vendor[s] who managed its IT infrastructure would be solely responsible for any actual over-deployment costs) (with additional corporate defendant Micro Focus per lawsuit arising after Attachmate had been acquired by UK-headquartered global software company Micro Focus); *Epic Systems v. Attachmate* (03/19/15–07/25/16, USDC WIDC) (223 pleadings filed); *Attachmate v. Health Net* (08/17/09-01/04/11 USDC WAWD); *Attachmate v. Public Health Trust of Miami-Dade County Florida* (08/20/09-09/30/10, USDC SDFL); *Attachmate v. Montefiore Medical Center et al.* (10/8/12–5/7/13 USDC WDWA); *Franciscan Missionaries of our Lady Health System v. Attachmate* (08/23/11-11/13/12, USDC LAMDC); *Wellspan Health v. Attachmate* (01/19/12–04/0 5/12, USDC PAMD); *Wellmont Health System v. Attachmate* (01/28/2013–07/30/2013, USDC TNED); *Northwest Community Hospitals v. Attachmate* (9/30/11–6/6/13 USDC ILND); *Union Hospital v. Attachmate* (02/19/14–05/07/14, USDC INSD); *Trihealth, Inc. v. Attachmate* 11/21/12-2/14/14 USDC OHSD); *University of Kansas Medical Authority v. Attachmate* (03/11/15–09/11/15 USDC KS); *Fairview Health Services v. Attachmate* (11/21/14-12/15/14, USDC MN); *The Mount Sinai Hospital v. Attachmate* (10/21/14–07/23/15, USDC SDNY); *Children's Hospital v. Attachmate* (07/14/15–09/21/15, USDC MDDC); *The Medical College of Wisconsin v. Attachmate* (02/05/15-04/12/16, USDC WIED). The lawsuits in which the software vendor is the defendant are "declaratory judgment" cases. In such litigations, a plaintiff requests adjudication (e.g., of an allegation of contract breach, intellectual property infringement, or other legal violation) by a specified third party (i.e., the defendant) who has claimed wrongdoing by that plaintiff. This process allows the accused party (here, health providers) to avoid uncertainty as to if, when, and on what terms the accusation will be resolved—and at a frequently lower cost, and perhaps in front of a more sympathetic jury, in its operational hometown.

[17] Per materials provided to the author by the University of Kansas Medical Center, per the author's open records research under the Kansas public information law.

[18] Per materials provided to the author by the Miami-Dade Health County Attorney's Office, per the author's open records research under the Florida public information law. This payoff was required per the negotiated settlement of software vendor Attachmate's lawsuit filed by the vendor in its headquarters hometown, Seattle, after 13 months of expensive litigation (*Attachmate v. Public Health Trust of Miami-Dade County & Univ. of Miami*, Case #: 2:09-cv-01180-JLR, USDC WDWA 8/20/2009-9/30/2010). In the mediation that preceded

8. Done Your "IT Spit-Swab Genetic Test"? (Or, Are You Open To The Idea That You Don't Know Your Own Innards?): Do You Know The Provenance & History Of Your Actual Code Inside?

What percent of the software on which your organization operates, was harvested from volunteers? What is the degree of dependency of daily health care delivery at your job on code crafted by independent, anonymous, pseudonyms, part-timing coders who believe that traditional, for-profit software creation is immoral, inefficient, or obsolete?

Specifically, to what extent have both your employer's immediate suppliers – and their one, two, and more supply chain links-removed tier upstream sub-suppliers – aggregated "open source" and "free" software into their solutions? And how much knowledge, current data, and risk management have your colleagues deployed to understand, identify, and manage the ongoing obligations of such no-fee but still-obligations-attached software?

While the unique and perhaps unexpected history, theory, and variations of free and open source software ("FOSS") are beyond the scope of this chapter (and, indeed the subject of many books, conferences, and other research),[19] every IT manager and steward (and also every C-suite and board leader) should recognize that:

---

the settlement, the vendor claimed it was due to $4,277,500 actual damages, plus $3.079,800 in prejudgment interest and reimbursement of approximately $160,000 in vendor's attorneys fees and other enforcement costs. (September 24, 2010 56-page mediation brief.)

[19] Understanding the history, variety, impacts, benefit, and risks of open source software now is necessary to any person claiming professional responsibility for, or familiarity with, modern information technology. Among the wealth of introductory resources:

A. Books: Professional "fluency" regarding FOSS now is as important for IT professionals as the historic book *The Mythical Man-Month*, which analyzed the inevitably phased, sequential nature of software design and development projects (and the consequent unavailability of acceleration and/or remediation by midstream addition of more people resources—since biology precludes making a baby by corralling nine women for one month). Consensus, canonical, mandatory "homework" for IT professionals:
   - Definitely includes *The Cathedral & The Bazaar* (subtitled "*Musings On Linux and Open Source By An Accidental Revolutionary*," and explaining the sociology, "value propositions," and culture of the open source movement) (Eric S. Rayman 1999, 2001)
   - Preferably includes multiauthor anthologies collecting reviews of various FOSS projects, changes, and successes: for example, *Open Sources 2.0—The Continuing Evolution* (OReilly Press 2006), *Open Sources—Voices From The Open Source Revolution* (OReilly Press 1999), and/or *Perspectives on Free and Open Source Software* (The MIT Press 2005)
   - and perhaps includes:
     The Success of Open Source (Stephen Weber, Harvard Press 2004) and
     Free Software, Free Society—Selected Essays of Richard M. Stallman (2002, collecting advocacy and analysis by the extraordinary, influential author of the General Public License and McArthur Foundation "Genius Award" 2).

B. Organizations/Websites: www.fsf.org (the original and most partisan advocate), www.opensource.org (which made "free" software more palatable to the business community), and www.linuxfoundation.org.

C. Publicly traded corporations' Disclosures: all tech vendors acknowledge the impacts of FOSS. Perspectives of particular vendor and their particular products and services can be found in the Annual Reports (e.g., "Form 10-K"), initial public stock offerings (i.e., "S-1" prospecti), and other official SEC filings include:
   1. H.I.T.-specific Vendors:
      - AllScripts ("... Open source license terms are often ambiguous, ... Therefore, the potential impact of such terms on our business is somewhat unknown. ...") (2/26/18 10-K, at www.sec.gov/Archives/edgar/data/1124804/000156459018003105/mdrx-10k_20171231.htm)
      - Athenahealth ("... Open source license ... restrictions or obligations that could be detrimental to our business, operating results or financial condition. Some open source software licenses

- In modern times, almost all software is "hybrid"—a varying, subtle, changing *blend* of proprietary, immediate-vendor-written and gathered, diverse, multiparty, Internet-distributed components, aggregated into a product, platform, or some amalgam thereof
- Restrictive licenses constrain certain later behaviors, for some FOSS code (e.g., any application, library, or tool released under a General Public License ["GPL"])
- By now, most software vendors and many experienced software customers (particularly in non-health industries) already have considered, designed, launched, assessed, and

---

automatically terminate upon any violation of their terms. … may require us to re-engineer portions of our technologies, discontinue use of such open source software, which could impact our ability to sell certain offerings that use that open source software, or result in infringement of third-party intellectual property, which could result in litigation and liability … no assurance that efforts we take to monitor the use of open source software … will be successful, and such use could inadvertently occur. …") (2/1/18 10-K, at www.sec.gov/Archives/edgar/data/1131096/000113109618000022/athn-20171231x10k.htm)

- R1 R.C.M. (formerly known as Accretive Health) (outsourcing services vendor, particularly for the Ascension hospitals network) ("… Consistent with common industry practices, we occasionally utilize open source software or third party software products to meet our clients' needs. …") (3/9/18 10-K, at www.sec.gov/Archives/edgar/data/1472595/000147259518000023/a201710k.htm)
- Cerner ("…*Many of our software solutions and technology-enabled services contain open source software that may pose particular risks to our proprietary software solutions and technology-enabled services in a manner that could have a negative effect on our business…*.") (bold and italics font emphasis in original) (2/12/18 10-K: www.sec.gov/Archives/edgar/data/804753/000080475318000006/a201710-k.htm)
- Mediware ("… we could be subject to claims by third parties, including competitors [who hold patents] and creators of open-source code, that we are misappropriating or infringing patents, confidential information or other intellectual property or proprietary rights of others. These claims, even if not meritorious, could require us to

  Spend significant sums in litigation
  Pay damages
  Develop noninfringing intellectual property
  Acquire costly licenses to the intellectual property that is the subject of asserted infringement.

  We may be unable to develop noninfringing products or services or obtain a license on commercially reasonable terms, or at all. We may also be required to indemnify our customers if they become subject to third-party claims relating to intellectual property that we license or otherwise provide to them, which could be costly. …") (9/11/12 10-K, at www.sec.gov/Archives/edgar/data/874733/000143774912009322/medi_10k-063012.htm)

2. Generic IT Vendors:
   - Red Hat (large, long-established Linux operating system software developer/publisher; June 4, 1999 and January 14, 2000 S-1's) (www.sec.gov/cgi-bin/browse-edgar?action=getcompany&CIK=0001087423&owner=exclude&count=40&hidefilings=0)
   - Cloudera (cloud; March 31, 2017 and September 15, 2017 S-1's) (www.sec.gov/cgi-bin/browse-edgar?company=cloudera&owner=exclude&action=getcompany)
   - MongoDB (database software; September 21, 2017 S-1) (www.sec.gov/cgi-bin/browse-edgar?company=MongoDB&owner=exclude&action=getcompany)
   - HortonWorks (BigData tools November 10, 2014 S-1) (www.sec.gov/cgi-bin/browse-edgar?company=Hortonworks&owner=exclude&action=getcompany)
   - Elastic N.V (Dutch search software vendor, filed September 5, 2018) (www.sec.gov/cgi-bin/browse-edgar?action=getcompany&CIK=0001707753&owner=exclude&count=40&hidefilings=0)
   - and many, many others.

iterated internal processes, training, risk decisions, and risk mitigation efforts, in order toenjoy the benefits but attempt to minimize and control the inevitable risks of such collectively created, web-circulated software (and to support and try to better enable compliance with their HIPAA, cybersecurity, and other obligations).

Software-specialist vendors and software users more experienced in lifecycle software management (i.e., most industries other than health) can be, have been, and are surprised, damaged, and distressed by belated FOSS discovery and wrangling.[20] So smart HIT managers act to manage FOSS deployment.

Some FOSS products, piece-parts, and tools have been identified as having cybersecurity vulnerabilities.[21] And later-surfacing, previously unknown deficiencies in hospital IT infrastructure have figured in financial claims by business partners whose operations were interrupted and allegedly damaged by unavailability of the hospitals' EHR and other data.[22] So prudent FOSS users—that is, every business—and their managers and leaders should upgrade their procurement policies, sourcing skills, IT teams, and insurance coverages to address the modern reality of free-baked-in-everywhere free and open source software.

9. Done Your "Advance Directives" Yet?: Prudent Prior Provisioning For End-Of-Relationship

When your supplier's gone, what will you do?

Do both your contracts and ongoing contract administration adequately prepare for the changes that likely result from your vendor's unilateral product or product-version termination (called "end-of-lifing" in the software industry), acquisition by another company (or,

---

[20] IT products vendor Cisco has been praised and revered for decades regarding its skills and track record for smoothly identifying and then absorbing other companies, via a savvy merger negotiation, due diligence, and "onboarding" process. Yet Cisco lots millions of dollars in marketplace value (i.e., the "market cap" of its issued stock) upon its public announcement of noncompliance with the GPL license by its just-acquired subsidiary LinkSys (developer/manufacturer of home WiFi routers and other consumer electronics products). Lack of awareness and/or license noncompliance by other IT and software vendors has been demonstrated in various intellectual property, antitrust, and other litigations (e.g., *Artifex Software Inc. v. Diebold Inc. & Premier Election Solutions* [10/22/08-6/25/09, USDC NDCA, 40 pleadings] [voting machines allegedly incorporating software distributed under GPL license, settled], *Ximpleware v. Versata, Ameriprise, United Healthcare et al.* [patent case, 11/5/13–6/22/15, 207 pleadings, USDC NDCA], *Ximpleware v. Versata, Ameriprise, & Aurea Software* [copyright case, 11/5/13-2/13/15, 143 pleadings, USDC NDCA], *CoKinetic Systems, Corp. v. Panasonic Avionics Corporation* [3/1/17-1/19/18, USDC SDNY, 38 pleadings before being confidentially settled], and others). Moreover, the frequency, subtlety, and significance of unnoted inclusion of, and possible noncompliance regarding, open source inside products and/or organizations' infrastructure are reflected by the fact that there is an entire industry of services and tools vendors whose sole focus is helping both IT vendors and other organizations audit (diagnose!) their actual, not-yet-identified open source utilization (and, often dependence). Such vendors include Black Duck Software (acquired December 2017 by publicly traded vendor Synopsys), Palamida (acquired October 2016 by Flexera Software), and others.

[21] For further details, see "2018 Open Source Security and Risk Analysis Report" by vendor Black Duck Software (available without charge at www.blackducksoftware.com/open-source-security-risk-analysis-2018?utm_medium=cpc%26utm_campaign=18_8_Global_PS_OSSRA%26utm_source=adwords&gclid=EAIaIQobChMImK-KwNLR3gIVhIzICh2-sQk4EAAYASAAEgJfkvD_BwE).

[22] For example, downtime during a ransomware attack triggered the *Surfside Non-Surgical Orthopedics v. AllScripts Healthcare Solutions, Inc.* litigation (which is still pending and unresolved at the time of this chapter's writing). Defendant AllScripts has asserted lack of financial responsibility in part (among other reasons) due to lack of awareness of cybersecurity holes in its selected products, an excusable ignorance shared by all users of the same technology, per belated discovery of a so-called zero-day flaw. ("… Plaintiff fails to state a claim for which this Court may grant relief: a zero-day, criminal ransomware attack is precisely the type of unforeseeable event that breaks the chain of causation. …," from November 7, 2018, defendant's reply brief supporting its motion to dismiss the pending purported class action lawsuit [1/25/18—TBD, USDC SDNY].)

increasingly for software companies, a software-focused private equity fund) and consequent overhaul, bankruptcy, or just inadequate performance? Adequately?

For example, abrupt, unexpected notification of shutdown was the bad news for dozens of Chicago hospitals, from the contracted operator of their data-sharing arrangement. "30 days from now, we'll be gone, but we'll ship you data tapes before then" was *not* adequate comfort for patient safety, HIPAA compliance, or quality concerns when a regional "HIE" infrastructure services vendor decided to close shop. As a result, the customer health providers quickly sued. Fortunately, the many surprised and impacted health provider organizations (i.e., HIE participants)[23] obtained a court-ordered injunction against being unilaterally "unplugged" and negotiated, belatedly, an acceptable process for data transfers, testing, and confirmation.

The moral from the frequency of such "commercial morbidity"? As other, older IT-using industries have long known, include in all significant contracts and enforce robust quality testing, both software source code escrowing[24] and other supply chain protecting terms. And clearly assign (i.e., define, in writing) and follow up on (e.g., include in annual performance reviews!) IT and procurement managers' responsibilities to assess and confirm the ongoing financial health, products and services availability, and safety of all key suppliers.

10. Knowing The Genetics of HIT ("We Don't Really Know" s Analytical Realism)

    "Your doctor knows best, and everything" as a patient's approach to surgical decisions, is a long-gone cultural artifact. Uncertainty and change are the only certainty in HIT (and overall evolution of the U.S. health industries, many argue.)

    "You don't know what you don't know," one hears.[25] HIT leaders seeking to improve risk assessment and mitigation (with consequent benefits to quality of care, plus employer financial results) should approach projects with humility, flexibility, and efforts to adjust postlaunch their processes, due to inevitable deficits and delays in their field vision.

    Congenital deformities often are discovered only belatedly, even in adult years. Defects in software and IT systems often are detected only long—many years—after their creation or installation.[26] Moreover, post-discovery remediation of errors in both HIT and non-HIT

[23] While the lawsuit was brought by the HIE as an individual legal entity and does not specify the number of impacted health providers, the plaintiff MCHC-Chicago Hospital Council ("MCHC") was comprised of approximately 140 hospitals and health care organizations per an October 9, 2016, Wikipedia entry (https://en.wikipedia.org/wiki/Metropolitan_Chicago_Healthcare_Council).

[24] Follow-up is necessary. Industry lore and some litigations confirm that too frequently a purchasing contract includes a vendor requirement of technology escrowing for the new customer's benefit—but it never happens. (e.g., *NavWorx, Inc v. Aspen Avionics & Accord Tech.*, Petition November 2, 2017, Dallas County, Texas District Court, following February 27, 2017, Strategic Purchasing Agreement).

[25] And theoretical physicists assert that any completely accurate observation is impossible, per modification of the phenomenon sought to be reviewed and analyzed (i.e., the Heisenberg uncertainty principle).

[26] For examples of latency between software customers alleged, and often proven or conceded, over-deployment of in-licenses (e.g., copyright infringements) and later discovery of same, only via vendors asserting audit rights included in original contracts, see the December 2017 article cited above in endnote #xiii_. Also, the $133,000,000 settlement payment by eClinicalWorks for fraud in purportedly achieving certification for Meaningful Use standards for its customers (thus aiding selling efforts), announced May 31, 2017, by the U.S. Department Of Justice, actually lay below public view for years, during investigation and prosecution. The litigation began September 29, 2011, per the discovery and protest by an IT administration employee at the Rikers jail in New York, via a sealed complaint (typical for so-called whistleblower cases under the False Claims Act) (i.e., *United States of America Ex Rel Brendan Delaney v. Eclinical Works*, Case 1:11-cv-04755-FB-MDG, USDC EDNY [Brooklyn] [dismissed 9/9/13, unsealed 2/9/15]), and only achieved results via a 2d case, by other, specialized litigators (05/01/2015—5/31/17, USDC VT, 26 disclosed pleadings).

projects regularly follow those initial discomforts by many years.[27] Also, many software bugs, disputes among the vendors, and other HIT challenges never receive press coverage.[28]

What to do, at least for projects of moderate or large duration, dollars, or impacts?

One possible best practice: "transplant" best practices from other, more mature IT settings. Assume that one does *-not-* possess perfection or omniscience in current HIT practices and contracts, rather than the converse (e.g., the teen bravado mantra assertion "I've got this!").

Why not learn from comparable, adjacent settings?

In particular, "graft" onto the body of your contracts particular terms designed to drive better visibility into, assessment of, and control of *mid-project* changes.

For decades, in long-term IT outsourcing agreements, customers and vendors have negotiated, implemented, and benefited from "governance" precision. Good-sized outsourcing transactions include binding provisions for ongoing, periodic, formalized critiques, cross-reporting, re-prioritization, and limited renegotiation. By contractually requiring (e.g., as an express precondition to interim payments!) quarterly, biannual, and/or annual measurement and written analysis of project stressors, deliveries, and forecasts, health providers can (and should) reduce the risks of belated, higher-cost, lower-flexibility realization of changed IT priorities, rippling technical modifications necessitated by third-party specification changes, subcontractor inadequate performance, or other challenges.[29]

Americans historically have heard, and like to believe, that their health system is the world's best. But as health providers increasingly depend on digital "blood" (software) and "oxygen" (data), as medical software becomes more robust and more interdependent, and as HIT leaders increasingly consider and recognize the gap between IT management practices and skills in non-health versus in health domains, hopefully health and HIT researchers, managers, and executives will adopt upgraded training and project management processes.

---

[27] Assumptions of system health can be unfounded, since dormancies in IT disputes are normal. For example, a dispute regarding proper interpretation of a 2008 claims data license between WebMD and Change Healthcare didn't not burst into litigation until 2017 (case 651775/2017 in Supreme Court of the State of New York, Commercial Division). Similarly, a Medicare software system overhaul was contracted in 2012, suspended in 2014, terminated in 2015, and only remediated in 2017 (by a $81,000,000 payment by the vendor, after $27,000,000 had been paid, for a $170,000,000 project, in the agreement between Computer Sciences Corporation [i.e., CSC, now reformulated as DXC Technology] and the State of Maryland, per www.baltimoresun.com/business/bs-md-medicaid-settlement-20180209-story.html and http://foxbaltimore.com/news/local/md-settles-with-computer-contractor-over-medicaid-failures [2012 award of $297,000,000 contract by the Maryland Department of Health and Mental Hygiene announced by vendor in press release available at www.dxc.technology/newsroom/press_releases/80126-csc_wins_contract_to_replace_maryland_s_medicaid_management_information_system]).

[28] For example, at this writing, no industry media coverage has surfaced of the early-stages *Cerner v. NextGen* litigation, which is not disclosed in SEC filings by either EHR vendor (and was discovered inadvertently by the author, via researching other litigation). The plaintiff asserts premature, unjustified termination of third-level technical support and software reselling rights granted in 2010 and 2015 to Siemens Medical Systems, acquired by Cerner in 2015.

[29] Similarly, the architectural, construction, and engineering industries regularly include project provisions for in-field, real-time post-contracting revisions of their blueprints, materials, and pricing (e.g., when necessitated by error, materials shortages, or unexpected weather). Some construction projects accelerate and pre-authorize, in advance, real-world on-site decisions and adjustments, by contractually specifying and legitimizing a formal "Owner's Representative" with defined powers to alert prior plans and specifications.

APPENDICES

Appendix A: HIT Project Categories

Ambulatory Electronic Health Record (EHR)

Chapter 33: All Automation Isn't Good
Chapter 34: Start Simple...Maybe
Chapter 35: It's in the EHR...but Where?
Chapter 36: All Systems Down...What Now?
Chapter 37: Weekends Are Not Just for Relaxing
Chapter 38: 104 Synergistic Problems
Chapter 39: What Defines "Failure"?
Chapter 40: Digital Surveys Don't Always Mean Easier

Inpatient Electronic Health Record (EHR)

Chapter 1: Build It with Them, Make It Mandatory, and They Will Come
Chapter 2: One Size Does Not Fit All
Chapter 3: Putting the Cart before the Horse
Chapter 4: Hospital Objectives vs. Project Timelines
Chapter 5: Clinical Quality Improvement or Administrative Oversight
Chapter 6: A Legacy Shortfall Reinforces a New Endeavor
Chapter 7: When Value Endures
Chapter 8: Usability Reigns Supreme
Chapter 9: A Mobile App That Didn't
Chapter 10: Disruptive Workflow Disrupts the Rollout
Chapter 11: Anatomy of a Preventable Mistake
Chapter 12: Failure to Plan, Failure to Rollout
Chapter 13: Fitting a Square Peg into a Round Hole
Chapter 14: Basic Math
Chapter 15: In with the New Does Not Mean Out with the Old
Chapter 16: First-Time Failures Ensured Later Success
Chapter 18: How Many Is Too Many
Chapter 19: Simultaneous Systems Migration
Chapter 20: Notification Failure

Chapter 21: Collaboration Is Essential
Chapter 22: Lessons Beyond Bar Coding
Chapter 24: Vendor and Customer
Chapter 26: Ready for the Upgrade
Chapter 27: Effective Leadership Includes the Right People
Chapter 29: Shortsighted Vision
Chapter 30: Committing Leadership Resources
Chapter 31: When to Throw in the Towel
Chapter 41: Push vs. Pull
Chapter 32: When Life Throws You Lemons, Make Lemonade
Chapter 44: Improved Population Management Requires Management

Community-Facing Technologies (Physician and Consumer)

Chapter 25: The Phone's On, but Nobody's Home
Chapter 41: Push vs. Pull
Chapter 42: Disconnecting Primary Care Providers
Chapter 43: Loss Aversion

Computerized Provider Order Entry (CPOE)

Chapter 1: Build It with Them, Make It Mandatory, and They Will Come
Chapter 2: One Size Does Not Fit All
Chapter 5: Clinical Quality Improvement or Administrative Oversight
Chapter 8: Usability Reigns Supreme
Chapter 9: A Mobile App That Didn't
Chapter 10: Disruptive Workflow Disrupts the Rollout
Chapter 11: Anatomy of a Preventable Mistake
Chapter 14: Basic Math
Chapter 16: First-Time Failures Ensured Later Success
Chapter 29: Shortsighted Vision
Chapter 30: Committing Leadership Resources
Chapter 31: When to Throw in the Towel
Chapter 33: All Automation Isn't Good

Electronic Medication Administration Record (eMAR)

Chapter 4: Hospital Objectives vs. Project Timelines
Chapter 10: Disruptive Workflow Disrupts the Rollout
Chapter 11: Anatomy of a Preventable Mistake
Chapter 12: Failure to Plan, Failure to Rollout
Chapter 14: Basic Math

Pharmacy IS

Chapter 10: Disruptive Workflow Disrupts the Rollout
Chapter 11: Anatomy of a Preventable Mistake
Chapter 12: Failure to Plan, Failure to Rollout
Chapter 14: Basic Math
Chapter 16: First-Time Failures Ensured Later Success

Infrastructure and Technology

Chapter 15: In with the New Does Not Mean Out with the Old
Chapter 17: No Other Phase Is More Important
Chapter 23: A Single Point of Failure
Chapter 24: Vendor and Customer
Chapter 26: Ready for the Upgrade
Chapter 19: Simultaneous Systems Migration
Chapter 25: The Phone's On, but Nobody's Home
Chapter 31: When to Throw in the Towel
Chapter 32: When Life Throws You Lemons, Make Lemonade
Chapter 34: Start Simple...Maybe

Laboratory Information Systems

Chapter 22: Lessons Beyond Bar Coding
Chapter 31: When to Throw in the Towel
Chapter 33: All Automation Isn't Good

Population Health & Analytics

Chapter 6: A Legacy Shortfall Reinforces a New Endeavor
Chapter 28: Culture Eats Implementation for Lunch
Chapter 40: Digital Surveys Don't Always Mean Easier
Chapter 42: Disconnecting Primary Care Providers
Chapter 44: Improved Population Management Requires Management

Appendix B: Lessons Learned Categories

Communication

Chapter 4: Hospital Objectives vs. Project Timelines
Chapter 5: Clinical Quality Improvement or Administrative Oversight
Chapter 6: A Legacy Shortfall Reinforces a New Endeavor
Chapter 7: When Value Endures
Chapter 9: A Mobile App That Didn't
Chapter 24: Vendor and Customer
Chapter 25: The Phone's On, but Nobody's Home
Chapter 26: Ready for the Upgrade
Chapter 29: Shortsighted Vision
Chapter 30: Committing Leadership Resources
Chapter 31: When to Throw in the Towel
Chapter 34: Start Simple...Maybe
Chapter 36: All Systems Down...What Now?
Chapter 37: Weekends Are Not Just for Relaxing
Chapter 42: Disconnecting Primary Care Providers
Chapter 43: Loss Aversion
Chapter 44: Improved Population Management Requires Management

Contracts

Chapter 26: Ready for the Upgrade
Chapter 38: 104 Synergistic Problems
Chapter 40: Digital surveys Don't Always Mean Easier

Data Model

Chapter 6: A Legacy Shortfall Reinforces a New Endeavor
Chapter 18: How Many Is Too Many
Chapter 27: Effective Leadership Includes the Right People

Chapter 33: All Automation Isn't Good
Chapter 42: Disconnecting Primary Care Providers

Implementation Approaches

Chapter 1: Build It with Them, Make It Mandatory, and They Will Come
Chapter 2: One Size Does Not Fit All
Chapter 3: Putting the Cart before the Horse
Chapter 7: When Value Endures
Chapter 10: Disruptive Workflow Disrupts the Rollout
Chapter 11: Anatomy of a Preventable Mistake
Chapter 12: Failure to Plan, Failure to Rollout
Chapter 15: In with the New Does Not Mean Out with the Old
Chapter 16: First-Time Failures Ensured Later Success
Chapter 22: Lessons Beyond Bar Coding
Chapter 24: Vendor and Customer
Chapter 28: Culture Eats Implementation for Lunch
Chapter 32: When Life Throws Lemons, Make Lemonade
Chapter 34: Start Simple…Maybe
Chapter 40: Digital Surveys Don't Always Mean Easier
Chapter 41: Push vs. Pull
Chapter 42: Disconnecting Primary Care Providers
Chapter 43: Loss Aversion
Chapter 44: Improved Population Management Requires Management

Leadership/Governance

Chapter 1: Build It with Them, Make It Mandatory, and They Will Come
Chapter 4: Hospital Objectives vs. Project Timelines
Chapter 9: A Mobile App That Didn't
Chapter 10: Disruptive Workflow Disrupts the Rollout
Chapter 11: Anatomy of a Preventable Mistake
Chapter 12: Failure to Plan, Failure to Rollout
Chapter 13: Fitting a Square Peg into a Round Hole
Chapter 17: Device Selection: No Other Phase Is More Important
Chapter 18: How Many Is Too Many
Chapter 21: Collaboration Is Essential
Chapter 24: Vendor and Customer
Chapter 26: Ready for the Upgrade
Chapter 27: Effective Leadership Includes the Right People
Chapter 28: Culture Eats Implementation for Lunch
Chapter 29: Shortsighted Vision
Chapter 30: Committing Leadership Resources
Chapter 31: When to Throw in the Towel

Chapter 32: When Life Throws Lemons, Make Lemonade
Chapter 34: Start Simple...Maybe
Chapter 35: It's in the EHR...but Where?
Chapter 36: All Systems Down...What Now?
Chapter 38: 104 Synergistic Problems
Chapter 44: Improved Population Management Requires Management

Project Management

Chapter 3: Putting the Cart before the Horse
Chapter 13: Fitting a Square Peg into a Round Hole
Chapter 17: Device Selection: No Other Phase Is More Important
Chapter 22: Lessons Beyond Bar Coding
Chapter 23: A Single Point of Failure
Chapter 24: Vendor and Customer
Chapter 26: Ready for the Upgrade
Chapter 38: 104 Synergistic Problems
Chapter 40: Digital Surveys Don't Always Mean Easier

Staffing Resources

Chapter 2: One Size Does Not Fit All
Chapter 4: Hospital Objectives vs. Project Timelines
Chapter 6: A Legacy Shortfall Reinforces a New Endeavor
Chapter 12: Failure to Plan, Failure to Rollout
Chapter 15: In with the New Does Not Mean Out with the Old
Chapter 16: First-Time Failures Ensured Later Success
Chapter 33: All Automation Isn't Good
Chapter 25: The Phone's On, but Nobody's Home
Chapter 29: Shortsighted Vision
Chapter 30: Committing Leadership Resources
Chapter 37: Weekends Are Not Just for Relaxing

System Configuration

Chapter 3: Putting the Cart before the Horse
Chapter 6: A Legacy Shortfall Reinforces a New Endeavor
Chapter 8: Usability Reigns Supreme
Chapter 14: Basic Math
Chapter 19: Simultaneous Systems Migration
Chapter 20: Notification Failure
Chapter 22: Lessons Beyond Bar Coding
Chapter 25: The Phone's On, but Nobody's Home

Chapter 27: Effective Leadership Includes the Right People
Chapter 33: All Automation Isn't Good
Chapter 34: Start Simple…Maybe
Chapter 35: It's in the EHR...but Where?
Chapter 42: Disconnecting Primary Care Providers

System Design

Chapter 3: Putting the Cart before the Horse
Chapter 7: When Value Endures
Chapter 8: Usability Reigns Supreme
Chapter 10: Disruptive Workflow Disrupts the Rollout
Chapter 11: Anatomy of a Preventable Mistake
Chapter 13: Fitting a Square Peg into a Round Hole
Chapter 16: First-Time Failures Ensured Later Success
Chapter 20: Notification Failure
Chapter 21: Collaboration Is Essential
Chapter 22: Lessons Beyond Bar Coding
Chapter 35: It's in the EHR...but Where?
Chapter 39: What Defines "Failure"?
Chapter 40: Digital Surveys Don't Always Mean Easier
Chapter 41: Push vs. Pull
Chapter 43: Loss Aversion

Technology Problems

Chapter 4: Hospital Objectives vs. Project Timelines
Chapter 12: Failure to Plan, Failure to Rollout
Chapter 14: Basic Math
Chapter 15: In with the New Does Not Mean Out with the Old
Chapter 19: Simultaneous Systems Migration
Chapter 23: A Single Point of Failure
Chapter 31: When to Throw in the Towel
Chapter 34: Start Simple…Maybe
Chapter 36: All Systems Down…What Now?
Chapter 38: 104 Synergistic Problems
Chapter 39: What Defines "Failure"?

Training

Chapter 2: One Size Does Not Fit All
Chapter 7: When Value Endures
Chapter 15: In with the New Does Not Mean Out with the Old

Chapter 16: First-Time Failures Ensured Later Success
Chapter 18: How Many Is Too Many
Chapter 22: Lessons Beyond Bar Coding
Chapter 28: Culture Eats Implementation for Lunch
Chapter 32: When Life Throws Lemons, Make Lemonade
Chapter 34: Start Simple...Maybe
Chapter 36: All Systems Down...What Now?
Chapter 39: What Defines “Failure”?
Chapter 42: Disconnecting Primary Care Providers

Workflow

Chapter 2: One Size Does Not Fit All
Chapter 3: Putting the Cart before the Horse
Chapter 5: Clinical Quality Improvement or Administrative Oversight
Chapter 7: When Value Endures
Chapter 9: A Mobile App That Didn’t
Chapter 10: Disruptive Workflow Disrupts the Rollout
Chapter 11: Anatomy of a Preventable Mistake
Chapter 12: Failure to Plan, Failure to Rollout
Chapter 16: First-Time Failures Ensured Later Success
Chapter 17: Device Selection: No Other Phase Is More Important
Chapter 18: How Many Is Too Many
Chapter 21: Collaboration Is Essential
Chapter 22: Lessons Beyond Bar Coding
Chapter 33: All Automation Isn’t Good
Chapter 38: 104 Synergistic Problems
Chapter 41: Push vs. Pull
Chapter 25: The Phone’s On, but Nobody’s Home
Chapter 40: Digital Surveys Don’t Always Mean Easier
Chapter 42: Disconnecting Primary Care Providers
Chapter 44: Improved Population Management Requires Management

Appendix C: Case Study References and Bibliography of Additional Resources

References

Aarts J. 2012. Towards safe electronic health records: A socio-technical perspective and the need for incident reporting. *Health Policy and Technology* 1(1): 8–15.

Abbott P, J Foster, H de Fatima, and P Marin Dykes. 2014. Complexity and the science of implementation in health IT—Knowledge gaps and future visions. *International Journal of Medical Informatics* 83: e12–e22.

Abouzahra M. 2011. Causes of failure in Healthcare IT projects. 3rd International Conference on Advanced Management Science, IACSIT Press, Singapore. IPEDR Vol. 19, pp. 46–50. www.axelos.com/best-practice-solutions/prince2.

Ash JS, NR Anderson, and P Tarczy-Hornoch. 2008. People and organizational issues in research systems implementation. Journal of the American Medical Informatics Association 15(3): 283–289.

Bakken S. 2001. An informatics infrastructure is essential for evidence-based practice. *Journal of the American Medical Informatics Association* 8: 199–201.

Berg M. 2001. Implementing information systems in health care organizations: Myths and challenges. *International Journal of Medical Informatics* 64: 143–156.

Berwick DM. 2003. Disseminating innovations in health care. *JAMA* 289: 1969–1975.

Black AD, J Car, C Pagliari, C Anandan, K Cresswell, T Bokun, B McKinstry, R Procter, A Majeed, and A Sheikh. 2011. The impact of eHealth on the quality and safety of health care: A systematic overview. *PLoS Medicine* 8(1): e1000387.

Boonstra A, A Versluis, and JFJ Vos. 2014. Implementing electronic health records in hospitals: A systematic literature review. *BMC Health Services Research* 14: 370.

Bradley EH, et al. 2004. Translating research into practice: Speeding the adoption of innovative health care programs. *Issue Brief (Commonwealth Fund)* 724: 1–12.

Chan KS, H Kharrazi, MA Parikh, and EW Ford. 2016. Assessing electronic health record implementation challenges using item response theory. *American Journal of Managed Care* 22(12): e409–e415.

Chapman AK, CU Lehmann, PK Donohue, and SW Aucott. 2012. Implementation of computerized provider order entry in a neonatal intensive care unit: Impact on admission workflow. *International Journal of Medical Informatics* 81(5): 291–295.

Chaudoir S, A Dugan, and C Barr. 2013. Measuring factors affecting implementation of health innovations: A systematic review of structural, organizational, provider, patient, and innovation level measures. *Implementation Science* 8: 22.

Cherry B, M Carter, D Owen, and C Lockhart. 2008. Factors affecting electronic health record adoption in long-term care facilities. *Journal of Healthcare Quality* 30: 37–47.

Committee on Patient Safety and Health Information Technology Board on Health Care Services. 2011. *Health IT and Patient Safety: Building Safer Systems for Better Care.* Washington, DC: Institute of Medicine.

Conn J. 2010. Grassley queries hospitals about IT vendors, 'gag order' contract clauses. Modern Healthcare. http://modernhealthcare.com/article/20100120/INFO/301209999/0#.

Damschroder L, D Aron, DR Keith, S Kirsch, J Alexander, and J Lowery. 2009. Fostering implementation of health service research finding into practice: A consolidate framework for advancing implementation science. *Implementation Science* 4: 50.

Ellis P, et al. Diffusion and dissemination of evidence-based cancer control interventions. www.ahrq.gov/clinic/tp/cancontp.htm Last Accessed on February 7, 2008.

Feldstein C, E Russell, and RE Glasgow. 2008. A practical, robust implementation and sustainability model (PRISM) for integrating research findings into practice. *The Joint Commission Journal on Quality and Patient Safety* 34: 4.

Fitzpatrick G, and G Ellingsen. 2012. A review of 25 years of CSCW research in healthcare: Contributions, challenges and future agendas. *Computer Supported Cooperative Work (CSCW)* 22(4–6): 609–665.

Foshay N, and C Kuziemsky. 2014. Toward an implementation framework for business intelligence in healthcare. *International Journal of Medical Informatics* 34: 20–27.

Freudenheim M. 2004. Many hospitals resist computerized patient care. *New York Times*, April 6.

Goodman KW, Berner ES, Dente MA, Kaplan B, Koppel R, et al. 2011. Challenges in ethics, safety, best practices, and oversight regarding HIT vendors, their customers, and patients: A report of an AMIA special task force. *Journal of the American Medical Informatics Association* 18(1): 77–81.

Green LW, and MW Kreuter. 1999. *Health Promotion Planning: An Educational and Ecological Approach.* Mountain View, CA: Mayfield Publishing.

Green LW, L Richard, and L Potvin. 1996. Ecological foundations of health promotion. *American Journal of Health Promotion* 10: 270–280.

Greenhalgh T, S Hinder, K Stramer, T Bratan, and J Russell. 2010. Adoption, non-adoption, and abandonment of a personal electronic health record: Case study of HealthSpace. *BMJ* 341: c5814.

Greenhalgh T, K Stramer, T Bratan, E Byrne, Y Mohammad, and J Russell. 2008. Introduction of shared electronic records: Multi-site case study using diffusion of innovation theory. *BMJ* 337: a1786.

Grol R, and J Grimshaw. 1999. Evidence-based implementation of evidence-based medicine. *The Joint Commission Journal on Quality Improvement* 25: 503–513.

Han Y, J Carcillo, S Venkataraman, R Clark, R Watson, T Nguyen, HR Bayir, and R Orr. 2005. Unexpected mortality after implementation of a commercially sold computerized physician order entry system. *Pediatrics* 116: 1506.

Hann's On Software. 2008. Hann's on software HL7 interface specification. Documentation version: January 4, 2008.

Harrison MI, R Koppel, and S Bar-Lev. 2007. Unintended consequences of information technologies in health care—an interactive sociotechnical analysis. *Journal of the American Medical Informatics Association* 14(5): 542–549.

Hughes RG. April 2008. Chapter 44: Tools and strategies for quality improvement and patient safety. In: RG Hughes, editor. *Patient Safety and Quality: An Evidence-Based Handbook for Nurses.* Rockville, MD: Agency for Healthcare Research and Quality. Available from: www.ncbi.nlm.nih.gov/books/NBK2682/.

Institute for Safe Medication Practices. 2007. High-alert medication feature: Anticoagulant safety takes center stage in 2007. ISMP Medication Safety Alert! www.ismp.org/newsletters/acutecare/articles/20070111.asp.

Institute of Medicine of the National Academies. 2011. *Health IT and Patient Safety: Building Safer Systems for Better Care.* Washington, DC: The National Academies Press.

Kaplan B. 1987. The medical computing 'lag': Perceptions of barriers to the application of computers to medicine. *International Journal of Technology Assessment in Health Care* 3(1): 123–136.

Kaplan B. 2001a. Evaluating informatics applications—review of the clinical decision support systems evaluation literature. *International Journal of Medical Informatics* 64(1): 15–37.

Kaplan B. 2001b. Evaluating informatics applications—social interactionism and call for methodological pluralism. *International Journal of Medical Informatics* 64(1): 39–56.

Kaplan B, and KJ Harris-Salamone. 2009. Health IT project success and failure: Recommendations from literature and an AMIA workshop. *Journal of the American Medical Informatics Association* 16(3): 291–299.

Kaplan B, and N Shaw. 2004. Future directions in evaluation research: People, organizational, and social issues. *Methods of Information in Medicine* 43(3–4): 215–231.

Kannry J, et al. 2016. The Chief Clinical Informatics Officer (CCIO): AMIA task force report on CCIO knowledge, education, and skillset requirements. *Applied Clinical Informatics* 7(1): 143–176.

Keenan GM, E Yakel, K Dunn Lopez, D Tschannen, and Y Ford. 2012. Challenges to nurses' efforts of retrieving, documenting and communicating patient care. *Journal of the American Medical Informatics Association*. PMID:22822042.

Kellerman A and S Jones. 2013. Analysis and commentary: What it will take to achieve the as-yet-unfulfilled promises of Health Information Technology? *Health Affairs* 32: 63–68.

Kling R and S Iaconno. 1988. The mobilization of support for computerization: The role of computerization movements. *Social Problems* 34: 226–243.

Kling R, H Crawford, H Rosenbaum, S Sawyer, and S Weisband. 2000. Learning from social informatics: Information and communication technologies in human contexts. Center for Social Informatics, Indiana University. http://rkcsi.indiana.edu/archive/SI/Arts/SI_report_Aug_14.doc.

Kling R, H Rosenbaum, and S Sawyer. 2005. *Understanding and Communicating Social Informatics: A Framework for Studying and Teaching the Human Contexts of Information and Communication Technologies*. Medford, NJ: Information Today Press. 107–108.

Koppel R, JP Metlay, A Cohen, B Abaluck, AR Locale, SE Kimmel, et al. 2005. Role of computerized physician order entry systems in facilitating medication errors. *Journal of the American Medical Informatics Association* 293(10): 1197–1203.

Lapointe L, M Mignerat, and I Vedel. 2011. The IT productivity paradox in health: A stakeholder's perspective. *International Journal of Medical Informatics* 80: 102–115.

Leviss J, and C Cole. February 2008. Physician leaders—Why the HIT struggle? *Presented at HIMSS Annual Conference—Orlando, FL.*

Lorenzi NM, LL Novak, JB Weiss, CS Gadd, and KM Unertl. 2008. Crossing the implementation chasm: A proposal for bold action. *Journal of the American Medical Informatics Association* 15(3): 290–296.

Markus ML and RI Benjamin. 1997. The magic bullet theory in IT-enabled transformation. *Sloan Management Review* 38(2): 55–68.

Middleton B, M Bloomrosen, MA Dente, B Hashmat, R Koppel, JM Overhage, TH Payne, T Rosenbloom, C Weaver, J Zhang, and American Medical Informatics Association. 2013. Enhancing patient safety and quality of care by improving the usability of electronic health record systems: Recommendations from AMIA. *Journal of the American Medical Informatics Association* 20(e1): e2–e8.

Novak J. August 28, 2012. *HIMSS Industry Solution Webinar: IT Projects Have a 70% Failure Rate: Don't Let Your Hospital IT Projects Fail.* Chicago, IL: HIMSS.

Nolan K, et al. 2005. Using a framework for spread: The case of patient access in the Veterans Health Administration. *Joint Commission Journal on Quality and Patient Safety* 31: 339–347.

Obama B. 2009. Address to Joint Session of the Congress, February 24, 2009. *Public Papers of the Presidents of the United States.* Washington, DC: Government Printing Office. www.gpo.gov/fdsys/pkg/PPP-2009-book1/pdf/PPP-2009-book1-Doc-pg145-2.pdf.

Ong K. 2011. *Medical Informatics—An Executive Primer*, 2nd ed. Chicago, IL: HIMSS.

Peel L and D Rose. 2009. MPs point to 'further delays and turmoil' for £12.4 billion NHS computer upgrade. *Times Online.* http://www.thetimes.co.uk/tto/news/uk/article1937417.ece.

PRINCE2. 2013. What is PRINCE2? www.prince2.com/what-is-prince2.asp.

Ratwani RM, A Zachary Hettinger, A Kosydar, RJ Fairbanks, and ML Hodgkins. April 1, 2017. A framework for evaluating electronic health record vendor user-centered design and usability testing processes. *Journal of the American Medical Informatics Association* 24(e1): e35–e39. doi:10.1093/jamia/ocw092.

Rogers EM. 1995. *Diffusion of innovations.* New York: Free Press.

Samal L, PC Dykes, JO Greenberg, O Hasan, AK Venkatesh, LA Volk, and DW Bates. April 22, 2016. Care coordination gaps due to lack of interoperability in the United States: A qualitative study and literature review. *BMC Health Services Research* 16: 143.

Saroyan W. 1971. *The Human Comedy*. New York: Random House.
Silverstein S. 2006. Access patterns to a website on healthcare IT failure. *AMIA 2006 Annual Meeting, Poster Session*, Washington, DC.
Simon SR, CS Soran, R Kaushal, CA Jenter, LA Volk, E Burdick, PD Cleary, EJ Orav, EG Poon, and DW Bates. 2009. Physicians' usage of key functions in electronic health records from 2005 to 2007: A statewide survey. *Journal of the American Medical Informatics Association* 16(4): 465–470.
Sittig DF, and H Singh. 2011. Defining health information technology-related errors: New developments since to err is human. *Archives of Internal Medicine* 171: 1281–1284.
Sittig DF, and H Singh. 2010. A new sociotechnical model for studying health information technology in complex adaptive healthcare systems. *Quality & Safety in Health Care* 19: i68–i74. doi:10.1136/qshc.2010.042085 [PMC free article].
Sperl-Hillen JM, et al. 2004. *Do all components of the chronic care model contribute equally to quality improvement? Joint Commission Journal on Quality and Safety* 30: 303–309.
Star SL, and K Ruhleder. 1996. Steps towards an ecology of infrastructure: Design and access for large information spaces. *Information Systems Research* 7: 111–135.
The 7 basic quality tools for process improvement. http://asq.org/learn-about-quality/seven-basic-quality-tools/overview/overview.html Accessed on January 19, 2018.
Ward R. 2013. The application of technology acceptance and diffusion of innovation models in healthcare informatics. *Health Policy and Technology* 2: 222–228.
Wright A, et al. 2018. Clinical decision support alert malfunctions: Analysis and empirically derived taxonomy. *Journal of the American Medical Informatics Association* 25: 496–506.
Zhang X, P Yu, J Yan, and I Ton A M Spil. 2015. Using diffusion of innovation theory to understand the factors impacting patient acceptance and use of consumer e-health innovations: A case study in a primary care clinic. *BMC Health Services Research* 15: 71.
Zhou L, CS Soran, CA Jenter, LA Volk, EJ Orav, DW Bates, and SR Simon. 2009. The relationship between electronic health record use and quality of care over time. *Journal of the American Medical Informatics Association* 16(4): 457–464.

Additional Resources

Alsid J, and J Leviss. March 3, 2012. Workforce development essential to Obama's health care IT initiative. Huffington post. www.huffingtonpost.com/julian-l-alssid-and-jonathan-a-leviss/workforce-development-ess_b_171556.html.
American College of Surgeons (ACS) on unintended consequences of EHRs: http://bulletin.facs.org/2018/09/ehrs-add-to-surgeons-administrative-burdens-the-acs-responds/.
Bakken S. 2001. An informatics infrastructure is essential for evidence-based practice. *Journal of the American Medical Informatics Association* 8: 199–201.
Brender J, E Ammenwerth, P Nykänen, and J Talmon. 2006. Factors influencing success and failure of health informatics systems: A pilot Delphi study. *Methods of Information in Medicine* 45(1): 125–136.
Byrne CM, LM Mercincavage, O Bouhaddou, JR Bennett, EC Pan, NE Botts, LM Olinger, E Hunolt, KH Banty, and T Cromwell. August 2014. The Department of Veterans Affairs' (VA) implementation of the Virtual Lifetime Electronic Record (VLER): Findings and lessons learned from Health Information Exchange at 12 sites. *International Journal of Medical Informatics* 83(8): 537–547. doi:10.1016/j.ijmedinf.2014.04.005. Epub April 28, 2014. PMID:24845146.
Daray MJE. 2009. Negotiating electronic health record technology agreements. *The Health Lawyer* 22(2): 53–160.
De Georgia MA, F Kaffashi, FJ Jacono, and KA Loparo. 2015. Information technology in critical care: Review of monitoring and data acquisition systems for patient care and research. *ScientificWorldJournal*. Article ID 727694. doi:10.1155/2015/727694.
Dhillon-Chattha P, R McCorkle, and E Borycki. 2018. An evidence-based tool for safe configuration of electronic health records: The eSafety checklist. *Applied Clinical Informatics* 9: 817–830.

Downing N, D Bates, and C Longhurst. May 8, 2018. Physician burnout in the Electronic Health Record Era: Are we ignoring the real cause? *Annals of Internal Medicine*. doi:10.7326/M18-0139.

Feldman SS, BL Schooley, and GP Bhavsar. August 15, 2014. Health information exchange implementation: Lessons learned and critical success factors from a case study. *JMIR Medical Informatics* 2(2): e19. doi:10.2196/medinform.3455. PMID:25599991.

Gawande A. November 12, 2018. Why doctors hate their computers. *The New Yorker*. Retrieved from http://www.newyorker.com/magazine/2018/11/12/why-doctors-hate-their-computers.

Glaser J. June 13, 2005. Success factors for clinical information system implementation. *Hospital and Health Networks' Most Wired Magazine*.

Grabenbauer L, R Fraser, J McClay, N Woelfl, CB Thompson, J Cambell, and J Windle. 2011. Adoption of electronic health records. *Applied Clinical Informatics* 2(2): 165–176.

Graham J, D Levick, and R Schreiber. 2010. AMDIS case conference: Intrusive medication safety alerts. *Applied Clinical Informatics* 1(1): 68–78.

Grassley CE. January 20, 2010. Grassley asks hospitals about experiences with federal health information technology program. Washington, DC: US Senate. http://grassley.senate.gov/news/Article.cfm?customel_dataPageID_1502= 24867.

Hersh W, and A Wright. What workforce is needed to implement the health information technology agenda?: Analysis from the HIMSS Analytics Database. *AMIA 2008 Symposium Proceedings*, Washington, DC, p. 303.

Hersh W, K Boone, and A Totten. 2018. Characteristics of the healthcare information technology workforce in the HITECH era: Underestimated in size, still growing, and adapting to advanced uses. *JAMIA Open* 0(0): 1–7. doi:10.1093/jamiaopen/ooy029. http://hcrenewal.blogspot.com

Institute for Healthcare Improvement. 2011. Failure modes and effects analysis tool. www.ihi.org/knowledge/Pages/Tools/FailureModesand EffectsAnalysisTool.aspx.

Institute of Medicine of the National Academies. 2012. *Health IT and Patient Safety: Building Safer Systems for Better Care*. Washington, DC: National Academies Press.

Jones SS, PS Heaton, RS Rudin, and EC Schneider. 2012. Unraveling the IT productivity paradox—Lessons for health care. *New England Journal of Medicine* 366(24): 2243–2245.

Kaplan B, and KD Harris-Salamone. 2009. Health IT project success and failure: Recommendations from an AMIA workshop. *Journal American Medical Informatics Association* 16(3): 291–299.

Keenan GM, E Yakel, K Dunn Lopez, D Tschannen, and Y Ford. July 21, 2012. Challenges to nurses' efforts of retrieving, documenting and communicating patient care. *Journal of the American Medical Informatics Association*. doi:10.1136/amiajnl-2012-000894.

Keenan GM, E Yakel, Y Yao, D Xu, L Szalacha, J Chen, A Johnson, D Tschannen, YB Ford, and DJ Wilkie. July 2012. Maintaining a consistent big picture: Meaningful use of a web-based POC EHR system. *International Journal of Nursing Knowledge* 23(3): 119–133.

Kilbridge P. 2003. Computer crash: Lessons from a system failure. *New England Journal of Medicine* 348(10): 881–882.

Koppel R, and D Kreda. 2009. Health care information technology vendors "hold harmless" clause: Implications for patients and clinicians. *Journal of the American Medical Association* 301(12): 1276–1278.

Kuperman GJ, RM Reichley, and TC Bailey. 2006. Using commercial knowledge bases for clinical decision support; opportunities, hurdles, and recommendations. *Journal of the American Medical Informatics Association* 13(4): 369–371.

Leviss J. 2011. HIT or miss: Studying failures to enable success. *Applied Clinical Informatics* 2(3): 345–349.

Leviss J, R Kremsdorf, and M Mohaideen. 2006. The CMIO—A new leader in healthcare. *Journal of the American Medical Informatics Association* 13(5): 573–578.

Maloney N, AR Heider, A Rockwood, and R Singh. October 27, 2014. Creating a connected community: Lessons learned from the Western New York beacon community. *EGEMS (Washington, DC)* 2(3): 1091. eCollection 2014. PMID:25848618.

Murff H, and J Kannry. 2001. Physician satisfaction with two order entry systems. *Journal of the American Medical Informatics Association* 8: 499–509.

Obama B. February 24, 2009. President Obama's address to congress. The New York Times [Internet]. Available from: www.nytimes.com/2009/02/24/us/politics/24obama-text.html.

Palmieri P, L Peterson, and L Bedoya Corazzo. 2011. Technological iatrogenesis: The manifestation of inadequate organizational planning and the integration of health information technology. In: JA Wolfe, H Hanson, MJ Moir, L Friedman, and GT Savage, editors. *Advances in Health Care Management*. Organizational Development in Healthcare, Vol. 10, pp. 287–312. Bingley: Emerald Group Publishing.

Paré G, C Sicotte, M Jaana, and D Girouard. 2008. Prioritizing the risk factors influencing the success of clinical information systems. *Methods of Information in Medicine* 47(3): 251–259. https://physicians-foundation.org/wp-content/uploads/2018/09/physicians-survey-results-final-2018.pdf.

Report by the Comptroller and Auditor General of the National Audit Office (United Kingdom): The National Programme for IT in the NHS: An update on the delivery of detailed care records systems. HC 888, Session 2010–2012, May 18, 2011.

RTI Health, Social, and Economics Research. 2002. The economic impacts of inadequate infrastructure for software testing final report. Gaithersburg, MD: National Institute of Standards and Technology.

Silow-Carroll S, J Edwards, and D Rodin. 2012. Using electronic health records to improve quality and efficiency: The experiences of leading hospitals. *Commonwealth Fund* 17: 1–40.

Sittig D, and H Singh. 2012. Electronic health records and national patient-safety goals. *New England Journal of Medicine* 367(19): 1854–1860.

The Standish Group. 1995. Chaos report. http://net.educause.edu/ir/library/pdf/NCP08083B.pdf.

The Standish Group. 2001. Extreme CHAOS. www.cin.ufpe.br/~gmp/docs/papers/extreme_chaos2001.pdf.

Stanford EHR white paper. http://med.stanford.edu/ehr/whitepaper.html.

Terpenning M, A Berlin, and J Graham. 2011. AMDIS case conference: Implementing electronic health records in a small subspecialty practice. *Applied Clinical Informatics* 2(2): 158–164.

Yackel T, and P Embi. 2010. Unintended errors with EHR-based result management: A case series. *Journal of the American Medical Informatics Association* 17(1): 104–107.

Index

D

E

N

O

P

Q

R

Printed in the United States
by Baker & Taylor Publisher Services